D0407888

TURBO-CAPITALISM

TURBO-CAPITALISM

WINNERS AND LOSERS IN
THE GLOBAL ECONOMY

Edward Luttwak

HarperCollins*Publishers*

To my wife Dalya

CONTENTS

ACKNOWLEDGMENTS

I am grateful for the direct help of my former research assistant David Leishman, now advancing as a doctoral student and teacher in agricultural economics. I am as grateful for all the indirect help I have received over many years from the directing, administrative and research staff of the Center for Strategic and International Studies of Washington DC, my only institutional affiliation. It has grown so large under the valiant leadership of Ambassador David M. Abshire, and so many have helped in one way or another, that I cannot thank individuals without indecent excess.

PREFACE

Perhaps it is because I am the son of an innovative capitalist manufacturer, and an entrepreneur on my own account, that I deeply believe both in the virtues of capitalism and in the need to impose some measure of control over its workings.

With the possible exception of nuclear weapons, capitalism is the most powerful of human inventions. As true an expression of the restless soul of European civilization as the urge to discover, create and conquer, capitalism has now spread to almost every part of the world. Traditional economics guided by unchanging practices, communist economies directed by bureaucrats, closed economies commanded by rulers or magnates have all been swept away, surviving only in isolated backwaters. Nothing can equal the unique ability of capitalism to convert simple human greed into infinitely varied productive energies. No purposeful central administration can pursue both efficiency and innovation as successfully as the relentless competition for profit and wealth unleashed by capitalism. No disciplined scheme can coordinate tasks and apportion supplies as harmoniously as the utterly spontaneous workings of capitalist markets, which need no scheme or discipline at all.

By displacing set work-routines or planned outputs with the ever-changing competitive production of goods and services; by replacing giving and taking among the entitled with buying and selling among people who might as well be perfect strangers and often are, capitalism transforms both ends of every traditional, bureaucratic, or patrimonial economy it conquers. With that, inevitably, much else is also transformed, from the ways of politics and government to private habits and personal tastes, from the patterns of family life to the very landscape of town and country.

Even Russia's very new and much-resisted capitalism has been strong enough to refashion the grimly monumental Moscow of Soviet days with shiny office towers, countless new shops, and restaurants and cafés and bars that illuminate the night of once-dark and somber streets. Less visibly, storeroom clerks have become the owners of shops and even international traders. Bureaucrats, party officials, secret policemen, scientists and all sorts of other state employees have become bankers, merchants, managers or even billionaire tycoons, often after an interval as traffickers, smugglers or even gangsters. This has changed mentalities, tastes and political preferences radically, sometimes more than once in very few years.

Even their poor and tentative rural capitalism has been strong enough to transform the Mayan villages of the emerald-green highlands of Guatemala. They now have shops and therefore shopkeepers, whose outlook must differ from their fellow Mayans who still live by cultivating the land. The tiny family plots, once apportioned by ancestral custom, are increasingly bought and sold for hard cash, allowing some villagers to enlarge their holdings while others are left landless. Once, the better or luckier tiller of the soil had the honor of giving or lending food to the hungry; now he sells his surplus for money – giving him a far greater incentive to work harder to grow more, though fewer grateful friends. Before, all were united in periodic misery or minimal abundance according to the vagaries of harvests, and all their mud and wattle dwellings looked the same; now concrete-block walls and corrugated-iron roofs proclaim that some have much more than others.

An economic force as strong as capitalism can only be controlled, if at all, by the counter-force of political power. But I do not believe that the Russian or Mayan or any other emerging capitalism should be controlled. If anything, they should be encouraged in every way. The relatively poor Russians, the miserably poor Mayans, and all in between that capitalism might uplift to a decent existence, have no other possible remedy. That is not true, however, of the mostly impersonal corporate and financial capitalism of the more affluent countries, where all other aims – social, political and even cultural – need not be sacrificed for a bit more efficiency, slightly more wealth – especially wealth so unevenly distributed.

True, there is nothing sinister or wicked about the aims of today's more advanced forms of capitalism. Profit and expansion are the proper ambitions of any capitalism. Much is wrong, however, about some of the methods which have now become routine. Abrupt mass firings are preferred to gentler retirements that may cost only slightly more or even less – because they drive up share prices, if only for a day of quick gains by the managers themselves. Plants that may sustain entire communities are closed without warning for the same reason, perhaps with no real effort to improve their efficiency instead. Rapid gain displaces larger, long-term benefits because managers are impatient to move on to the next and greater corporate slot, while there is less and less long-term ownership.

In the process, individual lives, families, communities, even entire regions are disrupted, sometimes wrecked. Hard statistics show that dismissed employees lose more than their jobs, often having their lives shortened by stress and humiliation, sometimes losing their marriages as well as mortgaged homes. Even booming economies are littered with ghost towns, or ghostly neighbourhoods that have lost their main or only source of jobs and income. Unstable jobs, even if truly well-paid, are not qualitatively the same as stable, career jobs; they only sustain immediate consumption, not the building-up of lives.

Few corporations would risk damaging the natural environment nowadays, for fear of harsh penalties. But many damage the human environment, suffering no penalties at all. It is perfectly true, however, that corporations are only responsible to their shareholders – fashionable talk of 'stakeholders' having no real substance after all. Corporations are not moral entities. They exist to earn profits, and so it should be. It is or should be the task of governments alone to control capitalism on behalf of the citizens they are supposed to equally represent. It is or should be the highest priority of governments to find ways of keeping the disruptions of capitalism within tolerable bounds, without sapping capitalism's marvellous creative energies.

In my student days at the London School of Economics during the early 1960s, and for almost two decades thereafter, the opposite problem existed: an excess of control over private-enterprise capitalism. Its competitive drive for constant improvement and growth, its unmatched ability to generate wealth potentially for all, were obstructed almost everywhere in the supposedly capitalist world. Private-enterprise capitalism was completely excluded from some of the most important industries in many countries. And capitalism itself was prohibited in the vast expanse under communist rule from East Berlin to the China coast.

In France, Italy and Spain especially, but also in Great Britain and elsewhere in Western Europe as well as in Australia, New Zealand, South Africa and much of non-communist Asia, there was much pervasive obstruction as well as outright exclusion. A great many industries described as basic, or strategic, or more poetically as 'the commanding heights', were dominated or totally monopolized by state-owned firms managed by bureaucrats or, worse, political appointees. Iron and steel, coalmining, aviation and most military production were prime candidates, but in almost all of those countries, electricity supply, telephone and telegraph services, railways, airlines, intercity bus fleets, and local mass transport were also under public ownership, national, regional or municipal. In some, private capitalism was displaced in yet more industries as varied as shipbuilding, chemicals and commercial banking, or even ice-cream production.

In the United States, there was little public ownership, but much public regulation – and very detailed too, with prices or tariffs set to the last cent by Federal, State or local commissions, boards and agencies for each service or product. Capitalist competition was totally excluded from regulated monopolies starting with Ma Bell, the country's only major telephone company. And it was severely restricted in a long list of other industries, from airlines along with all other inter-state transport, to Savings & Loan Associations, to natural gas output and pipeline delivery, and final distribution to factories and homes – with specified prices set from above for each gasfield, each transit, each locality, each class of user. If one adds the Pentagon's supervision of then vast military industries, and the Department of Agriculture's intrusive control of the largest of all industries, it can be seen that Americans were much more eager to celebrate private-enterprise capitalism than to allow its unfettered practice.

All this detailed regulatory control was meant to stabilize industries and employment, which was also a key purpose of outright public ownership as practiced in Europe and beyond. In Japan and eventually Korea and other East Asian countries, yet another way of controlling capitalism was found, not to stabilize industries at all but rather to force-feed and guide their fastest possible growth. This 'developmental' capitalism was privately owned but subsidized, assisted and *very* closely directed by powerful economic ministries.

Each non-communist country that did allow free enterprise in some spheres thus established its own version of controlled capitalism. And there was a spontaneous tendency for public ownership, market regulation and purposeful bureaucratic direction to increase over time. Larger firms, sometimes complete industries in trouble, were taken under the wing of government to protect employment, thus increasing public ownership. It became normal to subsidize money-losing state enterprises for years on end. Regulators and bureaucrats naturally tend to over-regulate and micro-manage if allowed to get away with it, which they often were. The only contrary tendency was the slow liberalization of international trade and foreign-exchange controls.

Capitalism was thus becoming distinctly over-controlled by the late 1970s. All too many corporations left in private but managerial hands naturally adapted to the political environment by themselves becoming more and more bureaucratic and politicized, a process in itself harmful to creative innovation, and even to plain hard work. Yet in most countries controlled capitalism was only on the verge of decline at the time, or perhaps only beginning to approach the culminating point of useful control beyond which decline would start.

But controlled capitalism had not been a failure overall. On the contrary, it had been a truly colossal success. From the end of the Second World War until the mid-1970s the American and European economies were uplifted by many years of rapid growth, bringing affluence from the relatively few to almost all. Japan famously grew even faster, though limiting its standard of living somewhat to invest in yet more growth. Nevertheless there too, as in entire regions of Europe, ancestral poverty gave way to a steadily increasing prosperity.

In the late 1970s the tendency to control capitalism was abruptly reversed. Ideology and fashion were important in dismantling the American system of regulations. Well-funded lobbying by interested parties eager to profit from deregulation was also important, perhaps more so. The consequences for separate industries were debated, not always in any depth. In each case, efficiency gains could be shown, and that was that. There was no serious national debate about the social desirability of deregulation as such, no attempt at an assessment of the combined impact on American society of all the separate deregulations.

In Europe ideology and fashion were also at work to diminish public ownership; in Europe, too, there was the very plausible expectation of more economic efficiency under private ownership. But in many cases it was the turning-away from decades of debt-growth and inflationary policies that forced the issue. Governments that accumulated public debt and printed money with abandon could always borrow or print a little more to cover the losses of money-losing state enterprises. Once deflationary policies became the norm, however, real money was needed – any subsidy paid out increasingly meant that some other government spending would have to be cut, including the kind of spending that wins votes.

Each country started dismantling controlled capitalism in its own way, at its own rate, for its own reasons, industry by industry. As each internationally competitive industry was unleashed in the United States or elsewhere, its gain in efficiency undercut prices or increased quality, or both, forcing the pace of decontrol for that same industry in other countries. Thus no country could stop the process by keeping its own controlled capitalism intact within its boundaries without paying an ever-increasing economic price. France did it, and paid. Japan did it, and it is paying very heavily at this time, in spite of the formidable efficiency of a few export industries that were never controlled, or only a little.

There was certainly no common forum where a broad international debate of the combined social and political and even cultural repercussions of dismantling controlled capitalism could be conducted. Even less could there be a joint international assessment of the consequences for each country and all. Economic efficiency would increase, to be sure. But what of societal inefficiencies? Yet there appear to be many, from regional impoverishment in a few cases, to almost universal community decline, family instability, and the resulting increase in the prevalence of crime. Hence the hard questions were never even asked, as successive privatizations and deregulations and globalizations were decided, releasing the unchecked powers of today's turbo-capitalism.

This book raises a few of those questions.

June 1998   Edward Luttwak
                                            Chevy Chase, Maryland

ONE

Winners and Losers

On penalty of suffering high unemployment and indeed long-term decline, the entire world is urgently being summoned to imitate the new ways of work and wealth of the American economy. New they certainly are. It was not until the end of the 1970s that today's roaring turbo-capitalism was unleashed by the abolition of anti-competition laws and regulations left over from the 1930s, by the technological innovations thus allowed, by the privatization of whatever could be privatized, and by the removal of most import barriers.

For individual Americans, the results have been spectacular, one way or another. Tens of thousands of acrobatic entrepreneurs and mere corporate managers, hundreds of thousands of bold or just lucky investors, have become multi-millionaires, billionaires or even multi-billionaires. Because many prefer to believe that great enrichment is justified by great personal achievement, the computer pioneers from Microsoft's Bill Gates down to ordinary software centi-millionaires are forever being cited as typical of the new ultra-rich. But many prospered hugely in newly deregulated industries from natural gas to commercial banking, simply by taking what was offered to them once restrictions were lifted. Others still did very well yet more easily in plain old trades, just by floating on a rising stock-market tide.

High achievement is rewarded, but so is mediocrity, given an indulgent board of directors. Lawrence Coss, chief executive officer of Green Tree Financial, concurrently appeared on two different 1997

1

Business Week rankings of US corporate chiefs: one for the highest earners of 1996 – he was number one at $102,449,000, or $280,682 per day including weekends and vacations – and one for the least effective in raising shareholder value.[1]

Some sixty million less enterprising Americans who were once paid rather well for routine work in unionized factories and corporate offices must now in effect compete every day with the labor-saving technologies which could replace them, and even with cheaper foreign labor. To keep their now perpetually insecure jobs, they and their unions have had to accept stagnant or even declining earnings and fringe benefits. By January 1997, with unemployment falling below 5 per cent in high boom times and emerging labor shortages here and there, the Chairman of the Federal Reserve, Alan Greenspan, worried aloud that this implicit bargain (job security for low inflation) would come to an end, bringing higher wages – not a worthy aim, but instead a dreadful prospect for America's official slayer of the dragon inflation. His fears were misplaced. Having increased by a mere 2.7 per cent – less than inflation – and thus fallen in real terms during the recovery year 1995, total pay and benefits increased by only 2.9 per cent even in the boom year 1996, and then by 3 per cent at the peak of the boom in 1997, only then finally gaining a fraction over inflation.[2]

Others among the sixty million less fortunate Americans have failed to keep or find industrial or office jobs, thus being driven into poorly paid selling, serving, guarding, handling, laboring and cleaning jobs. In so doing, the downwardly mobile have claimed for themselves all the traditional occupations of the underclass, whose non-workers in turn account for most of the 1.8 million people behind bars at the last count.[3] Another 3.7 million were on probation or parole awaiting trial, so that the criminalized total of 5.5 million accounts for 2.8 per cent of the adult population of the United States, twice the proportion of 1980 when turbo-capitalism was just getting started.

The causal link between turbo-capitalism and crime passes through the accelerated technical and structural changes that have eliminated

[1] As measured by stock price at year-end 1996, plus reinvested dividends over 1994–96 minus the year-end 1993 stock price. Jennifer Reingold, 'Executive pay' (annual survey), *Business Week*, 21 April 1997.

[2] Bureau of Labor Statistics, Employment Cost Index, quarterly releases, 1995, 1996, 1997. Re Greenspan: Robert D. Hershey, Jr, 'Pay report is noninflationary, relieving markets (for a while)', *New York Times*, 29 January 1997, page D1.

[3] Mid-year 1997. US Department of Justice, Bureau of Justice Statistics, *Correction Statistics*.

many *urban* industrial-type jobs. In the past, when the unskilled were still employable, it was enough to muster the energy and motivation to walk down the street to the nearest factory gate to be inducted for life into the economy. After that, mere inertia was enough to keep one's job and respectability.

As the economy has been transformed and nearby jobs have migrated away to suburbs, to non-union rural areas or abroad, or else have simply disappeared, many inner-city people have failed to become highly skilled cosmopolitans. Not everyone can find his or her own niche among the dazzling opportunities that turbo-capitalism offers, from foreign-exchange dealing on Wall Street or the City of London, to software writing in Silicon Valley or France's Sophia Antipolis and the better-paid professions. Unable to enter into the realm of work, they live on the fringes or in the core of criminal life, whether in America's inner cities or rural backwaters dotted with rusty trailer-homes, or in the run-down areas of Glasgow or Liverpool for that matter.

Another fifty million or so working Americans and their children have been living increasingly affluent lives. It is their prosperity that is so plainly visible in the ample houses of hundreds of suburbs across America, in the proliferation of luxury vehicles and pleasure boats, in palatial shopping centers and crowded holiday resorts. Many of them can live so well because they have high earnings in skilled trades or professions, in middle-high management, or by self-employment ranging from at-home consulting to the running of their own substantial business enterprises. Many Americans, however, live at an even higher standard than their incomes allow, because personal 'consumer' credit is so easily obtained. At the time of writing, the combined personal debt of all Americans has now reached the truly colossal level of five trillion dollars ($5,000 billion), almost nine-tenths of their total annual income. Perhaps it is the atmosphere of turbo-capitalism, with its transatlantic private jets and designer mansions, that encourages people lower down the income ladder to spend much more than they earn. In any case, consumption is at an all-time high as a proportion of income, and savings are at an all-time low: a mere 4 per cent.

Turbo-capitalism has been much less effective in actually increasing the earnings of ordinary people. Partly because really high earners have been receiving an increasing proportion of all incomes, and partly because there are now many more one-adult households, *median* family incomes rose by only one-twentieth during the nineteen years

1977–95 following deregulation. That miserably slow increase, just over one-quarter of 1 per cent per year, was evidently not enough to satisfy the heightened impulse to consume, and the result is the present mountain of personal debt, cause certain of a recession at a date as yet uncertain.

Richer Americans collect interest on trillions of dollars of deposits, bonds and mortgage loans. Yet because total savings by all Americans are so meager, the net foreign debt of the United States is fast approaching $1 trillion, the equivalent of several years of the country's economic growth. Foreigners hold hundreds of billion dollars of US Government bonds – the dollar notes circulating all over the world are not even counted in the debt – but the American economy is also uniquely attractive to industrial investors: where else is there both a very rich market and cheap labor? Mercedes and BMW are now producing cars in the United States with workers whose hourly cost is less than half of their German counterparts, yet both could sell all their local output just in California and a few more states.

More than content to see foreigners investing in the United States, themselves eager to invest abroad to benefit from higher interest rates, dividends or direct profits, utterly convinced as a matter of faith beyond any self-interested consideration that all obstacles to free trade should be eliminated, elite Americans do not merely approve of globalization. They treasure it as their only common ideology, almost a religion. Faithfully reflecting their priorities, seemingly indifferent to the protests of non-elite Americans damaged by imports, all recent US Presidents and their administrations have pressured governments around the world to remove any and all trade and investment barriers as rapidly as possible. They have also relentlessly advocated all forms of privatization and deregulation, without which free trade is mere theory, thereby automatically promoting the spread of turbo-capitalism, knowingly or not.

Turbo-Capitalism Conquers the World

Encouraged by the spread of the very American notion that whatever is efficient is automatically desirable, implying that nations exist to sustain economies rather than the other way round, propelled by justified fears that to resist it guarantees long-term economic decline, powerfully promoted by local interests eager to profit from it, turbo-capitalism is spreading far and wide outside the United States. Already broadly established in the United Kingdom, where Margaret Thatcher would claim to have independently invented it, turbo-capitalism is rapidly penetrating continental Europe from Germany to Greece, as well as eastern Europe to Moscow and beyond. It is sweeping away the remnants of discredited Latin American statism, and spreading through all the developing parts of Asia. Only in France and Japan does the attempt persist to defend old ways, secure jobs and high wages, and in both countries resistance is weakening by the day.

Everywhere it reaches, turbo-capitalism generates new wealth from all the resources released by the competition-powered destruction of inefficient practices, firms and entire industries that were previously state-owned, or subsidized, or protected by regulations or tariffs. Also destroyed, of course, are the secure jobs of the employees they once sheltered, while at the same time the architects and beneficiaries of change enrich themselves at an unprecedented rate, on an unprecedented scale.

There is only one Bill Gates who could afford to buy himself an aircraft carrier for every birthday. But all countries that have undergone turbo-capitalist change, from the United Kingdom to Argentina, from Finland to New Zealand, now have their new billionaires or at least centi-millionaires, as they all have their new poor. They are the unemployed or part-time employed, or poorly re-employed of no particular skill, who were once on the more generous and utterly secure payrolls of wasteful state industries and public utilities now privatized, of overstaffed bureaucracies now drastically reduced, or inefficient private businesses that could not survive the removal of the internal regulations and external trade barriers that once protected their inefficiency from both domestic and foreign competitors. Cities such as Buenos Aires, where a modest affluence was the norm, now contain hundreds of thousands of these new poor, but they are also to be found in some numbers in Helsinki or Auckland, as in the less fortunate parts of the United Kingdom.

Argentina is entirely typical of newly turbo-capitalist countries. It is no longer steadily declining from its original wealth, derived from colossal grain and beef exports, into long-term impoverishment masked by ever-expanding public employment and financed in great part by printing banknotes. Its youth already has many new opportunities in an expanding array of new enterprises, modern trades and technological professions, and will have many more opportunities in the future if all goes well, and no political explosion occurs to interrupt a very painful transition. For it is not only a lost generation of middle-aged unemployables that is paying the price of this crossing of the desert to a turbo-capitalist promised land. As in the United States and the United Kingdom, those who keep their jobs or find new ones must now do so for sharply differentiated earnings: stagnant or actually declining if in routine occupations; steady, rising, or even exploding if they have skills or talents that no computer or machine can replace, and that happen to be much in demand in Argentina or anywhere in the entire world.

Manual workers and routine clericals, whose relatively good wages used to be assured by Argentina's powerful trade unions regardless of productivity, now earn less, sometimes much less. Turbo-capitalism, however, is a destroyer of all privilege, not merely that of unionized workers. Shopkeepers who used to have their own little local monopolies are being displaced *en masse* by cheaper supermarkets and chain stores. The many trades sheltered by hard-to-get licenses or permits or exclusive social connections have been opened up to competition, reducing earnings in many cases. Even the employees of booming Buenos Aires investment banks now often earn much less than they did, for what was once an almost inherited occupation in the closed world of Argentine private finance must now be internationally competitive – and often enough their employer is now a foreign bank or investment house that recognizes no privileges of caste, race or family heritage.

Argentina is also typical of newly turbo-capitalist countries in that its overall economic progress has so far created many more losers than winners among its people. Losers have the vote in democratic countries, including Argentina nowadays. Were it not for the fact that most losers are also parents, who may reasonably hope that their children will be gainers one day, the voting booth would soon enough stop the advance of turbo-capitalism, and even reverse it. That is what happened in France in 1997, after an exceptionally informative election campaign, devoid of moralistic posturings on abortion or drugs, in which no accusations of sexual peccadilloes were traded, and which instead amounted to an accelerated course in today's brutal economic realities. Once it became clear that dismantling the French state-controlled economy might be of great benefit some day, but would meanwhile produce more losers than winners for many years to come, enough voters decided that they would be among the losers to assure a Socialist victory. And the new government's first act was to stop the imminent privatization of several state-owned industries. Matters were not so clear-cut in Japan's 1996 elections. There too a majority of voters spurned the champions of massive deregulation in favor of the more cautious Liberal Democratic party. Its leaders were just as insistent in promising deregulation, but their well-known obedience to Japan's bureaucrats suggested that they would do as little as possible to implement their promises, and that too very slowly.

It is not that most voters in either France or Japan ignore the merits of turbo-capitalism. They too want their countries to open up their economies to competition, some day. Just as the young and lusty St Augustine did when praying to be made chaste, they desire the ruthless economic discipline of turbo-capitalism – but not yet.

All rising forces evoke resistance, and so does turbo-capitalism. That turbo-capitalism comes from the United States – already over-powering in so many other ways, from teenage fashions to high politics – inspires confidence, but also awakens old resentments. European and Asian traditionalists bitterly resent the Americanization of their own countries, of their own children often enough, just as much as Latin America's surviving leftists. Ironically, however, the most powerful reactions to turbo-capitalism are likely to be caused not by the uncritical acceptance of American ways, but rather by their dangerously incomplete imitation. Countries around the world are importing turbo-capitalism without importing the two great forces that serve to balance its overpowering strength in the United States, and which induce most Americans to accept its harsh discipline and sharp inequalities.

Two Cheers for Nasty Lawyers

The first great force is the American legal system, with all its virtues and all its notorious peculiarities. One virtue is the exceptional ease with which ordinary people, even if quite poor, can resort to the courts in pursuit of private gain under the guise of 'damage awards': the wealth of many an American had its origins in a successful lawsuit. Another virtue is the government's activism in enforcing the laws that limit private business behavior in the public interest. To be sure, there are very few such laws in a country where private enterprise is so greatly celebrated. Those few laws, however, are often aggressively enforced.

Free markets have a natural tendency to become unfree, because they allow the most successful businesses to grow so large that they become monopolies, or near enough. Turbo-capitalism, of course, accelerates the process. As against that, the United States has the world's most stringent anti-trust (i.e. anti-monopoly) laws, often enforced with implacable determination.

If Microsoft had risen in the United Kingdom, to enrich the country by earning hugely from exports while requiring no imported raw materials at all, it would be treated as an industrial crown jewel, shielded by the establishment from any criticism or opposition, let alone anti-monopoly measures. Bill Gates would be Lord Gates of Windows, a life peer in the House of Lords.

A French Microsoft would have been become a veritable national institution, its products assiduously promoted by French commercial attachés around the world, its every need met by solicitous bureaucrats and attentive ministers. Very likely, the ministry of education would have established a special higher school to train software experts specifically to meet the company's personnel needs.

In Italy, Microsoft would be subsidized, protected and serviced at every turn by appreciative governments, with Gates a generous supporter of friendly political parties, and himself a dignified leader in public life as a Senator for Life.

A Japanese Microsoft would have been designated the country's one and only 'chosen instrument' in the global market for packaged software, just as Fujitsu is for mainframe computers, receiving very cheap finance on demand, marketing intelligence from the worldwide network of Japan Export Trade Organization offices, research support from state-funded laboratories throughout Japan, and of course immunity from any kind of anti-monopoly measures.

In the United States, by contrast, Microsoft has become the chief target of the anti-trust division of the Department of Justice, energized by the best and brightest young lawyers, doing their stint of government service before going on to the best law firms as specialists in defending corporations ... from the anti-trust division of the Department of Justice. As IBM had to, once it rose to dominate the big-computer industry, Microsoft has been forced to defend itself in the law courts from one accusation of monopolistic practices after another. First, in 1994 it had to sign a consent decree to avoid trial, renouncing some of its famously manipulative marketing practices. These included the 'bundling' at all-included prices of applications software (for word processing, etc.) with Microsoft's ubiquitous operating system, MS-DOS, later Windows, later still the aptly named Windows 95 (95 per cent of the world market), to destroy competitors who have to sell their own software separately, for money. Then in October 1997, the

Department of Justice asked a Federal judge to impose a one million dollar per day fine on Microsoft until it stops bundling its Internet Explorer 'browser' with the latest edition of Windows 95, to drive the separately sold Netscape Navigator out of business. In December 1997, it duly obtained that ruling. Microsoft, by then the dream client of several law firms, naturally appealed while continuing to prepare the launch of Windows 98. In June 1998 a Federal appeals court found in Microsoft's favor, striking down the prohibition against bundling, and sending the price of its shares above $100. But by then the Department of Justice and the attorney-generals of twenty States had filed a broader anti-trust suit against Microsoft, obtaining an early September 1998 trial date. Among other things, the Department of Justice was seeking a new prohibition, against Microsoft's insistence that computer manufacturers set their machines so that the first screen image is always the Windows 'desktop' opening page.

That Microsoft does much for the American economy is beyond doubt, yet it impresses the Department of Justice not at all. While each anti-trust accusation is ostensibly a matter of specific violations, and the government's lawyers duly ask for equally specific penalties or prohibitions, the truth is that the American interpretation of democracy does not tolerate any excessive concentration of power, no matter how it came about. In its days of great prosperity and huge cash reserves, General Motors could have become the Microsoft of cars by cutting prices low enough and long enough to drive Ford, Chrysler and Studebaker right out of the car business into other trades. Wisely, General Motors did no such thing, for a great victory in the marketplace would soon have become an even greater defeat in the courts. The government's anti-trust lawyers would have reacted to a GM monopoly by going to court to ask for its dissolution into several different companies under separate ownership – with every chance of success. That, after all, was how it all started at the beginning of the century, with the court-ordered break-up of Rockefeller's utterly dominant Standard Oil into separate companies, which have been competing with each other ever since.

Just as many countries have anti-monopoly laws without the will to enforce them, so too they have banking and stock-market regulations without also having investigators, regulators and prosecutors able and willing to enforce them. One exceptionally dramatic consequence of this gap between theory and practice was the Asian financial implosion of 1997.

Turbo-capitalism may or may not accelerate economic growth, but all three of its propelling forces accelerate the growth of finance. Although privatization is meant to achieve great things one day, in itself it adds nothing that was not there before by way of buildings, equipment, techniques or labor. Yet it immediately requires much financial activity, to 'securitize' assets into shares and bonds and then sell them, to obtain and grant bank credits, to raise project finance, and more. Deregulation likewise is meant to unleash competition that will increase efficiency in using material and human resources. In itself, however, it does not immediately increase those resources. On the other hand, enterprises liberated from restrictive rules are much more likely to use sophisticated financial services such as derivatives trading. Finally, some forms of globalization may only shift production from one country to another rather than increase it, yet all forms of globalization automatically require the exchange of foreign currencies, and may also call for the trading of futures contracts to hedge against exchange-rate changes, and perhaps more advanced swaps.

It follows that when turbo-capitalism arrives, banking of all kinds and stock markets grow much faster than the 'real economy' of farms, factories and shops. Businesses that never issued shares and bonds do so; stock exchanges are established or expanded, brokers multiply, banks are enlarged and new ones are created, along with investment houses, foreign-currency dealers, commodity traders and others. It follows too that much more needs to be done to enforce the law. If shareholders are to be protected, companies must be forced to reveal unfortunate truths in their prospectus, and executives must not be allowed to profit at their expense. If banks are to be protected, they must be forced to obey total safety limits in lending money, just as they must ensure that they know the actual financial situation of potential creditors, including their previous debts. If the public is to be protected, stockbrokers must not be allowed to rig the market, or to speculate at their clients' expense, or to favor some clients over others. And so it goes on, creating a need for up-to-date laws and procedural rules, enforced by a sufficient number of sufficiently skilled investigators, regulators and prosecutors, willing and able to do their job, undissuaded by bribes. That too is not enough, however. If mere bureaucrats are to confront well-connected corporate chiefs, tycoons, bankers and wealthy stockbrokers and financiers, they need the active political backing of their government and its leaders.

Indonesia, South Korea, Malaysia and Thailand are very different countries. Their initial troubles of 1997 were also different. What they had in common was that all four countries experienced very fast economic growth and even faster financial growth, without acquiring the bureaucratic apparatus needed to deter companies from lying to creditors and shareholders, to prevent banks from lending recklessly while borrowing abroad just as recklessly, and to ensure fairness in stock markets. Above all, there was no political will to enforce rules and laws. On the contrary, in all four countries the government itself, as well as individual leaders and their families, was deeply implicated in all that was going on: an explosion of bank credit to favored companies and individuals well beyond their capacity to repay the loans; an explosion of real estate and stock-market speculation, fed by more wildly imprudent bank loans; and an explosion of corporate and bank debt to foreign banks and investors.

To make matters very much worse, local banks mostly borrowed short term (it is cheaper) while issuing many long-term loans, so that to keep in balance they constantly needed to borrow new funds to replace the short-term debts they had to repay. Similarly, local big business that borrowed directly was like a man on a bicycle who must keep pedaling not to fall, because long-term investments in factories, equipment and office buildings were financed by short-term money in constant need of renewal. Moreover, with local capital scarce and local interest rates very high, American and European interest rates much lower, and Japanese rates ultra-low (1 per cent per year), both banks and big business borrowed dollar, yen and DM funds, which they would have to repay with their local-currency earnings. If the local currency declined against the dollar, yen or DM, the man on the bicycle would have to pedal that much harder to maintain his speed up a steeper slope.

All went well so long as all the news was good. That persuaded foreign banks to keep rolling over expired debts and eagerly lend more, and investors to keep investing; in fact they begged to be allowed to invest more (all four countries severely restricted foreign purchases of local shares). With that, the load carried by the man on the bicycle kept getting heavier. When Thailand drastically devalued its currency to remain export-competitive with China (which had devalued much earlier), the jig was up. It was the signal to sell off the currencies of Indonesia, Malaysia and then South Korea as well, to buy hard currency instead. That forced down the value of local currencies, causing yet more selling, and yet more falling. With that, the slope kept getting steeper for the cyclist because ever-bigger revenues in local currency were needed to repay the same amount of foreign-currency debt. It was obvious that many companies would not make it, causing their shares to crash, which in turn induced more investors to sell off their shares, which fell yet lower.

Not even the dogged investigators and determined regulators of the US Securities and Exchange Commission, the Federal Reserve and the Comptroller of the Currency were able to prevent the speculative explosion and crash of the savings and loan associations during the 1980s that had invested heavily in junk ('high-yield') bonds. But they did at least keep the larger commercial banks from joining in, and the SEC specifically continues to dissuade most companies and most stock dealers from most grosser forms of abuse most of the time. If Indonesia, South Korea, Malaysia and Thailand had done likewise, they would have avoided the financial collapse of 1997, and its consequences for their real economies by way of bankruptcies, unemployment and impoverishment.

That all four countries imported an American-style financial super-structure without importing an American-style understructure of laws, rules and effective enforcement was no accident: while their economies were politicized, their politics were commercialized. With the highest political leaders much engaged in business by way of their families, and the richest businessmen much engaged in politics, there was no possibility that lowly bureaucrats would feel free to investigate, expose, regulate and even prosecute their massive and conjoint violations of laws, regulations and ordinary prudence.

Two More Cheers for Greedy Lawyers

To resist monopolies and financial abuses in the public interest is fundamental, but big business is powerful in all sorts of other ways, all enhanced by turbo-capitalism. Abused consumers are fragmented, employees and suppliers are dependent, lesser competitors are out-matched. In virtually all countries, of course, there is some sort of civil law, and thus the possibility of resorting to the courts to seek redress. That, however, merely converts economic inferiority into legal inferiority in most cases. If mere consumers dissatisfied or perhaps injured by defective products, if employees treated badly, if suppliers subjected to extortion, or lesser competitors robbed by patents infringements try to sue in court for damages, they must contend with the talents and ample staffs of the leading law firms that big business can afford, and the prospect of endless delays and legal maneuvers if their case happens to be strong.

Justice may be blind, but she has her hand outstretched, and rich defendants can simply exhaust the resources of poor plaintiffs. That is an everyday reality all over the world, and it applies with particular force in the United States, which has the largest number of really big enterprises, and the weakest restraints of custom and tradition. Very few US corporations considering, say, mass dismissals would be inhibited by community disapproval, as their European or Japanese counterparts normally are. Few have a strong local identity to begin with, and fewer still act as veritable members of any local community, for all the vapid claims to that effect.

As against that, however, two peculiar features of the American legal system go a very long way towards redressing the balance. First, in contrast to the norm almost everywhere else, where the loser must pay the winner's legal costs as well as his own, American courts rarely order the payment of the winner's costs – and almost never do so if the winner has 'deep pockets'. The effect is to greatly reduce the risks of suing big corporations whose legal bills can easily run into millions of dollars. That in turn makes possible the second peculiarity, a practice prohibited or at least held unrespectable in most other countries: American lawyers are *routinely* eager to work for success ('contingency') fees alone, claiming as much as 25 or even 40 per cent of the winnings if monetary damages are awarded, nothing at all if the case is lost. Thus any plaintiff with a reasonable chance of winning substantial damages can very easily find lawyers to serve him at no cost, including some excellent ones with efficient offices and all required experts on retainer.

The unsurprising result is that big corporations, so greatly empowered by deregulation as well as by sheer magnitude and wealth, are constantly besieged by private lawsuits of every kind, energetically pressed by lawyers eager for their contingency fees. Dissatisfied consumers file many thousands of product-liability claims each year, often for huge sums; dismissed, demoted or insufficiently promoted employees file wrongful dismissal, maltreatment or sexual harassment suits, powerfully favored by numerous anti-discrimination laws if they happen to be women, or old, or handicapped, or the members of recognized racial minorities, all of whom collectively account for much of the entire labor force. Competitors, especially if much smaller and poorer, sue just as energetically on any number of grounds, from highly technical patent infringement suits to plain breach of contract, as do suppliers and clients. Shareholders sue chief executives and boards almost automatically if their stock abruptly goes down, charging malfeasance, misfeasance or nonfeasance with the aid of specialized trial lawyers who do nothing else.

Insurance companies are sued so frequently by dissatisfied claimants that their fate largely depends on the abilities of their legal departments. Road accident victims instructed by their lawyers to come into the courtroom with neckbraces or in wheelchairs easily evoke the sympathy of juries that will overlook clear evidence of drink and utter recklessness to show their compassion at the expense of automobile manufacturers and insurance companies. What product-liability lawyers can do is legendary, especially if they can tearfully appeal to juries with a widow and young orphans prominently displayed in the courtroom or, better still, the weeping parents of a dead child. Manufacturers whose cars, aircraft, boats, machinery, tools, food and drink or even toilet bowls are safely used by millions every day are almost routinely forced to pay triple punitive damages for defects not found by government inspectors, and certified only by lawyer-paid experts.

The American practice of jury trials even in civil cases, another great peculiarity, ensures that lawyers who can claim victim status for their clients can do very well even without tears, for in commercial disputes juries favor individuals over corporations, small corporations over large ones, and even very large corporations against those yet bigger, especially if they are 'from out of state' – for Texan juries, a corporation based in New York, London or even Tokyo is equally foreign.

Almost *two million* lawsuits against corporations are started each year in Federal and State courts, and business big and small must also contend with the suits pressed by local, State and Federal authorities, charging environmental, occupational safety, consumer protection, financial and, of course, anti-trust violations. One result of this ocean of litigation is to provide splendid incomes for a portion of the 700,000 lawyers who inhabit the United States, at least one of whom famously earned more than $1 billion for himself in a single case, by winning an epic multi-billion dollar award from Texaco. Total damage awards throughout the United States were last estimated at $150,000 million per year, of which at least one-quarter went to lawyers rather than their clients.

Another result, however, is the taming of big business in all sorts of ways. In truth, every kind of business is exposed to legal attacks powered by contingency fees, and small businesses are far more likely to be destroyed in the process. It is the biggest corporations, however, that have gained most in wealth and power from turbo-capitalism, not least through the opening of world markets, and it is their power that needs to be tamed to preserve the balance. When tempted to cut costs by cutting safety margins, their executives remember liability claims and refrain; when contemplating a high-handed imposition on suppliers or clients, they think of breach-of-contract suits and step back; when attracted by other people's technology, they recall what the jury did to the last big company accused of infringing the patents of an inventive small company; when top executives calculate how well they could do personally by manipulating the stock price just a little, they also calculate what a lost shareholder suit could cost them, even before the Securities and Exchange Commission gets into the act. Famously greedy American lawyers, ruthless in manipulating jurics, for whom plaintiffs are often mere puppets rather than respected clients, thus serve a higher purpose after all, by intimidating structurally greedy corporations.

There is also a personal dimension to the matter. Surrounded by deferential staffs, grandly transported in personal jets, courted by politicians in need of campaign contributions, by heads of universities proffering honorary degrees, even by foreign ministers and presidents eager to attract investments, the chiefs of the biggest US corporations could easily acquire Napoleonic pretensions. Their counterparts in Brazil or Mexico, those in some countries of Europe even, and until the crash of 1997 in Indonesia and Korea even more, can be Lords of the Universe among their retinues of secretary-concubines, servile retainers and obedient local politicians. Naturally they will not be stopped by trivial little laws or tiresome procedures from doing what they want to consumers, suppliers, lesser competitors or the environment. US corporate chiefs, by contrast, are forever consulting their lawyers to find out what they can legally do, in fear of those other lawyers out there, ready to drag them into court even when the government will not.

Finally, there is the little matter of the tax laws, and more especially of their enforcement. American conditions under turbo-capitalism greatly favor tax evasion. With most *commercial* regulations long since abolished (there are plenty of environmental and other regulations), with few permits or licenses required, the tax collectors have little information to go on. Moreover, the fiscal system relies very heavily on self-reported income taxes, as opposed to officially documented value-added or sales taxes. Finally, even though local, State and Federal authorities each collect their own revenues, there are very few different taxes in all as compared to many other countries. That alone favors evasion. Italians, by contrast, even if they fancy themselves champion evaders as many of them do, cannot avoid or evade paying a great deal of tax – much more than Americans in proportion to their incomes – simply because there are so many different taxes, more than a hundred of them.

If an American succeeds in underreporting his personal income tax without getting caught, he has solved much of his own fiscal problem. An Italian who does the same has just begun. To start with, value-added taxes are high and because all sales must be officially documented, successful evasion would require an entire chain of forgeries, difficult to manufacture and easily detected. Property taxes are also high, and virtually unavoidable – not for nothing do the Italian fiscal authorities define buildings as *immobili*. Then there are very costly annual permits, to use a car for example, which must be exhibited for all to see, as well as myriad of lesser license fees for such things as dogs, bicycles and television sets. And the list goes on.

In the United States, there is no need of such a multiplicity of taxes to capture revenues. It is not that Americans are especially honest, but rather that most of them are too frightened of the Internal Revenue Service to cheat on their taxes to any serious extent. Like its counterparts all over the world, the IRS imposes stiff penalties for bookkeeping errors that happen to favor the taxpayer. Unlike most of them, however, the IRS also routinely seeks prison sentences from Federal courts for deliberate tax evasion, and with considerable success. In very few countries – the United Kingdom is one – do convicted tax-evaders routinely end up in prison for years on end.

Because Americans who earn the very high incomes of turbo-capitalism cannot avoid paying taxes (*wealth* as such is untaxed), there is at least some redistribution going on by way of government spending. True, American income taxes are not very progressive nowadays. In contrast to top rates of 90 per cent or more in the past, the highest Federal rate is now only 38 per cent, and even in those places where local and State taxes are highest, the combined rate hardly exceeds 50 per cent. Nor does the government spend generously on the poor. Instead it is the old who benefit the most by way of free health care and pensions, given equally to old people who have nothing and to those who are very rich. Still, taxes are paid, and some are redistributed.

When turbo-capitalism penetrates more indulgent countries, however, their own new-made billionaires and millionaires can follow the traditionally rich who came before them in cheerfully evading taxes. Bribes reduce assessments and collections, often drastically. Corruption aside, fiscal administrations may be too inefficient and too vulnerable to political pressures to do their job properly, made exceedingly difficult in any case by the discreet transfer and deposit services offered by oh-so-respectable Western banks. Evaders who are not well connected may actually be caught in some cases, bribes and sheer inefficiency having failed to shield them. Even so, they hardly ever have to fear imprisonment. There are fines, of course, but fines alone are rarely enough to deter bold risk-takers, the very people who tend to benefit the most from turbo-capitalism. Thus very little of the new wealth is redistributed by way of taxes and public spending, instead accumulating without limit.

In these very different ways, some sort of equilibrium is maintained in the United States between the powerful engine of turbo-capitalism on the one hand, and the powerful brakes of the American legal system on the other. There is no such equilibrium where monopolies are unmolested or even protected by the state, where financial abuses are unchallenged, and where consumers, employees, suppliers and lesser competitors must face big business without the sharp weapon of the riskless, costless lawsuit.

Why American Winners Have No Fun

The second great force that persuades most Americans to accept the sharp inequalities of turbo-capitalism is the pervasive influence of Calvinist values. Although it was central to the faith of the Pilgrim Fathers and its tenets remain embedded in more than one form of Protestant Christianity, few Americans consciously believe in Calvinist doctrines in a religious sense. Yet a great many of them of all religions and none, who may know nothing at all about Calvinism as such, nevertheless act in accordance with its principles. How it came about that an almost forgotten religion should have left such a powerful non-religious residue is a very interesting question that has been much studied and debated. What is beyond debate is the enduring authority of Calvinist values. However often overlaid by transient moods, however often proclaimed dead and buried, they remain most vigorously strong just below the surface of American life, invisibly shaping both everyday choices and fundamental attitudes.

The Calvinist rules are quite simple, and binding. Rule Number

One is for high-earning winners. Rule Number Two is for the great mass of working people of varying affluence or poverty, but often losers in their own eyes. Rule Number Three is for the non-Calvinists among the losers, i.e. those who refuse to accept Rule Number Two, most of them poor.

The underlying Calvinist doctrine that governs Rule Number One – whereby earned wealth is no impediment to virtue, as Jesus reportedly said, but rather a sign of divine favor for the predestined – has long been forgotten. Yet its pervasive effect induces Americans to view the desire to become rich as most praiseworthy, and success in doing so as a *moral* achievement as well, for it is seen as the result of both sacrificial exertion in earning money, and self-denying restraint in spending it. Far from being viewed as self-seeking materialists, those who accumulate wealth are respected in rough proportion to the amount, so long as it is the fruit of their own individual efforts. As for the super-winners who earn the most fabulous amounts, they are greatly admired, more so than all other Americans, including the most famous war heroes. Dwight Eisenhower, President of the United States and before that the Supreme Commander who had risked the D-Day landings and then led the Allies to victory over Germany, was much admired, but was quite typical in his own deep admiration for the wealthy businessmen he first encountered in his White House days: they had made it on their own, without armies to fight for their victories.

Super-winners are respected and admired not only for what they do, but also for what they know, or rather for what it is assumed that they must know. They are often asked to pronounce on the great questions of the day, even if far removed from their fields of competence. During 1997, for example, both the champion software marketeer Bill Gates and the champion currency speculator George Soros were constantly and respectfully cited in the American media on a great variety of subjects, such as the conduct of public education, or the control of narcotics. Their interviewers assumed as a matter of course that the extent of their benevolent wisdom corresponds to the size of their incomes. That reverential attitude derives directly from Rule Number One, which goes beyond the moral justification of money making. Far from being condemned for greed, winners are held in the highest regard, and the greatest winners of all are almost in odor of sanctity.

There is, however, a puritanical catch: winners are not supposed actually to *enjoy* the wealth they accumulate. Instead they are obliged to keep working hard to become even richer, refraining from the leisurely and sexual diversions of their non-Calvinist counterparts of Europe, Latin America or Southeast Asia. With the exception of entertainers, high-paid athletes and a few eccentrics, high-earning Americans of working age conform to Rule Number One to a remarkable extent. Very brief holidays as well as outings and parties are allowed under the rubric of rest and relaxation, so as to prepare for yet more work, but that is all. The month-long holidays of their European counterparts are entirely unknown. Instead of the uproarious goings-on of the topless French Riviera, still today a summer gathering of Europe's seriously rich, for their American counterparts there are mostly the worthy encounters of Martha's Vineyard, where public issues are much discussed and little is drunk, the grim pursuit of physical fitness in such places as Aspen, Colorado, the anxious social rituals of Palm Beach, Florida, and much playing of golf, tennis and skiing. Even at play, Calvinist winners contrive to enjoy themselves as little as possible. Not coincidentally, their cold-weather Caribbean refuges feature almost uneatable food. In the most expensive residential clubs of the Bahamas, where a 'room' may include a private pool and two bedchambers with baths en suite, very elegant restaurants facing magnificent beaches serve deep-frozen fish deeply fried in heavy oil, tinned mushroom soup and pre-cut salads covered in thick sauce poured straight from the bottle. A European clientele would protest and flee. Their wealthy American clientele dutifully eats without complaint.

They may not be classic Puritans, constantly oppressed by the thought that somebody, somewhere, may be having a good time, but the Calvinist winners are certainly puritanical for themselves. When American businessmen travel to Paris or Tokyo, they often embarrass their hosts by engaging in the exotic practice of bringing wives along, which automatically rules out the customary forms of relaxation after the day's work is done. Back at home, very few American super-winners avail themselves of the secretarial concubines and trophy mistresses that denote the rank elsewhere; at most they may have trophy wives, not at all the same thing.

The disdain for pure enjoyment even on holiday is so strong that the Aspen Institute and its many imitators have made an industry out of it. High-earning winners as well as the hereditary rich are invited to Aspen and other such resorts not to gambol and play, but rather to participate for large fees or larger donations in earnest 'seminars', where the world's grimmest problems are gravely dissected. There

19

may be fun on the side all the same, but always with the reassuring thought that one is really there for the seminars, on pollution, drugs, world hunger, wars and others such.

There is a far more important catch to Rule Number One, yet another reflection of long-forgotten Calvinist doctrine: because wealth is a divine reward for *individual* effort and self-restraint, it should not be passed on to children and descendants, but instead should be given away to pay for 'good works'. In the past, rich Americans used their money to establish schools, universities, hospitals, orphanages and refuges for the deserving poor. Nowadays they establish charitable foundations that pursue all manner of aims, from radical political causes to the protection of plant life in Madagascar.

Warren Buffett, by far the most respected financier in the United States, its second-richest citizen by all accounts, and obviously determined to do his duty as a role-model, has publicly declared that he will pass no money at all to his children or their families – he means to give it all away for charitable purposes. Bill Gates, America's certified super-winner and richest citizen, has announced that he intends to give away 95 per cent of his wealth. Warren Buffett is an extreme case – as befits one so keen to be an example to others. In reality, few Americans disinherit their children. But there is incontrovertible evidence that rich and ultra-rich Americans are uniquely reluctant to pass on their wealth intact to their children, preferring to give much of it away: the existence of some 40,000 foundations with combined assets of roughly $225,000 million testifies to that.

The overall effect of Rule Number One is to legitimize both morally and socially the accumulation of wealth. The further effect of the rule is to reduce envy greatly, and thus its political or even violent expression. Why should the poor envy those who enrich themselves, if they neither enjoy their wealth nor keep it all for their own families? All that is left to envy is the satisfaction of hard work, the moral rewards of charitable gifts and bequests, and social prestige. That is still quite a lot, of course, but not enough to inspire violent hatred, or even the ordinary political forms of resentment.

Why American Losers Accept Their Fate

Rule Number Two, for the economy's losers, reflects exactly the same Calvinist doctrine as the first rule, but in reverse: failure is the result not of misfortune or injustice, but of divine disfavor. Just as the ability to become very rich is next to sanctity, an inability to do so is next to sin, indeed almost sinful in itself. Many Americans who may be rather affluent, but who cannot earn whatever amounts of money they consider adequate and proper, are oppressed by a powerful sense of guilt. Living in a country that so greatly respects and admires high-earning winners, losers find it hard to preserve their self-esteem.

A great many merely lead lives of quiet desperation, searching for distractions, eager to immerse themselves in whatever will take their minds off their failure, from vehement religion to televised sports. Others remedy despair with addiction, to drink, to drugs and to food above all, the only fully legal addiction, and hence very widespread. At the beginning of the twentieth century, a well-rounded belly, barely contained by a sober waistcoat, nicely accented by a gold watch-chain was the mark of the winner. President Taft was only the most prominent of the 300-pounders at the top of American society. Fashions change. Along with cigarette smoking (cigars are fashionable once again), obesity has become the most common attribute of the contemporary American loser. Americans are much fatter than Europeans, let alone Japanese. But this is an average of extreme deviations: American winners are usually thin, often unnaturally so, the result of severe diets and frantic exercise, while the poor are often very fat, making it even harder for them to find tolerably good jobs in a country where fatness equals failure. Less legal addictions have even worse consequences. Low self-esteem caused by low income sets off a vicious circle of what the caring professions call 'dysfunctional behavior', which further reduces income.

Beyond its repercussions for individual lives, Rule Number Two has powerful political consequences. More than any other factor, it explains why the United States has never had a significant socialist party: losers blame themselves rather than the system, they hate themselves instead of resenting the winners. It explains why no major presidential candidate has even tried to challenge the sharp inequalities of turbo-capitalism. The result is that in a country which is literally of the winners, governed by winners for winners, the losers have no political expression of their own. Nobody denies that to them – it is the losers themselves who want so much to identify with winners that they deny their votes to any candidate who tries to represent their interests. So, many losers vote for one or another of the winners' candidates; others prefer not to vote at all, not only because of lethargy or ignorance (as the winners always say), but simply because they have nobody to vote for. In recent national elections, almost half of all the eligible voters of the United States did not bother to cast their vote.

True, there are also plenty of non-Calvinists among the losers; mostly they are actually poor rather than just under-achievers by their own estimate. It is for them that there is Rule Number Three: those who do not accept Rule Number Two, who are not paralyzed by guilt and who are too uneducated to express their resentment legally, are destined to end up behind bars. Strict laws that prohibit many things that are allowed or at least tolerated in other countries; very strict enforcement; and long prison sentences, including an abundance of forty, fifty and sixty-year terms as well as mandatory life sentences without parole, all implement Rule Number Three very effectively. Only the sadly impoverished and chaotic Russian Federation has as great a proportion of its citizens in prison as the affluent and well-governed United States – 1.8 million at the last count. Not surprisingly, by 1998 crime was reportedly in sharp decline in many American cities, in seeming vindication of the ultra-tough policing of New York's Mayor Giuliani and of all his emulators in cities across America. The miracle had other explanations as well: a temporary dip in the population of youths with the ageing of the baby-boom generation, and the displacement of crime to the suburbs, where perpetrators and victims have both moved in large numbers. But in large measure, crime was bound to fall because so many potential offenders are already locked up.

There is a definite process at work, an almost inevitable sequence. Because of Rule Number Two, no political party or no presidential candidacy can emerge to express the envy and resentment of non-Calvinist losers, those who refuse to join the majority in blaming themselves for their condition, turning any bitterness they feel inwards, against themselves. The educated among non-Calvinist losers have other choices – the teaching profession at every level harbors great numbers of them – but for the uneducated there is only one possible form of expression: to break the law, by engaging in criminal activities such as murder, armed robbery, violent assault, rape and the smoking of marijuana in pipes or home-made cigarettes. Arrests across the United States for that crime alone – simple possession of soft drugs for personal use – were running at some 400,000 a year by 1995, almost one-third of the 1.5 million drug-related arrests, which in turn account for one-tenth of the 15.1 million arrests for all offenses excluding traffic violations.[4] And drug arrests are disproportionately likely to lead to prison sentences. At the last count, almost 300,000 people were imprisoned for drug offenses alone, with many more sentenced for something else as well.

A few were behind bars for the big-time smuggling of large quantities of hard drugs, but the vast majority were in for petty street sales, or even the simple possession of tiny amounts of marijuana if they were unlucky in choosing their jurisdiction. Because the act of smoking the leaves, stem or resin of *Cannabis sativa* plants does not strike the heart and conscience of all humans everywhere as a self-evident crime, some District Attorneys vigorously prosecute marijuana possession, seeking jail terms, while others seek only fines, and others still do not prosecute at all. Following their lead, some police departments devote great efforts and some ingenuity to the task, such as blackmailing students into becoming informers; others will arrest only those who blatantly smoke marijuana in public, and others still contrive to ignore even that. The same variance applies to street sales, treated as a major crime in some places, almost ignored in others. Capricious enforcement and capricious prosecution reflect the arbitrary quality of drug prohibitionism.

Yet reformers who argue that the American 'war against drugs' has failed, including Mr George Soros in one of his benevolent roles, are missing the point. It is true that the intended aim, to eliminate addiction, is an impossible fantasy given the infinite range of possible addictions even if every one of the classic drugs were to disappear. It is true that costly efforts to intercept imported drugs are entirely futile, except perhaps as a form of protectionism for home-grown crops and synthetics. And it is true that the cinematic 'drug busts' of the Drug Enforcement Agency, FBI and police forces everywhere only serve the interests of competing suppliers, just as eradication efforts overseas merely shift production from one place to another. All these things are true. But they do not settle the issue. To lock up 400,000 non-Calvinist losers for drug offenses alone, and at least as many again for drug-connected crimes, is a very major contribution to the total of 1.8 million successfully removed from circulation, most of them male, most of them young, most of them poorly educated, and more than one-third of them Blacks, the least Calvinist of the American poor. Should drugs be decriminalized, as Mr Soros and many others

---

[4] Department of Justice, Federal Bureau of Investigations, *Uniform Crime Reports, 1995 Summary*, 13 October 1996.

would wish, on what grounds could non-Calvinist losers be locked up?

With an extraordinary proportion of the potentially most restive, young, male population behind bars, crime rates have been plunging, with obviously beneficial consequences for public order. As it is, American inner cities, with their high concentrations of turbo-capitalism's losers, are in a state of permanent low-level insurrection, which makes them dangerous ground both for Whites and for middle-class Blacks, who are far more likely to have reasons to visit them. Were it not for the incarceration of so many young males, inner-city slums would be not only denied areas, but sources of serious gang attacks on the more fortunate city districts and nearby suburbs. Had the population of South-Central Los Angeles not consisted predominantly of children, women and old people, had it included a normal proportion of young males, it is much more likely that Beverly Hills would have been burned down during the Rodney King riots of 1992. Everyday life in New York, Chicago, Boston, Atlanta and other large cities would be far more dangerous than it is, if their populations were not significantly altered by the mass imprisonment of the non-Calvinist losers who are most likely to be violent.

The three rules are interconnected, in what one might call the 'Calvinist system', in which winners diminish envy by self-restraint, most losers blame only themselves for their fate, and both vent their frustrations by demanding the harsh punishment of rebellious losers. The State of Idaho, much larger than England with its 83,557 square miles of beautiful mountains and lush valleys extending to the Canadian border, its vast ranches and thriving new high-technology industries in its few small cities, achieves Calvinist perfection. Of its 1.2 million people, 95 per cent of them white, very few are poor and fewer still are a burden on public assistance, if only because there is a ceiling of $276 per month per family, regardless of size, on State welfare payments, which are also subject to a lifetime limit of two years. And the good people of Idaho need have little fear of crime as they go about their self-reliant, hard-working, church-going lives, partly because they are so good, and partly because few law-breakers are at liberty to disturb their lives. All the usual crimes are punished with long prison sentences: with parole for good behavior abolished in one of several waves of increasingly severe legislation, the *average* time actually served in Idaho's prisons by all inmates (78 per cent non-violent in 1996) is 44 months. Not all would be considered outright criminals elsewhere, but writing unfunded checks, driving drunk, driving without a valid license and the possession of any amount of any narcotic are jail-time felonies in Idaho. Prisons are expensive, but while total spending for the poor amounted to some $15 million in 1997, $200 million were found in the State budget to build a new prison – to be privately managed by a for-profit contractor, of course.[5]

The Perils of Incomplete Imitation

Americans are natural-born missionaries, unencumbered by excessive skepticism. Products of a nation defined by abstract ideas rather than race, religion or culture, they are constantly advocating some new idea or other. When they believe in something, even if they only started believing it that very day, Americans immediately want to convert the entire world to their latest enthusiasm. In the past, that has been true of any number of fad diets, and of fundamental democratic ideals, of cigarette smoking when the world still had to be converted from pipes a century ago, and of stringent smoking prohibitions most recently. Each time, there is not merely a cold intellectual certainty that the only truth has finally been found, but a passionate desire to have it universally recognized.

At present, almost all elite Americans, with corporate chiefs and fashionable economists in the lead, are utterly convinced that they have discovered the winning formula for economic success – the *only* formula – good for every country, rich or poor, good for all individuals willing and able to heed the message, and, of course, good for elite Americans: PRIVATIZATION + DEREGULATION + GLOBALIZATION = TURBO-CAPITALISM = PROSPERITY. Business people all over the world mostly agree with them – only a few, in a few countries, have some reservations. Wall Street professionals and their colleagues in stock exchanges from the City of London to Tokyo, from Milano to Santiago de Chile, and as far afield as Harare in Zimbabwe, enthusiastically agree without any reservations whatsoever, and so do millions of wealthy or hopeful investors. Increasingly, political leaders almost everywhere also accept that simple formula for economic success, ensuring its ever wider application in one country after another. The result is that Argentina, Brazil, Chile and so on through

[5] Timothy Egan, 'As Idaho prospers, prisons fill up while spending on the poor lags', *New York Times*, 16 April 1998, p. 1; p. A16.

the alphabet have been importing a dangerously unstable version of American turbo-capitalism, because the formula is incomplete.

The first thing missing, as we have seen, is a legal system – not just laws on paper – that enables the government itself and even the economically vulnerable to tame big business somewhat, enough at any rate for coexistence. Always needed, this counterweight is now indispensable to offset the power of wealth released by turbo-capitalism. All countries have their legal systems, of course, and some include serious obstacles to all forms of business, big, medium or small, by way of onerous requirements for permits, licenses and procedures. Very few, however, provide effective instruments for the enforcement of anti-monopoly laws, for the control of financial abuse by banks and stockbrokers, and for comprehensive tax collection. Still less do they allow consumers, suppliers and lesser competitors to employ the law to contain the overpowering strength of big business. Some of the missing laws have been legislated in some countries – consumer protection laws in the American style are spreading globally – others will no doubt be enacted. What cannot be done by the simple will of parliaments is to construct the bureaucracies that will actually enforce laws old and new against those best placed to resist them.

The other counterweight missing from the formula is just as indispensable and even more difficult to acquire: the three Calvinist rules. In some cultures, functional equivalents are already present. Japan, for example, has its own rendition, which requires modesty in winners, and persuades losers that their work – any work at all – is as worthy as that of any winner. It is enough to watch the deportment of the baggage porters at Narita airport to know that Japan's all-work-is-equal myth remains in good working order. In lesser degree the Chinese share similar attitudes, as do other Asian cultures in various ways.

So far, however, in too many countries undergoing turbo-capitalist change, the winners enjoy their wealth all too visibly, are enormously eager to enrich their children, and they give away very little, except to the Church. As for the losers, what they feel is not guilt but bitter resentment. And neither group is filled with the moral certainty required to punish losers who break the rules. The record of the US economy suggests that it might take twenty years or more for the new wealth of turbo-capitalism to begin to seep downward. Will the less fortunate of Argentina, Brazil, Chile and the rest of them wait that long? Or will the irresistible force of turbo-capitalism collide with popular opposition?

TWO

What is Turbo-Capitalism?

Its advocates use no such term. They simply call it *the* free market, but by that bit of short-hand they mean very much more than the freedom to buy and sell. What they celebrate, preach and demand is private enterprise liberated from government regulation, unchecked by effective trade unions, unfettered by sentimental concerns over the fate of employees or communities, unrestrained by customs barriers or investment restrictions, and molested as little as possible by taxation. What they insistently demand is the privatization of state-owned businesses of all kinds, and the conversion of public institutions, from universities and botanic gardens to prisons, from libraries and schools to old people's homes, into private enterprises run for profit. What they promise is a more dynamic economy that will generate new wealth, while saying nothing about the distribution of any wealth, old or new.

They call it the free market, but I call it turbo-charged capitalism, or turbo-capitalism for short, because it is so profoundly different from the strictly controlled capitalism that flourished from 1945 until the 1980s, and which brought the sensational novelty of mass affluence to the peoples of the United States, Western Europe, Japan and all other countries that followed in their paths.

Extremes converge, so it is not all that surprising that the new turbo-capitalism has much in common with the Soviet version of communism. It too offers but a single model and a single set of rules for every country in the world, ignoring all differences of society, culture and temperament. Controlled capitalism, by contrast, was controlled very differently in the United States, Western Europe and Japan, though in each case the aim was to set some limits on competition, sacrificing some of its bounties to stabilize industries and the lives of those who depended on them.

In the United States, the country of lawyers and big business, competition was strictly regulated by law in a long list of industries from airlines to natural gas, and by the market power of dominant corporations in several more. Either way, stable industries provided stable, well-paid employment, though top managers had to be content with meager salaries – in those days, very few chief executives earned more than thirty times as much as line employees, a miserably low ratio by current standards.

In Western Europe with its strong guild traditions, where democratic socialism set the post-1945 agenda even for non-socialist governments, competition was restricted only in the retail trades, the professions and a few industries including agriculture, but virtually all employees were shielded from competitive upheavals by stringent labor laws. While the American version of controlled capitalism protected corporations from each other and their employees only indirectly, the European version focused directly on the welfare of employees, by favoring strong trade unions, by making it very difficult to dismiss anyone, and by imposing all manner of obligations upon employers, from paid maternity leave to guaranteed severance payoffs of at least one month of pay for each year in the job. Beyond that, 'welfare state' programs assisted all citizens, with free or heavily subsidized medical care, non-contributory old-age pensions for those who had failed to participate in national-insurance schemes, and long-term unemployment benefits. The generosity of these programs varied from country to country, ranging from the heights of Germany and Sweden, where the long-term unemployed still now receive enough money to enjoy lengthy annual holidays abroad, to the relative austerity of Spanish provisions. But the average European was certainly better protected than his American counterpart even in the 1960s, when American per capita incomes were still much higher.

In Japan, where elite bureaucrats imposed their own sense of national aims on both corporate managers and consumers, weak industries were protected, rising industries were encouraged, and all sectors of the economy were directed to assure full employment, as they still are today, for all the recent talk of deregulation.

According to the enthusiasts of today's turbo-capitalism, all three

Three Versions of Controlled Capitalism

The West European Model

Aim: to shield weaker groups from adverse market forces.

For all employees: no dismissals without proven misconduct, severance payoffs start at 1 month's pay/year worked, 4 weeks of paid vacation, extra pay for overtime – all guaranteed by law (more negotiated by unions). France: 35-hour week.

For trade unions: strike breaking with non-union labor forbidden; 'closed shops' allowed. In larger German companies, unions must be represented on boards of directors.

For agriculture: subsidies and protection from foreign competition. Individual farmers assisted by aid programs.

For shopkeepers: strict licensing – to limit/prohibit competition from new shops, specially large-scale discount stores and supermarkets.

For 'strategic' industries: protection from foreign competition by state ownership or licensing; support by direct subsidies and preferential purchasing.

Comprehensive public assistance for aged, disabled, unmarried mothers, long-term unemployed; largely free health care for substantially all residents.

The Japanese Model

Aims: full employment, industrial leadership.

For shopkeepers: large-scale stores and supermarkets strictly limited in number and location. No-discount supplier contracts allowed. Competition not on price but quality.

For farmers, fishermen: high production subsidies; protection from foreign competition by tariffs, quotas, de facto import bans. Support payments.

For traditional straw, wood and leather artisans: protection from cheaper East Asian imports; local 'cultural' subsidies and concessionary facilities.

For favored high-technology industries: research and development subsidies, generous government orders, protection from imports.

For processing industries disadvantaged by higher energy/raw material costs: informal protection from imports, by preferential intra-group purchasing.

For airlines, railways, bus lines, ferry services: restrictive licensing.

The American Model, 1930s–1970s

Aim: shield sectors from 'disruptive' competition.

Under Federal or State laws, regulatory bodies set tariffs for air, rail, truck, bus and pipeline transport to prevent price cutting. Telecommunications are regulated monopolies. Natural gas and oil well-head prices are set by adjudication. Commercial and savings banks (S & Ls) subject to mandatory deposit rates (no rate competition allowed). Inter-state banking forbidden, to protect small local banks.

Agricultural production is subsidized. Export subsidies. Aid for small farmers.

Many industries are oligopolies subject to anti-trust restraints: 'price leadership' stops price cutting.

---

methods boiled down to pernicious government interference, which was bound to cause grotesque inefficiencies and slow economic growth. Yet, to their great and continuing embarrassment, growth under all three methods was much more rapid in the 1950s, 1960s and 1970s than it is today. Evidently there was not all that much inefficiency, or perhaps there was, but it was outweighed by the hidden advantages of stability: secure incomes sustain families that save more, providing more capital for others to invest, and they also invest more themselves, in the human capital of their children. But it is easy to prove that uncompetitive practices are inefficient, while the chain of consequences that runs from social stability to economic growth is far more complex, and passes through certain psychological linkages that are alien territory for economists.

In the United States, as in Western Europe and Japan, it was accepted without question that free-market competition was the best way of doing business. In all three it was recognized that the constant striving of profit-seekers to exploit natural, human, capital and knowledge resources as efficiently as possible does not merely earn wealth, but actually creates it out of nothing. As more profitable enterprises outbid less profitable ones for the employees, properties, capital and technical expertise they need to expand, unused, under-used or misused resources are recycled to increase the value of the goods and services produced by the entire economy. Always dynamic and often brutal, with its bankruptcies and industrial downfalls that engulf people, communities and entire regions, 'creative destruction' is the very engine of capitalist prosperity, the source of its constant innovation. Unless unprofitable practices, firms and industries are destroyed by competition, releasing resources with which new enterprises can be created, there can be no economic growth at all except to the small extent that population growth increases the labor force, new techniques are invented, or more natural resources are found.

That was the secret of capitalist success never uncovered by the KGB's many spies. The Soviet Union's grossly overmanned factories, filled with antiquated machinery producing outdated goods, its grossly overmanned farms, dotted with abandoned tractors rusting away for the lack of simple repairs, and its grossly overmanned service sector of decrepit shops, rotting warehouses, shabby cafeterias and miserable public transport were all monuments to the inadequacy of investment and innovation on its own, without creative destruction.

The Soviet Union certainly invested enormously in both infra-structures and machinery for its factories and farms, strangling the

30

supply of housing and consumer goods to do so. Along with all that capital investment, there was plenty of new technology too, some stolen by spies, much more of it developed by Soviet scientists and engineers, who were world leaders in some critical fields, such as metallurgy. Even more technology was purchased from the West with the foreign exchange earned by oil, timber, diamond and fur exports. To acquire technological innovation in bulk and very rapidly, Soviet ministries bought complete factories from the West, with all their equipment from assembly lines to hand-tools, and with the detailed know-how of Western technicians.

With vast natural resources and a well-educated population, the Soviet Union thus had everything it needed to achieve a broad prosperity, except for just one thing: there was no creative destruction at work, no competitive market pressure that would drive unprofitable factories, farms and shops out of business, releasing their labor, capital and properties for better uses. A brand-new plant imported whole from Italy would manufacture modern cars on automated production lines, alongside old plants that turned out badly outdated cars with ten times as many employees per unit of output. But the new plant could not expand to innovate the entire industry, because it was not free to borrow and invest more capital and hire more employees, both being assigned by the bureaucrats in charge – to old and new plants alike. With competition absent, old car plants, along with every sort of obsolete activity, stayed in business forever, each keeping its share of capital and labor, and indeed getting more of both year after year. The overall result was to waste the world's largest store of natural resources, huge amounts of capital that left the population in poverty, and the skills and talents of a vast labor force.

It was in the full knowledge of its supreme value that competitive destruction was nevertheless controlled in the United States until the 1980s, as it still is to a diminishing extent in Western Europe, and much more so in Japan.

Controlled Capitalism

American politicians venturing abroad during the Cold War years were forever preaching the boundless virtues of free enterprise to errant foreigners everywhere; they never tired of repeating the central truth that markets can be cleared only by the free interplay of supply and demand – Adam Smith's 'invisible hand' – so that all attempts to impose prices by government order are bound to fail, leaving wasteful surpluses if set too high, or else causing shortages and black markets if set too low. And yet, until the 1980s, in the United States itself the following industries were all strictly regulated by Federal, State or local boards, commissions, bureaus or departments, gatherings of bureaucrats, politicians and assorted worthies, who set fares, tariffs or other sorts of prices with their own very visible hands:

- airlines
- inter-state trucking
- inter-state bus lines
- inter-state railroads
- telephone and all other telecommunications
- commercial banking
- savings and loan (S & L) associations
- almost 90 per cent of agriculture
- natural gas and
- almost every electricity, gas, water and sewerage utility

Anyone reading the thick volumes that record the hearings of the Texas Railroad Commission, which by virtue of some ancient law of *circa* AD 1936 was empowered to set the well-head prices of natural gas (and of each type of petroleum condensate), will come across 'fair' or 'reasonable' or 'customary' prices, and sometimes even fair, reasonable *and* customary prices, but never plain old *prices*, as per the free interplay of supply and demand, etc.

The same was true of all other boards, commissions, bureaus or departments with price-fixing powers. All existed for one reason only: not to protect consumers from overcharging, but to protect producers from undercharging, from 'cut-throat' price competition – that is, genuine free-market competition – by which successful enterprises can increase their sales, eventually driving less successful enterprises towards extinction. The American system of regulated industries squarely obstructed 'creative destruction', the very engine of capitalist progress. But it was done for a purpose that seemed worthy enough: to stabilize entire industries and the jobs of all who worked in them, from the telephone operators of Ma Bell to the farmers who were shielded from the explosive volatility of commodity markets by guaranteed minimum prices for their bushels of wheat.

Eastern Airlines could compete as much as it wanted with National Airlines on the New York–Miami route, but only by offering – or just claiming – better cabin service, meals and so on, not by fare cutting. Identical air fares were ordained for both airlines by the Civil Aviation Bureau, whose staff engaged in recondite cost-plus calculations to set its own 'just' fare for the route, as for all routes in the United States. Because no airline could take away their New York–Miami business by offering cheaper fares, both Eastern and National were essentially secure, and in turn the providers of secure, well-paid jobs. In the absence of improvident remarriages or other costly vices, an airline mechanic could own a house and pay for the college education of two or three children, an impossibility for many pilots nowadays, let alone mechanics.

On the other hand, the chief executive officers of Eastern and National, as of all airlines, were essentially administrators. They therefore received million-dollar salaries that would evoke the ridicule and contempt of their successors – the acrobats who run today's deregulated airlines, perpetually caught up in fare wars, always only a slow season away from bankruptcy. Each of them demands at least a hundred times a mechanic's salary, if not twice that – a level somewhat more easily achieved because the pay of airline mechanics has declined somewhat in the two decades since deregulation. Also penalized, of course, were the passengers, who had to pay the set fare or else travel by car, bus or train because there were no discount fares or discount airlines.

Because Eastern and National were still private firms, for all their detailed regulation, with shareholders who would dump their holdings if profits and dividends were too low, and because gross incompetence would still lead to bankruptcy, both still had to be reasonably efficient. But they certainly did not have to pursue extreme cost-cutting measures to survive. When a Valuejet airliner crashed in 1996, it was discovered that the aircraft in question had been bought second-hand from Turkish Airlines, and was almost twenty-five years old; that essential loading and maintenance work had been contracted out to the lowest bidder; and that the aircrew was recruited among those willing to work for very little: my maid earns $24,000 a year, while Valuejet co-pilots were paid $25,000. None of these practices would have been conceivable before the deregulation that started in 1978, let alone allowed.

Similar arrangements prevailed in all other regulated industries. Savings and loan associations, for example, were ostensibly free to compete as they wished – except that the interest rates paid to depositors and the mortgage rates paid by borrowers were fixed nationwide. That made it impossible for any one S & L to grow by offering higher rates to depositors and/or charging lower interest rates on its loans. Some S & Ls grew nonetheless, by achieving superior administrative efficiencies that reduced their costs, allowing them to attract more customers by adding branches, offering better service or simply advertizing. Before they were deregulated in the 1980s, S & Ls were famous for their 3–5–6 rule: 3 per cent paid to depositors; 5 per cent charged to mortgage borrowers; on the golf links by 6 p.m.

In exchange for ample but unspectacular salaries, S & L managers were only required to administer prudently the money they took in from depositors. They did not have to be hyper-enterprising financial acrobats or even especially talented in money matters. It was not a lack of enterprise that becalmed the trusty providers of America's home mortgages, but severe restrictions that kept them out of anything resembling a speculative venture.

In the 1980s, after deregulation, S & Ls became much more famous – for their colossal bankruptcies. Left free to attract deposits by paying higher interest rates, a new breed of acrobatic S & L managers did so with a vengeance, attracting huge amounts by offering three or four times the measly 3 per cent of regulated days. Naturally they increased their own pay and bonuses in proportion, no longer earning twenty times as much as ordinary tellers, but a hundred, two hundred or three hundred times as much. At that point it only remained for them to find borrowers who would pay even more interest than the very high rates paid to depositors. Aspiring home-owners could not pay such rates, of course, but real-estate speculators did, and so did hotel speculators, gambling casino speculators and even more generous crooks, who did not bother actually to buy any real estate or build any hotels, casinos or anything else.

Even crooked speculators were in short supply, so it was fortunate for the hyperactive S & L managers that there was a very easy solution at hand: they simply bought 'high-yield' bonds from Drexel and other Wall Street issuers of their ilk, undeterred by their more common name of 'junk bonds' and their formal description as 'not-investment-grade' bonds, guaranteed only by the dubious credit of corporations that were unable to raise money from prudent lenders. In the end, it was only the stodgy S & Ls that survived, while the taxpayer had to refund hundreds of billions of dollars to depositors in hundreds of failed S & Ls. Thousands of humble employees lost their jobs. Most managers of bankrupt S & Ls, on the other hand, were able to keep their winnings from the boom years.

But so long as the American system of regulated industries endured, the world's loudest advocates of free-market capitalism practiced its opposite in large degree. In theory, that was true only of the specific industries that were officially regulated, each under its own specific law. They were important enough: along with Federal, State and local governments, their employees accounted for one in every four working Americans. But other important industries were in practice regulated as well, not by law but informally, by a handful of leading corporations that effectively dominated the entire sector, and sometimes by a single giant with a monopoly or near monopoly. Thus office machinery and computers were run by IBM; aluminum by Alcoa; steel by the aptly named US Steel; paints and many other chemicals by Dupont; airliners by Boeing and Douglas; pharmaceuticals by Merck and a few other giants; detergents and hygiene products, cigarettes and canned foods by a few each; motor vehicles – the largest of all industries – by General Motors; and oil, gas and petrochemicals by the five sisters that acted as one: Exxon, Texaco, Mobil, Chevron and Amoco.

Had the United States lacked strong anti-trust laws, often aggressively enforced, these giant corporations could have exploited their market power to squeeze consumers, lesser competitors and suppliers. As it was, to avoid prosecutions and the resulting bad publicity, they followed an unwritten code, the business equivalent of good table manners. Instead of illegally consorting with lesser competitors to fix prices, they simply *published* their own prices, counting on the prudence of everyone else to accept their 'price leadership'.

In the automobile industry, for example, Ford and Chrysler were in theory free to act as they liked. In practice, they had to raise and lower prices in step with GM, with very little leeway. To try to sell comparable models at higher prices than GM would diminish their sales and erode profits, with large outright losses guaranteed if the price gap were significant. To sell comparable models for less would trigger even bigger GM price cuts in retaliation, with equally disastrous results. Neither Ford nor Chrysler could possibly win a price war against GM's vast treasury, which could sustain enormous losses for years on end. Yet GM could not use its mountains of cash to drive Ford and Chrysler into bankruptcy by below-cost pricing. That would only lead to anti-trust prosecutions by the Department of Justice, which were very likely to end in the forced sale of one or more GM divisions – and in those days Chevrolet, Buick, Oldsmobile and Cadillac were still largely self-sufficient from design to production, and therefore all too easily separable. In other words, the automobile industry was just as regulated as natural gas, except that GM tacitly did all the regulating by what it did, and by what it very carefully refrained from doing.

Once the 'dominated' sectors and the aerospace and military contractors largely controlled by the Pentagon were added to the long list of industries and utilities regulated by law, not much was left exposed to genuine free-market competition in the United States: mostly shopkeeping, the eating and lodging trades, textile mills and garment workshops, the small machine-shop end of the engineering sector, the laboratory end of the chemical and electronic sectors, the local end of food processing and a few others. The small businesses of these fragmented industries typically had little capital, no market power at all, and a high mortality that became higher whenever the economy slowed down. Many of the jobs they offered were at the minimum wage, with few fringe benefits or none, while even their best-paid jobs were precarious – no business can guarantee employment beyond its own life span.

At the same time, because small businesses in unregulated industries had to be highly competitive to survive at all, they were more efficient overall than big business, and far more innovative. Most famously, the entire personal-computer industry came out of the legendary garage workshops of Silicon Valley. Less famously, the humble garment business invented the phenomenon of designer clothing, which turned some humble workshop and one-room showroom operations into very large enterprises spanning the globe. In these and other ways, the more fortunate small-business owners could exceed the moderately high salaries of the managers of regulated big business, with some doing far better than that. All that has happened since deregulation is that these same conditions have spread into virtually all parts of the American economy, and increasingly into the global economy.

The Retreat of the State

That capitalism, unobstructed by public ownership, government regulations, cartels, monopolies, effective trade unions, cultural inhibitions or kinship obligations, is by far the most productive system ever devised on this earth is a very old truth now disputed only by a few Western academics. That capitalism achieves growth as well as it does because its relentless competition destroys inefficient structures and methods, thus allowing more efficient structures and methods to rise in their place, is simple economics that all understand. And, finally, that rapid structural change can inflict more disruption upon working lives, firms, entire industries and their localities than individuals can absorb, or the connective tissue of friendships, families, clans, elective groupings, neighborhoods, villages, towns, cities or even whole nations can withstand, is another old truth. In fact it was already discovered and thoroughly examined in Germany well before the end of the nineteenth century, though grave warnings of what too much disruption might do to German society, and thus to German politics, went unheeded.

What is new about turbo-capitalism is only a matter of degree, a mere acceleration in the pace of structural change at any given rate of economic growth. But that, as it turns out, is quite enough to make all the difference. Structural change, with all its personal upheavals and social disruptions, is now quite rapid even when there is zero growth, becoming that much faster when economies do grow. The machine turns fast, grinding down established ways and their human relationships even when the economy is not growing at all; and it reaches Ferrari-like acceleration even when the economy advances at steamroller speeds.

The most obvious cause of accelerated structural change (turbo-capitalism) is the worldwide retreat of the state from the marketplace. There has been a wholesale abandonment of public ownership, central planning, administrative direction and most forms of regulatory control, with all their rigidities inimical to structural change, innovation, economic growth, individual dislocations and social disruptions alike. Having first been discredited intellectually, each of these devices to subject private economic behavior to public control has been rejected politically in one country after another, if not by popular opinion then certainly by the dominant elites. As each one was judged a problem rather than a solution, the usual remedy was not some mythical 'third way' compromise, but wholesale abolition; each time that happened, a new driver of change was unleashed, adding its own impulse, large or small, to turbo-capitalism all over the world.

Public ownership: from Argentina to Zambia with the entire communist world in between, the state or local ownership of business enterprises and infrastructures was after 1945 widely accepted as the guarantor of the public interest. It is now seen as a guarantee of bureaucratic inertia or plain idleness, technical stagnation and even simple theft. The remedy is privatization, by outright sale to locals or foreigners, by the sale of shares to the public – which may leave the old bureaucrats in charge as managers, usually with much higher pay – or in some cases by the transfer of shares to employees, who often quickly sell them to private investors. The effect in each individual case is to inject the energy of profit-seeking into the business, insofar as shareholders actively safeguard their interests, and more certainly when there is one private owner; the overall effect is to add activity to the financial superstructure, including the stock market.

Central planning: once viewed as the assured highway to prosperity through focused investment, it is now known to be systematically wasteful, simply because no group of mere humans can guess next year's demand for every one of hundreds of different polymers, not to mention two or three million other items from tower cranes to toothpicks. Unable to get it right except by accident, the planners are bound to order too much production of some things, wasting resources, and too little of others, causing shortages that may cripple the production of other items, or else leave consumers undersupplied, inducing them to resort to theft from state stores, and then black-market dealings to optimize their theft. In the process, honest people are turned into law-breakers, and forced to consort with those who would be criminals under any system. The remedy is abolition. Its effect is to release individual managements from bureaucratic dictates so that they succeed or fail in the market, allowing the entire economy to respond to local and foreign demand with neither wasted surpluses nor shortages.

Administrative direction: once gloriously successful in Japan, Korea and Taiwan, at least helpful in France, a famous failure in 1960s Britain, and ineffective or corrupt, or ineffective *and* corrupt, almost everywhere else, it is now being abandoned (slowly) even in Japan, having been abandoned long ago almost everywhere else. In this weaker, more flexible form of central planning, government officials set industrial production targets to let suppliers prepare for future demand, they set priorities to induce banks to lend money to favored industries, and they designate specific enterprises as 'chosen instruments' to be helped by the government to compete in the world market. One form of such help is to keep out foreign competition, to allow the chosen instrument to accumulate investment capital by charging high prices in the home market. The remedy is to abolish administrative direction in whole or in part, and its effects are to enhance the flexibility of the entire economy, and to break down trade barriers.

As for regulatory controls, they do not in truth cease to increase in number because even if steam locomotives need no longer be prevented by speed limits from causing cows to abort, more recent technical novelties often evoke regulation, and some positively demand it: for example, to allocate cell-phone frequencies. But *commercial* regulation, as opposed to health and safety and environmental regulations, has definitely retreated and continues to do so. With that, efficiency increases, once-secure enterprises are exposed to the opportunities and perils of competitive markets, and employees, once equally secure, no longer are.

Another broad, obvious and indeed overrated cause of accelerated structural change is 'globalization', the much-celebrated unification of the puddles, ponds, lakes and seas of village, provincial, regional and national markets into a single economic ocean. With that, the once sheltered markets of those puddles, ponds, lakes and seas are exposed to the tidal waves of change of global trade, and of yet more volatile global finance with its massive flows and backflows of capital.

Although the internationally negotiated removal of merchandise import barriers, investment controls and licensing restrictions on services always attracts attention and controversy, a great many factors have been at work to unify once separate markets. One is the advent and rapid geographic spread of reliable, cheap and instant telecommunications, which ease the formation of new commercial relationships both materially and psychologically; to rely on a sub-contractor for a vital component is far more easily done if its managers can be reached instantaneously, every time.

Another is the reduced incidence of transport costs, because of the waning material content of commerce; a big part of the price when pig iron or even steel plate is traded, freight is downright insignificant for shipments of electronic components, even if the ship in question is actually an aircraft. Moreover, transport as such has become cheaper, with larger aircraft, more automated ships, better harbors and more roads, notably rural roads in many parts of Asia and Latin America, if not Africa.

Still another impulse to globalization is the widespread diffusion of up-to-date technologies for the production of export goods or components, even within otherwise backward local economies. Last, but perhaps first, is the hammering down of once very diverse consumer preferences into a uniformity of tastes, achieved by fashions carried around the world by transnational mass media imagery, and advertising.

The overall effect of globalization is that any production anywhere can expand enormously if it is competitive, far beyond the limits of the local market. With that, the world's resources are being used more efficiently. More can be produced – much more in many cases – than in the days when economies were more self-sufficient, i.e. more likely to be wasteful of locally abundant resources much in demand elsewhere, more likely to be hindered by the high local price of resources cheaper in other places. By the same token, however, any production anywhere and the related employment can be displaced at any time by cheaper production from somewhere else in the world. Life in the global economy is full of exciting surprises, and catastrophic downfalls.

From Tradition to Contracts

A further cause of accelerated structural change has none of the visibility of globalization, has little to do with either politics or technology, is hard even to identify and almost impossible to measure: the breakdown of long-term customary commercial relationships, their replacement by arm's-length, one-deal-at-a-time, pure supply and demand, *contractual* relations.

It is a very old story in the United States, a very new one elsewhere. When I was a child in Milano, Italy, one did not drive to anonymous supermarkets or chain stores selected each time for their presumed combinations of price and quality. Bread was bought from *the* bakery, meat from *the* butcher, vegetables and fruits from *the* greengrocer. There was only one of each on our street, and just as they were our only suppliers, we and our near neighbors were their only possible clients. Shopkeepers did not have to guess and gamble when stocking up, for they could anticipate quite closely the rhythms of demand through the seasons, and day by day. Neither did they have to watch their competitors' prices, to match them to the exact cent; the full-page advertisements of American newspapers, listing items one by one to allow comparison shopping, could not exist in that world. By the same token, shopkeepers could not hope to expand beyond the narrow limits of their strictly localized markets. Nor could they sell their goods without serving their clients as individuals, accommodating their moods as well as their specific needs, which included informal no-interest credit in poorer parts of town.

This state of affairs did not abrogate the mechanics of supply and demand: if any of our shopkeepers had demanded unreasonably high prices, it would have been enough to stroll over to the next street, or the one after that, to find a competitor. But neither did pure market relationships obtain. Shopkeepers and their clients were not just sellers and buyers, they were also neighbors acquainted with each other's families and bound by mutual obligations. Clients did not feel free to shop elsewhere because their custom would be missed, even if they did not have to pass the particular shop on their way home with tell-tale bags in hand. Nor did shopkeepers knowingly sell substandard goods to distracted buyers or children sent to fetch, because they would have to face them or their mothers on the next day, and the day after that, and for years to come. And in meeting their own needs, for shoemaker, tailor or dentist, they would rely more often than not on their own neighbor-clients. Till this day, the same kind of customary relations persist all over the world, wherever the typical American combination of motorized customers and anonymous super-markets and chain stores has yet to arrive.

More important, what was true of shopkeepers and their clients in my street in Milano remains true till now of large-scale commercial relationships in many parts of the world, though Japan is still perhaps the purest example of the type. Firms do not constantly shop around to find the cheapest possible sources for everything they buy, as theory would prescribe. Instead they have their established suppliers, with which they are linked by a web of mutual obligations. For suppliers, it means that they must do their best to meet their clients' specific needs even if inconvenient, accommodating their standards, accepting their rhythms of production, anticipating capacity requirements at their own risk, and never, ever, trying to exploit temporary shortages to extract higher prices.

For their part, the firms they supply will not promptly abandon them just because they receive a better offer from some other source – often perforce it would be a foreign supplier, outside the circle of mutual obligations that keeps domestic competitors at bay. Instead of being simply dropped, the established supplier is kept informed all along, and given enough time to try to match the competition, perhaps with the help of equipment loans or technical assistance; any data incautiously proffered by the intruder would be handed over too, of course. Firms likewise expect their own clients to remain faithful to them, and accept the obligation to serve them accordingly, not merely effectively but loyally.

From one intermediate supplier to another, to the final assemblers or packagers, the chain of mutual obligations runs forward to tied wholesalers that both get and give credit, and so on down to the sub-distributors that deliver the most minute quantities to the smallest shops, each serving mostly its own circle of loyal, known clients. Written contracts would be out of place here and are almost unknown, unless a foreign entity is involved somewhere along the line. All is agreed face to face on each side's word alone, or simply pre-ordained by custom, although naturally there are invoices and receipts. If for some reason a contract is written – and then almost always informally, few Japanese firms have legal departments or lawyers on retainer – it is not enforced by resorting to the courts or formal arbitration, except in rare and extreme cases. Instead, commercial disagreements have to be resolved by mutual concessions, or at most by the informal mediation of available higher-ranking figures, because quarrels disturb the entire system, so that both sides are discredited almost regardless of the merits of their own case.

Again, through it all, the pure logic of supply and demand, the pressures of competitiveness, cannot be ignored or suppressed. But they are definitely tempered by a great and natural reluctance to break customary and personal relationships all along the chain. Nor does it end there. It extends both below to employees, from whom a familial degree of loyalty is demanded in exchange for jobs that are assured even through the worst downturns, and above to banks and large international trading companies.

Each has its own circle of firms that will not look elsewhere for credit or export outlets, while themselves expecting not merely loans on commercial terms or effective services, but loyal support in good times and bad, and outright indulgence with overdue loans if need be. That is how the Korean debt crisis of 1997 came about. Known by different names in different countries – Japan's *kereitsu* and Korea's *chaebol* sound much more exotic than they are, for the same practices are common in Europe as well – these informal associations that ultimately bind everyone involved, from employees at the base to the heads of banks at the top, are revealingly thought of as 'families' rather than corporate groupings by their participants.

Informal associations have stood as stubborn barriers to the spread of turbo-capitalism in more ways than one. Very specifically, imports of goods and services are kept out by the closed circle of established relationships among sellers and buyers all along the chain. Wholesalers tied to domestic firms will not handle competing imports, and without them there is no access to their distributors and sub-distributors, which are essential to reach the final points of sale. Nor will firms turn to rank outsiders for insurance or banking services, any more than they are ready to replace domestic supplies with imports. All that does not exactly stop globalization cold – on the contrary, it positively encourages exports as the only way to exceed the limits of a domestic market largely pre-empted by other people's closed circles. But to the extent that foreign goods and services are kept out, globalization is one-sided, and therefore of much weaker effect in forcing structural change.

Another impediment to turbo-capitalism is of broader effect. There is no competition to drive it without a free market, no free market without arm's-length dealings, and none of the latter without *contractual* relations, as opposed to customary or even emotional relationships. Because written contracts are almost unknown within each 'family', because those inside have few dealings with outsiders, there is a great reluctance to enter into written contracts, very little of the required legal expertise, no inclination to limit oneself to contractual requirements when fulfilling felt obligations, and even less to perform beyond them – just because words were once written on paper. When outsiders insist that contracts be respected regardless of circumstances, angry disbelief is the usual response, followed by sheer outrage if lawsuits are threatened. Both are combined if the outsider imagines that normal dealings can continue on other matters, or with a different division of the same company, or with a different company of the same group, while legal proceedings on the dispute continue to unfold. Normal operating behavior in the United States, very rare in Europe and Latin America, such practices are unknown in Japan or the rest of Asia.

It is pleasing to think that lawyers are thereby kept out, but so are domestic or foreign suppliers or buyers outside the magic circle, which can neither rely on trust alone, lacking any long prior relationship, nor have real contracts to provide a ready-made framework of mutual relations. However, there is more to it than that. Cold-blooded, truly arm's-length and therefore purely contractual relations exemplify the entire spirit of turbo-capitalism. Likewise their absence exemplifies the 'familial capitalism' of Asia and beyond, as one might label it. Just as the former is enabled to drive relentless change – because necessary relations can instantly be defined along the way by contracts alone – the latter inherently resists change, insofar as it entails the erosion, injury or outright severing of established human relationships.

What is now aiding the worldwide spread of turbo-capitalism is the accelerated breakdown of familial capitalism. In Asia it is happening most dramatically. Once the financial crash of 1997 abruptly ended the flow of indulgent bank credit, and much rigorous credit too, a myriad of long-established industrial and commercial linkages were also cut off, as firms and individuals, employers and employees had to scramble to survive, either inside or outside 'family' circles. In Europe and beyond it is happening more gradually, but everywhere more and more clients insist on shopping around, undeterred by any loyalties to subcontractors or vendors, just as more and more suppliers disregard old clients to serve profitable new ones, and more and more employers treat employees as disposable inputs in the American style, insofar as the local laws allow. Employees naturally reciprocate insofar as they have choices. On the street of my childhood in Milano, Italy, the business of the surviving shops is much diminished, as bulk shopping is done by car, in whatever anonymous supermarket is offering the best deals – and few are now deterred by the disapproving gaze of fruitseller or butcher. Everywhere familial capitalism is rapidly retreating, and turbo-capitalism rapidly advancing.

The Victory of the Computer

A seemingly narrower, ultimately more important cause of accelerated structural change is the rather sudden arrival of the long-awaited, much-delayed, *big* increases in the productivity of offices that computers and other electronics were supposed to bring long ago. In factories of all kinds, computerized machine tools and other forms of automation gradually increased productivity over the years in step with their introduction – indeed, it had to be so, because otherwise the successive investments would not have been made. The same was true of purely routine clerical work, such as the processing of payrolls, which was taken over by computers from the 1960s even in less advanced countries. By contrast, more and more electronic machinery was introduced into *administrative* offices – a big part of any modern economy – without apparently increasing their productivity anywhere near as much. Banks, insurance companies, corporate offices of every kind and size – all places where decisions have to be made to do the job, even if within the narrowest guidelines – took in more and more equipment without seemingly reducing their need for white-collar employees. What was true of both physical production and clerical work was not true of administration, where salaries are higher and the potential for saving overhead costs was much greater.

Then, in the 1980s, it finally happened. Perhaps it was simply a matter of generational change. By then even senior managers had learned to use personal computers and the rest of the electronic machinery, allowing them to recognize their uses, abuses and non-uses. That opened the way for cost cutting by dismissals. One of the first moves in many corporations was to compel junior managers to rely entirely on machines instead of secretarial help, and secretarial companionship. Next, local-area computer networks were used to allow managers at the next level up literally to oversee, right on their own screens, the work that their underlings were doing or not doing. That introduced to office work, even of administrative level, the same transparency as industrial assembly-line work, with the same immediate visibility of inefficient procedures, inefficient habits and inefficient employees. The result was to raise the productivity of office employees – and expose them to the workplace dislocations and mass dismissals that have long been the lot of blue-collar industrial workers in advanced economies.

Right through the 1990s, with the US economy booming, one famous corporation after another has announced white-collar job eliminations. They call it 'restructuring' or more fancifully 're-engineering the corporation', and duly decorate the proceedings with the most recently fashionable management-consultant verbiage – those catchy, suggestive yet profoundly shallow slogans coined by the authors of the latest business-book best sellers. Expensively proclaimed with evangelical insistence by authors on the corporate lecture circuit, the slogans are repeated with great solemnity by their understudies in corporate 'workshops' and 'retreats' to audiences of deferential, bewildered employees.

This, however, is mere background music. The real cost savings that Wall Street anticipates by bidding up the shares, thereby not-coincidentally rewarding mass-firing top executives who have stock options, come not from the management-consultant verbiage, but rather from a whole cascade of displacements: of telephone-answering secretaries by voice mail interactive recordings; of letter-writing secretaries by computer word processing, faxboards and email; of filing secretaries by electronic memories; of clerical supervisors with nobody left to supervise; of junior administrators by automated processing; of administrative supervisors with nobody left to supervise; and of middle managers no longer needed to supervise dismissed clerical and administrative employees. This is why businesses whose sales are rising are nevertheless not adding white-collar positions, while businesses whose sales are level are reducing them, and businesses in decline are eliminating them *en masse* – by the tens of thousands when they are sick giants, such as IBM, GM and AT&T.

Economists have long deplored the very disappointing productivity gains in the administrative superstructure of advanced economies, in spite of the proliferation of computers and other office electronics. This was particularly irritating to the fraternity because the goods-producing industries – whose productivity did keep increasing – are of diminishing significance, so that lagging productivity in offices was lowering the numbers for the economy as a whole. Those economists need fret no longer: white-collar productivity is finally increasing at a fast pace, allowing employers to cut costs – that is, rid themselves of employees – just as fast.

Adaptation ... and Frustration

There may be other explanations for the acceleration of structural economic change. What counts is the result: the competition-driven creative destruction of outdated skills, trades, firms, entire industries is now apt to span years rather than a generation or two – often very few years. The same rapid pace of change that increases global prosperity, that allows poorer nations and regions to catch up, while offering opportunities to enterprising people everywhere, also brutally exceeds the adaptive limits of individuals, families and communities.

When the sons and daughters of American steelworkers, British coalminers or German welders can no longer find jobs in the parental trades, becoming instead software-writers, teachers, lawyers or shop assistants, few have reason to complain; many can only celebrate their good fortune. With normal generational change, gradual economic change that spans a generation is usually accommodated quite easily. But when the same process of change works so fast that steelworkers, coalminers or welders must themselves abandon lifetime proclivities to acquire demanding new skills on penalty of chronic unemployment or unskilled low-wage labor, the outcome is often failure and frustration.

Of course, nothing could be more outmoded, out-of-date, and

hopelessly *passé* than to weep over the travails of steelworkers, coal-miners or welders, all of them leftovers of the classic industrial working class. What has happened to white-collar employment under turbo-capitalism is less easily disregarded: the more highly skilled minority has done very well, the less skilled majority has suffered an actual loss of earnings, and for both any given job is more precarious than before – even when jobs in general are abundant. No statistics can measure the *security* of employment, a subjective feeling in any case. Just as subjective is the claim of leading economists that the surprisingly weak pressure for higher pay in the United States during the boom years of 1994–98 was due to the fears of employees and unions that jobs would go elsewhere, or simply disappear, if pay were to increase. What the wage statistics do show is that the mass of less skilled white-collar employees has done poorly in the US economy.

Back in the early 1980s, when trade union officials were bitterly complaining that American workers were being extruded from well-paid industrial employment into minimum-wage 'hamburger-flipping' jobs, lusty free-market enthusiasts silenced them by pointing to the rapid increase in 'money-flipping' jobs in the financial sector – banking, insurance, financial services and real-estate dealing. That is where the debate ended – much too soon. By the end of 1992, when union leaders had long since given up complaining, more than 4.9 million Americans were listed as 'non-supervisory' employees in the financial sector, a well-paid lot one would assume. In fact their average earnings were only $10.14 per hour, as compared to $10.98 for rank-and-file workers in manufacturing. Five years later, in December 1997, the average hourly earnings of manufacturing workers had reached $13.62, while their white-collar counterparts in banking, insurance, financial services and real estate were still behind them at an average of $13.46 an hour.[1] If any disemployed industrial workers did equip themselves with the obligatory red suspenders to seek their fortunes on Wall Street, they would have found the rewards sur-prisingly modest.

At a time when it is forever being explained that it is silly to worry about manufacturing in the age of 'services', it remains a fact that service employees throughout the US economy are paid much less than their counterparts still holding industrial jobs. In retail trade, for example, a category that includes everything from department stores

---

[1] US Department of Labor, Bureau of Labor Statistics, *Employment, Hours and Earnings, United States, 1909–90*, vol. 1, pp. 3–4; id., 1990–95; id., BLS net data.

to street-corner news stands, rank-and-file employees earned an average of $8.50 per hour in December 1997, only 60 per cent of what their counterparts in manufacturing were earning. This was the result of a slight recovery after years of falling real wages, a decline masked by inflation. Measured in constant 1982 dollars, the average hourly earnings of retail employees went down year after year from a peak of $6.20 in 1978 to $5.07 in 1990, only rising again – at a glacial pace – when the economy was booming to reach $5.21 in December 1997.[2]

The retail trade is full of married women who work part-time and of youngsters still in school who work only at weekends and during holidays. That can be expected to depress earnings, and it does. It is true that many retail employees receive commissions that may not be reported to the collectors of labor statistics. Yet the proposition that the pay of ordinary employees in the service sector has declined still holds. Neither part-timers with modest demands nor commissions are to be found in transportation and public utilities (including airlines, railways, bus services, urban mass transit, trucking and power companies). Average hourly earnings for ordinary, non-supervisory employees in that entire sector amounted to $15.14 in December 1997, substantially more – in fact $1.68 more – than the average in manufacturing, but substantially less than those same employees had earned in the 1970s in real dollars. Their earnings too peaked in 1978 (not coincidentally, it was the start of a period of high inflation) at $11.18 per hour in constant 1982 dollars, as opposed to $9.27 in December 1997, at the height of the boom.[3]

In the great and varied mass of service jobs, there are predictable highs, such as in film making, computer and data processing, and commodity brokerage, and equally predictable lows in the hotel/motel and eating trades, security-guard work, etc. But while the average hourly earnings of *all* non-farm, non-government, non-supervisory employees throughout the US economy stood at $12.51 in December 1997, the average for those in 'goods-producing' sectors (mining, construction, manufacturing) was $14.18. In other words, the new service economy pays less well than old-fashioned industries in which people still make things.

White-collar employees with advanced computer skills and other abilities that are much in demand have fared better than the mass of

[2] Ibid.; BLS net data.
[3] Ibid.; BLS net data.

plain managers. Their decline is definitely a structural trend. With 'lean and mean' downsized corporations dominant in every industry, and traditional 'satisficing' corporations (moderate dividends, steady, slow growth) almost extinct, top managers as a class earn very much more than before, while middle managers earn less. You do not ask the boss for a raise at a time when every management consultant is telling every boss that the key to higher profits is to cut overhead costs, by firing employees who do not personally 'add value', starting with expensive middle managers. People in sales add value, people in production add value, but managers do not add value; they only supervise those who do, in ways that can be substituted, and not only by machines.

Long-distance telephone companies, for example, used to have a great number of sales people to hunt for customers by direct solicitation over the phone. In most cases, customers were not so much hunted as poached, from other long-distance companies. It was not easy work, and a strong dose of motivation was needed to succeed. It was the task of junior managers to ensure that the calls were not perfunctory (customers heard 'this conversation might be monitored for quality control') and of middle managers to supervise the supervisors. It was then realized that if sales employees were dismissed and rehired as self-employed contractors working for commissions, the motivation problem would be solved without any need for supervising managers.

Other industries have other forms of 'out-sourcing', but the result for the former managers involved is the same: dismissal. The great mass of not-so-young middle managers forced out of their jobs floods the market, making it difficult for them to find comparable employment elsewhere. Some can overcome the addiction to the corporate life and start their own businesses, and a few have already graced the pages of business journals as entrepreneurial wonders not born but made, by the shock of unemployment. Some adjust undramatically if painfully, by accepting whatever middle-class jobs they can get, normally with reduced pay. Others are much worse off. The 50–55-year-old male, white, college-educated, ex-corporate employee and former exemplar of the American dream, still perhaps living in his lavishly equipped suburban house, with two cars in the driveway, one or two children in $20,000 per annum universities (for tuition, board and lodging), who now exists on savings, second and third mortgages and scant earnings as a self-described 'consultant', has become a familiar figure in the contemporary United States.

They still send out resumés by the dozen. They still 'network', i.e.

beg for jobs from whomever they know. They still put on their business suits to commute to 'business' lunches with more fortunate friends, until that too peters out in mutual embarrassment. They still solicit employment agencies, overloaded with such applicants even in the boom years of 1996–7. But all their efforts collide with the reality that what has made US corporations more efficient since the 1980s is precisely the reduction of the managerial overhead, including the wholesale elimination of fifty-somethings who failed to make it to the top, but whose salaries are rather high, and whose age pushes up health insurance costs. It is chiefly by being mean to their own most vulnerable employees that corporations become lean.

Beyond all anecdotes there are statistics that quantify the downward slide of the entire population from which middle managers are drawn in the US economy. The median earnings of *all* males in the 45–54 age bracket with four years of university or other higher education – some two million Americans, all but 150,000 of them white as of 1992 – actually peaked in 1972 at some $55,000 in 1992 dollars; their earnings then stagnated until 1989, when a sharp decline set in to $41,898 by 1992.[4] In reality, two sharply divergent turbo-capitalist trends have been at work: the sensational increase in the earnings of the top 1 per cent of all managers, and a decline in the earnings of their less fortunate colleagues.

Money and Love

The retreat of the state, globalization and the computerization of office work are all spreading worldwide, but very unevenly. Sometimes events move rapidly, as in Eastern Europe after 1989, in the lands of the former Soviet Union after 1991, and in South-East Asia and Korea after the financial collapse of 1997. Mostly, however, the trends that are advancing global turbo-capitalism are gradual, and they still have very far to go – even in the United States, telephone services are not yet fully deregulated. Elsewhere, the advance has just begun. In South Korea, for example, the effective control of the largest firms by banks that are themselves controlled by the government – a system that, along with protectionism, certainly blocked turbo-capitalist change very effectively – was not dismantled until 1998, under orders

---

[4] *The New York Times*, 11 February 1994.

from the International Monetary Fund, acting as a front for the United States and Japan.

So far, it is chiefly in the United States and Britain that matters have progressed far enough to reveal the actual consequences of turbo-capitalism, good and bad, expected or otherwise. It is entirely certain, however, that what has already happened in the United States and Britain is happening, or will happen, in every other half-way modern economy in Europe, Asia and Latin America, because all are exposed to the same transforming impulses.

One expected, eagerly sought consequence has duly materialized: the increased efficiency that comes from more competition. All over the United States and in Britain too, large and small firms are producing more goods and services with less – less labor above all, but also less rented floorspace and less energy. Hence higher profits come from both ends – more revenue from increased sales and lower costs per unit too. Nor is the result more unemployment, because of a second consequence neither expected nor sought: over many years, real salaries and wages have declined for many employees, though they did not know it because inflation made it seem that pay was holding steady or even increasing.

Cheaper labor in turn allows a great proliferation of services that would have been unprofitable otherwise. Free to dismiss employees at will, with no legal prohibitions, penalties or high severance costs to stop them (that is what is meant by a 'flexible labor market'), employers do not hesitate to hire. At the time of writing, unemployment in the United Kingdom is much lower than in the rest of Western Europe, where wages are generally higher, and labor markets are mostly inflexible. As for the United States, its official unemployment rate is currently below 5 per cent, a wonderfully low level in these days of global excess capacity, high unemployment and deflation.

Another unexpected consequence of turbo-capitalism is the explosive increase in the incomes of the highest earners: the top 5 per cent now receives a much larger share of all incomes than it did before, more than one-fifth of late. With the decline of incomes in the lower half of the pyramid, the combined result is a sharp increase in income inequality, and an even greater increase in wealth inequality, because top earners save much more in proportion, and invest their savings more profitably.

Many people *feel* that inequality is a bad thing, but in standard Anglo-American economics – the only one around at present – it is not a problem, but rather part of the solution. Competition, which must be a good thing because it propels the engine of prosperity, is itself propelled by the incentive of higher rewards for more successful competitors, which automatically implies more inequality, other things – including taxes – being equal. The greater the difference in rewards, the stronger the incentive, the more intense the competition, the greater the resulting prosperity. To resist differences in rewards in the name of equality is therefore to resist prosperity itself. And cutting taxes on the highest incomes is the fastest way of increasing the incentive to compete, thus increasing prosperity. That inequality too increases is inevitable, and hence not worth deploring unless one is also willing to deplore prosperity. These few propositions provided much of the entire intellectual basis of what is called Thatcherism in the United Kingdom. It did not even need a name in the United States, where Ronald Reagan's 'supply-side economics' included several further steps, promising more prosperity, more government spending *and* a balanced budget by cutting taxes to induce the rich to become richer – thus eventually raising *taxable* incomes so much that lower taxes would yield more revenue, a reality by 1998.

Turbo-capitalism also has consequences outside the realm of economics, as we have seen. Its material benefits can only come from structural changes that increase efficiency. These changes, however, must necessarily change working lives too, inevitably affecting families as well; if that happens on any scale, communities too must change. In the most fortunate of all possible circumstances, *all* those changes might be greatly welcomed in themselves, with working lives enhanced by higher pay and/or more satisfying work, families made more affluent, communities enriched. Even so, however, the pure mechanism of change would inflict a cost, for it would reduce the emotional capital of individuals, families and communities, simply because the moss of human relations can only grow over the stones of stability, not the perpetually shifting sands of structural change.

In that regard as well, the lives of Americans in the age of turbo-capitalism are both promise and warning. Their generalized material affluence, their opportunities to achieve, are accompanied by a generalized emotional solitude. Too many changes of residence or work left successive tenuous friendships behind, having already dissuaded their deepening by the anticipation of departures to come. And lives on the go are mostly incompatible with the upkeep of intense family relationships beyond the confines of the home.

There is a lot of lonely space not only between but inside the ideal dwellings of the American dream, the veritable mansions of the richest suburbs, which could house parents, grown children and their children in familial communion if only all were poor enough, but which mostly house only one ever-so-busy male and as busy a female, with surviving parents in their own retirement abodes, distant children pursuing their budding careers, and few friends, whose degree of loyal commitment might rate them as mere acquaintances in other climes. In the amplitude of America, change brings individual opportunities, accelerated change brings greater opportunities, and a greater solitude is the price.

THREE

Glories and Downfalls of the Global Economy

Pragmatic common sense in examining and solving problems one by one is the Anglo-Saxon virtue. To uncover connections between seemingly unrelated spheres of human life is the vice of Germanic social philosophers and others of their ilk. But sometimes vice must prevail. Consider three sets of numbers.

First, on 10 August 1995, the Boeing Co., premier manufacturer of passenger airliners as well as sundry advanced weapons, was so highly regarded by analysts and investors that its shares were quoted at $65 on the New York Stock Exchange, seventy-seven times as much as its last-declared earnings. That enormous 'multiple' as stockbrokers call it, implied an equally enormous faith in Boeing's future prospects – a faith that was misplaced, for the stock would descend to $43 in 1997, after first briefly rising to $70. The shares of its nearest equivalent, McDonnell-Douglas (since bought by Boeing), were by contrast selling at only fifteen times earnings in August 1995, while the ratio for that great battleship of corporate America, General Electric, was only nineteen.

Second, in that same week, a survey of members of the International Association of Machinists and Aerospace Workers – a union which then represented 34,650 of Boeing's employees, almost all of whom regard themselves as belonging to the middle class – showed that just over 20 per cent thought their own job was 'somewhat secure', while over 50 per cent declared themselves 'not secure'.[1] They were right and wrong: right because over the next two years Boeing first 'downsized' its union employees to 28,000, only to hurriedly hire them back again, and more besides to reach 38,000 by year-end 1997. And the game of firing and hiring continues still, for the worst of reasons.

Third, 4.9 million people were under some form of 'correctional supervision' in the United States as of 1995, with some 2.8 million out on probation, 671,000 on early-release parole, 958,704 in State prisons, 95,034 in Federal prisons and some 446,000 in local jails, making a total of one incarcerated American out of 189 men, women and children, as compared to the already very high 1980 ratio of one to 480. Those numbers, already exceedingly high, were nevertheless destined to rise yet more. A mere two years later, by mid-1997, the grand total had increased to 5.5 million, with 1.8 actually in prison and the rest on probation or out on parole.[2] It is now projected that these numbers will increase further, to reach two million by 1999.

Explanations of the first number (the price of Boeing shares) were uncontroversial at the time, and readily obtained from any number of stockbroker 'buy' notices, all running in the same herd, as usual. As they correctly noted, Boeing was a beneficiary of turbo-capitalism's globalization twice over. With Tupolev and Yakovlev[3] having lost their old Soviet-sphere monopoly, Boeing now sells airliners to a truly worldwide market – literally to almost every airline of significant size. Thus Boeing's revenues are not captive to the boom–bust cycles of continental, let alone national economies, not even to the wild gyrations of US airlines, which alternate between frantic orders and abrupt cancellations. When Japan is in recession, China may still be booming; when South-East Asian orders are drastically reduced, Latin America and Europe are in expansion. Overall, the sum total of exports is more stable than the volatile home market, where US airlines are ingloriously surviving deregulation by cut-throat fare wars, extreme cost cutting (in-flight meals compete with those of Aeroflot at its mythic worst), abrupt shifts from expansion to contraction, repeated transits through court-controlled ('Chapter 11') bankruptcy –

---

[1] *Aviation Week & Space Technology*, 14 August 1995, p. 21.

[2] US Department of Justice, Bureau of Justice Statistics. 1995 figures are as of 31 December 1994; 1997 figures are mid-year estimates.

[3] Soviet-era design bureaus (led by aviation pioneers A.N. Tupolev and A.S. Yakovlev) whose designs were produced by a variety of plants. They are now organized as integrated private companies.

and by what hurts Boeing: the sudden cancellations of options or even firm orders.

Globalization serves Boeing the other way as well, as a buyer rather than a seller. Whenever a duly certified producer somewhere around the world can offer an airframe sub-assembly, or even a single panel, at a lower cost than one of its own plants, or one of its US vendors, Boeing's manufacturing costs are reduced by that much, less the small and still diminishing contracting, communication and transport costs of such 'offshore procurement'. While insistently demanding US Government diplomatic support in its quarrels with the Franco-German-British Airbus Industrie consortium, and with the European Union's anti-monopoly commissioner, Karel van Miert[4], Boeing has eagerly transferred as much work as possible to cheaper subcontractors overseas.

Beyond that, total Boeing costs were still being reduced back in 1995 by the continuing advance of computerization, and the reduction of employee payrolls it allows. At the design and development stage for new airliners, or for altogether more frequent modifications, lots of expensive design-engineer hours were replaced by the ever more complete application of computer-assisted design, now available in three dimensions to check the fit of solid forms, and with stress and thermal dynamics included as well. The '777' was Boeing's first airliner fully engineered 'in the computer' rather than through the lengthy and costly traditional sequence of mock-ups, prototypes, pre-production trial aircraft, testing and final detailed development. A billion dollars at least of engineering hours were thereby saved, one billion dollars less for Boeing's and outside engineers, a billion dollars more for shareholders and top executive salaries, bonuses and stock options. As for the humbler task of controlling inventories of parts and tools, it was fully computerized long before 1995. What was new and still being refined, however, was the computerization of component production and final assembly, to read the design automatically, and then feed a myriad of detailed work-specifications directly to machinery that was itself computerized. With that, more than design-engineering hours were saved; machine-shop and assembly-floor workers were being dismissed by the thousand, even as Boeing was receiving a flood of orders in what was becoming the biggest commercial aviation boom in history.

[4] Van Miert protested the Boeing/McDonnell-Douglas merger and demanded assurances that Boeing would stop signing exclusive supply contracts with US airlines – which shut out Airbus.

At the same time, the computerization of administrative work that was then emptying corporate office-buildings throughout the United States was no less advanced in Boeing's various offices. There too, telephone-answering secretaries were being replaced by voice mail, letter-writing secretaries by word processing, and filing secretaries by digitalized records, with the consequent redundancy of supervisors all the way up to medium–high executive levels.

With reductions in both factory-floor workers and engineers, both clericals and managers, Boeing succeeded in laying off some 45,000 employees between 1992 and 1996. It was all this job cutting that aroused so much enthusiasm on Wall Street, where costs were projected as declining even as sales revenues were projected as rising, in step with the great upsurge in airliner orders. Nobody stopped to wonder if production and thus revenues might not be undermined by the mass-firing of highly experienced workers. For those who bought Boeing shares, it was a costly mistake.

Booming Sales, Insecure Jobs

The explanation of the first number, the 1995 valuation of Boeing at seventy-seven times earnings – that is, the fact that Boeing was seen as a leading beneficiary of technology-powered, globalizing turbo-capitalism – also explained the second number, which measured the acute insecurity of Boeing employees. They had, and have, every reason to feel that their jobs are individually precarious even in the best of times, because Boeing has joined other American corporations, large and small, in firing employees not only when sales are down and the balance sheet demands it, but quite deliberately even in prosperity, and in Boeing's case, more egregiously still, even when in urgent need of more production.

On 16 December 1997, at a time when Boeing was struggling in much confusion with a huge backlog of overdue deliveries, which resulted in losses in the previous quarter after a $1.6 billion charge, chief executive officer Philip M. Condit announced that 12,000 jobs would be eliminated as soon as the situation was stabilized. Industry experts were amazed: the company was failing to meet its monthly target of 39 aircraft per month with 38,000 factory-floor workers, yet it was proposing to increase deliveries to 43 aircraft per month with only 26,000 workers. Technology progresses, to be sure, but not that fast. Perhaps Mr Condit was possessed of a secret remedy of his own, but Boeing had already astonished the industry by contriving to turn the unprecedented sales boom of 1995–97 into financial loss. Ironically, Boeing having dismissed too many skilled workers to service the airline orders pouring in, its only rival, Airbus Industrie, found itself in a position of decisive advantage because strict European labor-protection laws had prevented it from drastically cutting its own labor force.

However, there were no doubts about the policy in Wall Street. The market players in the New York Stock Exchange responded with immediate enthusiasm to Condit's announcement, bidding up the depressed Boeing stock by $1.69 a share to $50.63 for a while, though it soon fell sharply once again. This immediate response, by stock analysts and brokers who equate mass firings with brilliant management without bothering about the details, was of course the entire point of the exercise. Job cuts that will actually be implemented over a period of years – if they occur at all – are announced all at once to impress a stock market that equates them with guaranteed profits to come. So powerful is this conditioned reflex that Condit's gambit actually worked, even though at that very time Boeing was so short-handed because of previous mass firings that it was paying $7,500 bonuses to lure ex-workers back into its plant![5]

In theory, it is just the objective force of technology-driven 'creative destruction' that is at work: new, more efficient machines or methods displace less efficient ones, releasing labor that will eventually increase the world's total production of everything, once it is re-employed elsewhere. In theory too, by making Boeing more efficient, the US economy as a whole is made that much more efficient.

In practice, transient management fashions, tough-guy posturing and self-serving motives play a large role – perhaps even larger than that of creative destruction. Quite often employees are dismissed simply because at that particular time a senior executive happens to be especially eager to show himself as especially 'hard-nosed'. Harry C. Stonecipher, now Condit's newly appointed number two and likely successor as Boeing's president and chief operating officer, is entirely representative of the type. In a notably sympathetic report on Boeing's troubles,[6] Stonecipher is praised as someone who 'enjoys a reputation as a no-nonsense, tough guy manager'. Another compliment is attri-

[5] Lawrence Zuckerman, 'Boeing to raise output and then cut jobs', *New York Times*, 17 December 1997, p. D2.

[6] Tim Smart, 'Boeing's big stall', *Washington Post*, 18 January 1998, pp. H1–H12.

buted to a stock analyst at Credit Suisse First Boston: 'Harry is a hard guy ... What he promises, he generally beats up enough people to do it' – the convoluted syntax itself reveals the eagerness to find a Clint Eastwood in an inoffensive corporate functionary. Stonecipher's own words, as cited in the article, are perfectly in character: 'We have to win on the cost side of the equation ... in some cases we have the ball on the tee but we don't have the courage to swing the club.' Needless to say the 'we' in question is really a polite way of saying 'they', i.e. Boeing's management before Stonecipher's no doubt providential arrival.

In the wake of Boeing's 1997 acquisition of the giant McDonnell-Douglas corporation, and of Rockwell International's military units, almost 200,000 employees are now exposed to Mr Stonecipher's club. And judging by his remarks, Mr Stonecipher is not even contemplating the possibility of expanding Boeing's potential and product line by capitalizing on the many skills of its enlarged employee rolls. That might yield great results in both civilian and military markets, but it would certainly require much more effort by management than the standard three-step cost-cutting approach:

1. Keep all of the huge backlog of rich Pentagon contracts acquired with McDonnell-Douglas and Rockwell, which generate a massive flow of progress payments long before delivery.
2. Get rid of as many of their employees as possible, along with Boeing's own 12,000, to cut operating costs.
3. Rely on Wall Street to react favorably to the gap between current costs and current revenues, without worrying about Boeing's ability to produce as contracted.

Evidently, the 1970s fashion for 'human resources management-plus', to make the most of the sum total of employee skills by finding market outlets for their products, is entirely *passé*. It has given way to a suitably desexed North American substitute for Latin American *machismo* – the cult of the hard-faced executive who gets rid of lots of employees without sentimental hesitations. Thus the genuine logic of cost accounting is overlaid by mere fashion, albeit powered in many cases, if not at Boeing, by the very real rewards of stock-option millions for top executives who can impress the market for long enough to exercise their options to buy shares at pre-fixed values below the market price. Meanwhile, many US corporations and not only Boeing have been paying a very stiff price for having 'let go of' (no meretrix was ever more meretricious) too many valuable employees, while simultaneously alarming and depressing those who remain, inducing some of the best to seek less fickle employers.

Evidence that something other than sound business practice is at work can be found in the spectacular growth of 'temporary-help agencies', which rent labor by the day, week or month, and whose best customers are often yesterday's proud downsizers. Typical of this trend is the huge regional telephone company Pacific Bell. Long a provider of lifetime careers, so long as telephone services were still strictly regulated by the Federal Communications Commission, Pacific Bell dismissed more than 11,000 people between 1991 and 1995, only to be forced to hire 4,200 contract workers by 1996, many of them its own former employees. One such, interviewed by a veteran *New York Times* labor reporter,[7] originally went to work for the old regulated Pacific Bell at the age of 18, straight out of high school, was earning $30 per hour in net pay by late 1995, was abruptly dismissed at the age of 41, and was rehired six months later at $40 net per hour, plus the agency's commission, but without health or pension benefits. Another ex-employee was less fortunate. Having lost her $30 per hour job at the age of 44, she was rehired through an agency contract at $20 per hour, again with no health or pension benefits. Eight out of ten of the 900–1,000 contract workers supplied to Pacific Bell on an average day by its largest agency provider were reportedly former employees, now left unassisted with health care for themselves and their families, and unprovided for their retirement.

A 1995 Labor Department study estimated that some 17 per cent of five million listed contract employees were working for their former employers, the likes of Xerox, Hoffman-LaRoche, Delta Air Lines, Digital Equipment and Chevron. Likewise, an American Management Association survey of 720 newly downsized companies showed that 30 per cent had rehired former employees, almost always without giving them their former health and pension benefits.

How much loyalty, devotion or mere performance beyond the strict letter of specified requirements is to be had from dismissed, rehired employees, one cannot know. Still, it is rather unlikely that many of them would emulate the proverbial Toyota worker who ends his shift, changes to street clothes, drives home from the plant, prepares to sit down for dinner, and promptly rises again to return to the plant,

---

[7] Louis Uchitelle, 'More downsized workers are returning as rentals', *New York Times*, 8 December 1996, p. 1.

because it had just occurred to him that he might have misplaced a tool that the next shift might need. Such an anecdote may seem mawkish, yet advanced forms of industry are full of fragile processes that require an extreme degree of attentive care merely to function, from sterile computer-chip plants vulnerable to tiny particles of dust, to highly automated car production-lines whose every stoppage is very costly. There is no way of measuring the ultimate consequences for growth and profitability of running corporations with presumably embittered employees, and rehired ex-employees. But adverse consequences there must be, at least for jobs that are more than purely mechanical, less than fully transparent.

None of this is at all likely to impress US senior executives; 'caring' management that actively tries to avoid layoffs and offers periodic retraining to enhance both loyalty and skills has feminine undertones wholly out of place in the present neo-Darwinian climate – it is the respect of other corporate machos that they crave. In any case, the language of stock-option profits is far more persuasive than even the most conclusive of studies that shows the merits of having a stable and contented workforce. Boeing for its part set out in 1995 to ramp up production again as the world's leading aircraft maker, while concurrently announcing its intention of sending production overseas. This precipitated a ten-week strike by the International Association of Machinists and Aerospace Workers that was to cost no less than $2 billion in lost output – far more than many years of 'offshore procurement' might have saved.

Ultimately, however, the decisive fact is that, except for particular specialties, the US labor market is chronically oversupplied in all sorts of high-skill categories from engineers and physicists to accountants, in addition to the unskilled, whose utter uselessness in a 'high-tech' economy is by now well established. President Clinton's first Secretary of Labor, the well-known academic and acclaimed author Robert Reich, has made an entire career out of mourning their fate, while at every turn disclaiming any intention of interfering with the divine processes of the market – he too takes it for granted that American society exists to service the needs of the economy, and not the other way around.

At the end of 1997, at the peak of boom times, unemployment in the United States remained above 4.5 per cent, counting only those who registered, a wonderfully low number compared to the ruinous 10–12 per cent of most of Western Europe, but nevertheless just enough to make jobs critically scarcer than job-seekers, in most categories, in most parts of the country. Corporate managers accordingly feel free to treat their labor force as disposable, counting on the ease of recruiting replacements if and when needed. It was unfortunate for Boeing that when it had to recruit frantically in 1996–97 to make up for its previous mass firings, its major plants happened to be located in Washington State and Kansas, both areas of exceptionally low unemployment at the time, and where Boeing has a long-established reputation as the most unreliable of employers.

'Out-sourcing' – All the Way to China

Technology-driven, or merely technology-inspired, job eliminations are undoubtedly greater by far, but the incoming side of globalization makes a far from trivial contribution. By running persistently large trade deficits in manufactured goods with China, Japan and indeed most of East Asia, the United States imports not only cars, garments, shoes and sundry fripperies, but also unemployment and/or somewhat lower wages – though, of course, wages are set by the local US labor market, not in head-to-head competition with less productive, lower-paid workers overseas. Nevertheless, every time Boeing succeeds in cutting costs by purchasing abroad, jobs migrate there at the expense of local workers, to the greater benefit of its shareholders, top executives and all those employed overseas. For at its present stage, globalization enriches industrializing poor countries, impoverishes the semi-affluent majority in rich countries, and greatly adds to the incomes of the top 1 per cent on both sides who are managing the arbitrage.

In the purely theoretical context of a fully globalized economy – with no barriers to limit capital or technology movements, and no localized services, whether of doctors or cleaners – there would only be transport differentials between the wages of equally productive Bangladeshi and US workers, as for any other commodity. None of the above is true as yet: the productivity gap remains large in most cases, and in any case localized personal services continue to increase in importance, and could hardly disappear in any circumstances. However, it is a fact that US wages have been slowly converging with Third World wage rates, having long since already fallen much below German and Japanese wages, not counting superior fringe benefits – the month-long paid summer holidays of European blue-collar workers that routinely allow them to travel abroad are mere fantasy for their

American counterparts with their average of two weeks. Eventually, the next stage of globalization should relaunch the advanced economies with the demand of newly affluent ex-Third World countries, but those now being impoverished in advanced globalizing economies will have to wait a generation for the turnaround.

The cheapening of American labor, Ph.Ds very much included, is no longer news. Few US politicians find it necessary even to mention the trivial little statistic that the real hourly net pay of more than seven out of ten American employees has been stagnant or declining ever since the 1970s. How this is compatible with the slow but incontrovertible increase in affluence recorded by median income statistics and visible all around is no mystery. Household incomes have increased in the United States because many more wives work than before, and because working hours per employed person have actually increased. That lower wages can be offset by more labor is not the best of testimonials for the world's most advanced rendition of technology-powered, deregulated, globalizing turbo-capitalism.

The fall in US unemployment, in spite of continuing corporate mass-firings, is due to the superior flexibility of the American economy compared with rigid-wage Europe, as everyone knows. American banks as well as individual venture capitalists are willing to lend on future earnings, instead of demanding the guarantee of sizeable assets in hand; this is especially important in allowing young people to start new businesses. At the time of writing, my 22-year-old son has joined three friends of the same age in starting a new outdoor-adventure niche magazine with borrowed money; thus four new-made college graduates entered the labor market as employers rather than job-seekers, of themselves in the first instance, of others too if the magazine succeeds. Up to now, it is not the sort of thing that many young Europeans, let alone young Japanese, would feel free to try, even if unsecured capital were available. Flexibility is also a state of mind, both enhanced and required in turbo-capitalist conditions.

On the other hand, what labor flexibility mostly amounts to in the United States is the *in*flexibility of the individual constraints that force many Americans to accept low-paid work below their potential, in order to earn sooner rather than better. Hence jobs in marginal commercial services such as telemarketing (selling by unsolicited phone call, for commissions only) and in marginal personal services of the dog-washing-in-your-home variety can expand *ad infinitum*. Domestic service, too, is increasing after generations of decline, as marriages of young professionals committed to lifetime careers, scarcely interrupted by childbirth, produce more and more households that need and can afford servants. One constraint is that Americans must be self-supporting in extreme degree, because they cannot rely on the help of their families once they are declared to be adults. Forget the cousins that unemployed Andalusians or Greeks can count on, or the Italian parents that stand ready to help till death – in contemporary America, not even brothers and sisters help each other. Another constraint is the six-month limitation on government assistance for the unemployed, as compared to twelve or even twenty-four months in Western Europe – a mechanism easily perverted to be sure, which dissuades some people from working even when there are jobs to be had.

Europeans envy the abundance of American jobs, but many of them would not envy American wages. The arithmetic of work in turbo-capitalist conditions is paradoxical: total national income has been increasing for two decades at an average rate of just over 2.5 per cent; and yet, as better-paid corporate employment from factory floor to executive suite is replaced by often marginal service jobs, the hourly earnings of the bottom 70 per cent of all working Americans have remained stagnant or actually declined.

Betting the Company

On top of all the broad economic trends working against them, Boeing employees must also contend with the peculiarities of the airliner business. One peculiarity is that in certain markets, most notably China, Boeing must co-produce or purchase locally to be able to sell its aircraft at all, even when lower costs do not induce it to do that anyway. Another is that the risk capital needed to plan, design and engineer an entirely new airliner is large enough to strain even Boeing's gigantic resources. There has been much talk of an all-new 600-seat super jumbo, but the development cost would be so large that for Boeing it would amount to betting the company; it would court bankruptcy should the aircraft fail to sell promptly and well enough to rapidly pay back the capital outlay. By contrast, Boeing's rival, Airbus Industrie, formerly a consortium but now a unitary company, is the quintessential 'geo-economic' phenomenon of our times, exemplifying the logic of conflict in the grammar of commerce. Airbus has all the trappings of a big-time corporation, but in truth it has been the chosen instrument of the French, German and British governments, now cooperating to conquer market share in the airliner business, instead of competing to conquer colonial territories as they did a century ago. Airbus has been able to engineer its airliners with money from the French, German and British treasuries, so that the very notion of risk was irrelevant, until recent US–European Union trade negotiations finally set some limits on the subsidies it could receive.

Having no such access to public money, Boeing seeks to reduce its exposure by acquiring risk-sharing partners. Thus a 20 per cent share of the latest 777 airliner was conceded to a government-backed Japanese consortium of Mitsubishi Heavy Industries, Kawasaki Heavy Industries and Fuji Heavy Industries, which can participate in every phase from initial design to marketing, for years to come. Consequently, 20 per cent of the work of designing, engineering and manufacturing the 777 was irrevocably lost to Boeing's employees, including the factory-floor members of the International Association of Machinists and Aerospace Workers. This was part of the background to the 1995 strike. Boeing's solid argument is that 80 per cent of something is far better than 100 per cent of nothing. The counter-observation is that, while Boeing does not hesitate to 'out-source' at home or overseas whenever it is cheaper to do so, the Japanese consortium keeps its full 20 per cent manufacturing share at home, even though Japanese labor costs are now higher than in the United States. The Japanese seem to believe that the economy exists to serve society and not the other way around, so that the last margin of cost-efficiency *can* be compromised, in this case to promote the development of an industry deemed important for the country's overall advancement. And for that purpose, in addition to reasonable commercial gain, Boeing has given the consortium one of the century's best bargains: in exchange for a 20 per cent investment, it can acquire expertise in 100 per cent of the airliner business.

Even as Boeing's top executives and all shareholders are leading beneficiaries of globalization, the great mass of its employees find themselves in a now affluent but endangered tract of the global economic ocean. For one side, Boeing has been losing market share and its employees have been losing jobs to Airbus Industrie, which can afford to be an altogether more reliable employer, courtesy of French, German and British taxpayers – its accumulated losses may have exceeded $20 billion but at the last count (year-end 1997) Airbus Industrie claimed a backlog of 671 airliners on order, as opposed to Boeing's 568. On the other side, Boeing is now in the business of handing over market share (and thus further jobs) to its risk-sharing partners. Moreover, Boeing employees must in effect compete with other plants worldwide for their own work, for without higher productivity and/or union 'give-backs', the company will out-source whatever it can. Finally, as we have seen, Boeing employees are eliminated with abandon because of downsizing decisions that owe nothing to globalization, the peculiarities of the airliner industry, joint-venture partnerships or Airbus Industrie.

The acute sense of insecurity uncovered by the union's 1995 survey was therefore abundantly justified, in spite of the upsurge in aircraft orders that started just then and continued until the Asian financial crash in late 1997. True, Boeing workers thrown out – and 12,000 are under threat at the time of writing – could no doubt find an abundance of other jobs, but in the main they would be in lower-paying services, the mixed blessing of the dynamic US economy. For employees of a premier corporation that pays everyone rather well and also provides good health care and pension benefits, this is a devastating downfall entailing the possible loss of high-mortgage homes, the withdrawal of children from college education, and stress-induced sickness too, without Boeing's health-insurance benefits to pay for it. Almost all Boeing employees emphatically view themselves as belonging to the middle class, but that is a conceit as precarious as their jobs.

It is at this point that the explanation of the third set of numbers comes within sight. It has long been noticed that the technology-driven American version of turbo-capitalism condemns the less skilled to a lifetime of stagnant or declining earnings. Less noticed is another consequence – the poaching away or outright elimination of many of the low-paid but undemanding jobs that once allowed underclass strivers to rise into the working class. What has not been pondered, even to its first and most obvious implications, is that the upheavals and disruptions of turbo-capitalism, with its accelerated structural change, condemn many working Americans of *all* skill levels to lives of chronic economic insecurity. As entire industries rise and fall much faster than before, as firms expand, shrink, merge, separate, downsize and restructure at a pace never seen before, their employees at all but the highest levels must go to work each day not knowing if they will still have their job on the morrow. This uncertainty persists even when unemployment is below 5 per cent, as it is at the time of writing, for the prospect of finding another job of one kind or another is nowhere near as reassuring as a high degree of confidence in being able to keep the job one already has.

This is true of virtually the entire employed middle class, professionals very much included. They lack the formal safeguards of Western Europe's employee-protection laws and prolonged unemployment benefits. They lack the families in good working order that much of the rest of humanity still relies upon to survive hard times. And they lack the substantial liquid savings of their middle-class counterparts in all other developed countries. Hence most working Americans must rely on their jobs for their entire and immediate economic security – a condition taken for granted in the United States, but most unusual in other developed countries. Meanwhile, the unskilled of the underclass have largely become economically useless, which means that the United States has spectacular crime rates and that virtually every city has its 'no-go' areas, where intruders can easily become victims of the permanent Black *intifadah*, of which the sensational exculpation of the athlete O.J. Simpson is as much an expression as the occasional riots.

The further impoverishment of the unskilled means that the United States is on its way to acquiring the income-distribution characteristics of a Third World country, with a truly very rich top 1 per cent, and a significant minority (roughly 12 per cent) which remains below the official poverty line even though fully employed, forty hours a week, fifty weeks a year. In New York State, whose economy is very dynamic and especially turbo-capitalist – it contains Wall Street, after all – income distribution has predictably become even more unequal than in the United States as a whole. In 1996 the average income of the richest one-fifth of all households was almost twenty times higher at $132,390 than that of the poorest fifth at $6,787. Only in Washington DC was the ratio even more extreme at 28.2, while the averages for the United States as a whole were $117,499 and $9,254, a ratio of 12.7.[8] In New York State, moreover, the average income of the top-earning fifth of all households increased by 46 per cent between 1978 and 1996, while that of the poorest fifth of all households actually declined by 36 per cent – partly because of family breakdown trends that leave statisticians counting more single parents with children as 'households', but also because of declining earnings at the bottom of the economy that play their own large role in breaking up families.

The underclass, much filmed, much discussed and much deplored, but less than 5 per cent of the adult population, mostly does not vote

[8] Blaine Harden, 'New York richest get richer, poorest poorer', *Washington Post*, 19 December 1997, p. A3, citing Center on Budget and Policy Priorities data.

at all, provides no campaign funding and can express its resentments, if at all, only by individual acts of criminality and occasional mini-pogroms. They fall under Rule Number Three of the Calvinist system, in contrast to the working poor and semi-poor who obey Rule Number Two, silently accepting their lot because they feel guilty about their failure to succeed.

The New Prohibitionism

By contrast, the economic insecurity that coexists with affluence or semi-affluence for the vast majority of Americans is expressed politically whenever there are elections, Presidential, Congressional, State-level or local. They vote, or more than half of them do, at least in Presidential elections, and in the upper ranges they also contribute to election campaigns. The 1992 defeat of the otherwise unblemished President Bush, in the immediate aftermath of a spectacular military victory, was proof positive that no sitting President can be re-elected when unemployment approaches the levels that Western Europeans tolerated for years.

This is not enough, however, to express the resentment of the middle-class majority – not over poverty, which is not their lot, but in reaction to their widespread, low-level, chronic economic insecurity. There is no need to be a dead social philosopher to recognize the connection between what a turbo-capitalist economy is doing to most Americans, and the increasingly intolerant climate of contemporary American life. Visitors to the United States nowadays often point out that more and more things are legally or socially prohibited in the Land of the Free. Even as American democracy flourishes and is increasingly emulated as far afield as South Korea and Bolivia, it is an increasingly illiberal democracy.

In the absence of any plausible theory that suggests another course, the insecure majority makes no economic demands. It accepts without question the unchallengeable sovereignty of the market, and the absolute primacy of economic efficiency over almost any societal purpose. Instead it vents its anger and resentment by punishing, restricting and prohibiting all that can be punished, restricted and prohibited. America's own perfectly democratic, mostly non-racist and certainly unwarlike improved substitute for fascism nevertheless contains the essence of the original item: the non-economic expression of economic dissatisfactions. The cause-and-effect connection between the two, needless to say, is entirely unrecognized.

One symptom is the insatiable demand for stricter laws, longer prison sentences, mandatory life sentences for repeat offenders (with no discretion left to the court), mandatory life sentences without possibility of parole, many more death sentences and prompter executions. Until recently, the death penalty had either been abolished by legislation or was simply in abeyance in the great majority of States; in recent years it has been legislated again, and is regularly applied in thirty of the fifty States, including New York State. In twenty of the fifty States, juveniles can now be sentenced to death from the age of sixteen, though with execution delayed till the exact date of the condemned's eighteenth birthday. It is illegal to buy cigarettes or any beverage containing more than 1 per cent of alcohol at the age of sixteen, but one may be sentenced to death. Not all are satisfied, however. In 1998, debate started in California over the merits of lowering the minimum age of sentencing to fourteen, inevitably evoking competition: in New Mexico there is talk of imposing death sentences from the age of thirteen. With that, there is growing impatience with the long delay prior to execution. Even sharper has been the pressure for harsher forms of detention, including in the South a reversion to chain-gangs, so that once again prisoners in striped or arrowed uniforms work alongside rural roads, though no longer chanting as in the classic film renditions. Democracy really does work in the United States, and politicians including Bill Clinton obey the popular will. The result is a great mass of new Federal and State legislation that is adding rapidly to the number behind bars; as of 31 December 1994 there were already 1.4 million people in prisons. By mid-1997 the number had increased to 1.8 million, with further increases projected. This is the third Calvinist rule at work. And it works all the better for the fact that those who demand so much punishment honestly believe that they are only expressing righteous indignation against crime, and purposefully seeking protection against its violent perpetrators. That perhaps one-half of all prisoners were sentenced for selling drugs to consenting adults, for possessing drugs for their own use, or for other non-violent offenses including tax fraud, belies the protective justification.

However, this is only the most blatant expression of a much broader urge to prohibit and punish. In theory, America is in the grip of a *kulturkampf*, a cultural war, between permissive liberals and 'family-values' conservatives. In practice, self-defined liberals and all but the libertarian fragment of the conservatives[9] are tacitly collaborating to delegitimize anything and everything that can then be prohibited by laws or social disapproval. At first sight, each prohibition has its own independent justification, valid for left or right, or sometimes both:

- Smoking – for health reasons; for by-standers as well, under the heading of secondary inhalation or passive smoking.
- The eating of rich foods by those already fat, apt to evoke expressed disapproval in public eateries in the United States – for health reasons again, notwithstanding the demolition of the purported correlation between chubbiness and any adverse effects.
- Any sort of flirtation, however amiable – as sexual harassment, or even rape presumptive in many a university.
- Actual sex, if non-marital – because of HIV infection, which stubbornly remains statistically insignificant among non-injecting heterosexuals, in spite of hugely alarmist projections, yet is vociferously presented as a terrifying danger to schoolchildren across America.
- Pornography – to safeguard public decency, of course, notwithstanding inconveniently strong safeguards of free speech in the US Constitution. These are now circumvented by judicial rulings that affirm 'community values', lately applied not only in the incorrigible rural South against the likes of *The Tin Drum* of Gunther Grass, but also – most amazingly – against the pornography emporia of Times Square, Manhattan.
- More pornography, on the Internet – subject of an urgent, high-priority intervention in 1996, not coincidentally an election year, by President Clinton himself in favor of the V-chip, a device that allows the exclusion of naughty pixels.
- Topless bathing, universal on the Côte d'Azur, widespread elsewhere and narrowly confined to a diminishing handful of US beaches – for reasons of prudery masquerading as morality.
- All manner of speech and jest – to safeguard the wounded sentiments of potential victims under an infinity of rubrics: racism, sexism, ageism, handicapism, the sanctity of all religions. A joke with a sexual theme, or a mere sexual allusion perhaps unintentional, can now cost the job of a senior executive by simple accusation, because employers rightly fear the million-dollar

[9] Exemplified by Milton Friedman, recipient of the Nobel Prize for Economics and a tireless campaigner against drug prohibitionism.

lawsuits of aggrieved parties, charging responsibility for 'operating' a sexist workplace.

- And drugs, of course, arguably to be decriminalized if only because drug enforcement is totally ineffectual, arguably to be strictly prohibited on health grounds, but now so harshly punished that every year hundreds of thousands of young lives are seriously prejudiced by arrest records, which preclude many a profession if even the simple possession of a few grams of marijuana is charged.

It is no coincidence that prohibitions multiply when the middle classes are especially insecure. It has all happened before, and there is absolutely no need of a Gestapo when there are so many eager volunteers to do the job, by pursing lips, narrowing eyes (just ask anyone who smokes in public), loud disapproval, threatened or actual lawsuits and, even more consequentially, voting for the least tolerant candidate available.

In the past, everything would have been done more simply by the harsh persecution of a suitable racial or cultural minority, preferably obviously distinct by appearance, skin color or dress. That minority alone would have paid the price for the declining *relative* incomes of most Americans, and the insecurity of many more in the brave new economy of unlimited competition and endless structural change, which offers splendid opportunities to financial acrobats, and which keeps so many Americans awake at night fearfully wondering what the morrow will bring. With the persecution of minorities ruled out by untouchable constitutional guarantees, by many specific laws and chiefly by the force of fashion, the unexpressed fears of insecure bread-winners can find their outlet only in the prohibition of all that can be prohibited, and in harsh punishment of all those who can be criminalized.

Intolerant Justice, Unjust Tolerance

It is interesting to compare the state of freedom in the United States and in Italy, a country of extensive public ownership (only now being reduced by privatizations), pervasive regulations, very strict job protection laws, severe licensing restrictions on commerce, strongly supportive extended families and high savings rates. Few Italians have the range of opportunities that Americans enjoy; few Italians have to fear for their economic security from day to day.

In the United States, the freedom of the individual from arbitrary arrest and detention is effectively safeguarded by constitutional guarantees that no police officer or prosecutor can ignore. In Italy, by contrast, the many pretty words of the 1946 Constitutional Charter do not prevent magistrates from ordering arrests on vague charges, or from keeping people in prison for interrogation at their leisure, for weeks or months. On the other hand, Italian public opinion is not pressing Parliament to enact stricter criminal laws with mandatory prison sentences, or to reintroduce the death penalty, abolished in 1946. As a practical matter, Italian courts are far more reluctant to impose prison sentences for non-violent crimes than American courts, and when prison sentences are imposed, they are much shorter on average. For these reasons too – in addition to a lower incidence of arrests and successful prosecutions – only 50,476 Italians were in prison in April 1998; there would have been some 470,000 at American rates, a huge difference.[10]

As for the climate of ordinary life, while Americans are increasingly restricted in their personal choices by both legal prohibitions and social pressures, Italians remain broadly tolerant of each other's proclivities and tastes. In the absence of widespread economic insecurity, there is no great urge to punish and prohibit. Although most people find it boring, even the hardest of hard-core pornography is freely available at street-corner news-stands for its small clientele, and nobody seems to object to the nudity common in advertizing and frequent on open-channel television. Public figures can conduct their private lives without being terrorized by the fear of exposure, for even if politicians are caught out by scandal sheets with extra-marital companions, male or female, that is where matters end, with no serious media willing to take up the story, no expulsions and no resignations. Less prominent individuals benefit from a like indulgence in a climate not so much permissive as simply relaxed.

If the new style of prohibitionism is an expression of economic insecurities, one would expect it to spread to other countries that embrace turbo-capitalism. And that has indeed happened, most notably in Britain, where the Tories increasingly stressed 'family values' in step with their liberalization of the British economy during the 1980s under Margaret Thatcher, and even more in the 1990s under John Major – finally and completely wrecking their chances in the election of May 1997 for that very reason, because of an

[10] *Espresso*, 25 June 1998, p. 56, Table.

embarrassing number of sexual scandals among Major's ministers.

There has always been a repressive strain among the Tories, with a vociferous minority in favor of strict censorship, still longing for the good old days of corporal punishment, and still loudly calling for the restoration of the death penalty at the Conservative Party's annual conference. But until the 1980s, the dominant strain was characterized by the ingrained tolerance of the more aristocratic wing of the party – one does not call for censorship while drinking champagne aboard a yacht on the French Riviera. In contrast, Margaret Thatcher and John Major's New Tories, who believed in both free markets and social repression, were predominantly of modest middle-class origins.

When Tony Blair's free-market New Labour won the 1997 general election by a landslide, in great part by openly embracing Thatcherite economics with a light dusting of low-cost social concerns and vague mutterings about 'stakeholders', it ignored an entire tradition of internationalist socialist liberality in favour of the other Old Labour strain, provincial, low-Church, puritanical and repressive. It naturally struck a stringent 'family values' stance, and talked a lot about law and order, and the need to build more prisons. The Home Secretary, Jack Straw, an enthusiast for more prison sentences, longer sentences and stricter prison regimes, is also seemingly much preoccupied with film and video censorship. When Lord Birkett, one of the two vice-presidents of the British Board of Film Censors, was to replace the Earl of Harewood as its head in December 1997, Jack Straw personally intervened to block Birkett's elevation. With Lords Harewood and Birkett already greatly suspect (they belong to the champagne-in-the-French-Riviera set), to his 'intense annoyance' Jack Straw had just discovered that the BBFC had relaxed its norms on sex videos without consulting the Home Office and himself.[11]

The offense to public morals was indeed very grave: the BBFC had given an R18 certificate, which allows sale only in licensed sex shops, both to the American-made *Batbabe*, a variation on the Batman motif, 'said to contain 30 minutes of sexual intercourse', no doubt a shocking surprise for the innocent buyers, and to the British-made *Ladies Behaving Badly*, whose very title is redolent of an entire British tradition of prudery. Had the BBFC not intervened, both tapes could have been seized under the 1984 Video Recordings Act, and the perpetrators could have been sent to prison for up to two years, or

---

[11] Philip Johnston, 'Straw to change cast at board of film censors', *Daily Telegraph*, 9 December 1997, p. 13.

fined an unlimited amount of money for their full-frontal attack on Britain's purity. Naturally, Customs and Excise complained against the BBFC's liberality, and so did the police, much concerned with the upkeep of the obscenity laws, as always. Jack Straw was thus determined to appoint a new head for the BBFC who would comply with New Labour's priorities, which are exactly the same as those of the New Tories, exemplified by Julian Brazier, appropriately enough MP for Canterbury, and President of the Conservative Family Campaign, who demanded a BBFC President 'genuinely concerned' with hardcore pornography.

The same coincidence between the admission of turbo-capitalism and the exclusion of sexual wickedness that went unnoticed when jobs were still secure is reproduced elsewhere – even in countries as permissive as Belgium, the country of on-the-highway rural sex stations, complete with ladies in *déshabillé*. There, as in the United States and many other places, the advance of repressive prudery is spearheaded by outrage at child pornography and the sexual use of children, horrible crimes to be sure, but fortunately rather rare and always localized. Yet each episode sets off wide-ranging investigations that serve as diversionary attacks, whose goal is to overwhelm residual liberality before getting at the real objectives of the offensive – ordinary adult pornography, ordinary adult sex.

During the period of high employment and taken-for-granted personal economic security that ended in the 1970s, sex along with much else was progressively decriminalized, ever more broadly accepted within families, and viewed with increasingly untroubled equanimity by most people. Eventually, the doing and displaying by way of word, imagery and deed became overdoing and excess, stimulating a normal corrective reaction, slightly accentuated by the concurrent ageing of advanced populations. But this was rapidly overlaid by far more powerful prohibitionist and punitive urges, unleashed by the insecurities of turbo-capitalism, bringing us the likes of Jack Straw and his hunt for naughty video-tapes, all his American counterparts – every County judge and sheriff is his own Jack Straw – and, far more sadly, the grim cruelty of locking up more and more bad and semi-bad people at great cost to make them worse.

Thus *free markets* and *less free societies* go hand in hand, with the insecurities of the former expressed in all the possible forms of repression that today's conventionalities still allow: no anti-Semitism, the old tried and true standby to deflect resentment away from predatory elites; no racism, of course, which would 'shock and horrify'

Messrs Blair and Straw as they went about their business of expressing decency from every pore; and no *public* torture, for what daily goes on in prisons by way of standard operating procedures is not reckoned as such. This still allows lots of punishment and the prohibition of whatever can be prohibited, from tobacco to sex. In the meantime, the blatant contradiction in the remedies of both Democrats and Republicans in the United States, both Labour and Conservatives in Britain, passes unobserved: they all want a yet more dynamic turbo-capitalism *and* the protection of ancient 'family values'. In the words of the mail-bomb 'Unabomber' killer (later identified as Theodore H. Kaczynski, now imprisoned for life):

> The conservatives [add Labour, and US Democrats] are fools: they whine about the decay of traditional values, yet they enthusiastically support technological progress and economic growth. Apparently it never occurs to them that you can't make rapid, drastic changes in the technology and the economy of a society without causing rapid changes in all other aspects of the society as well, and that such rapid changes inevitably break down traditional values.[12]

[12] From 'Industrial society and its future', *Washington Post*, 2 August 1995.

FOUR

The Microsoft Mirage

There is nowadays only one economic orthodoxy, taught by almost all academic economists, happily celebrated by turbo-capitalism's winners, and accepted by almost all political leaders worldwide. It depicts the present workings of the American economy as a huge success, exemplified by the phenomenal rise of the 'New Titans' of the information age: the legendary twins Microsoft and Intel, and their lesser emulators such as Apple, Novell, Cisco, Oracle, Bay Net, Sun Microsystems, Sybase, Adobe Systems, Amgen, Cirrus, Informix, Intuit, Cordis, Am.Online, Autodesk, MBC Soft, Picturetel and Peoplesoft. Most of them did not even exist twenty years ago. The combined value of their shares, albeit fluctuating, now greatly exceeds that of the unfashionable old-style giants of US manufacturing, General Motors, Ford, Boeing, Dupont and Kodak. The phenomenal capital value of the New Titans is easily explained: they enjoy extraordinarily high profit margins on their sales. Instead of manufacturing a car at a unit cost of, say, $12,000 for sale at $18,000, they sell the accumulated result of past research at ten or twenty times the unit cost. Microsoft is the limiting case, for it nets some $200 or so for every package of software, whose unit cost for plastic and cardboard does not exceed a few dollars.

In the course of their advance from small beginnings to their present heights, the New Titans have made several billionaires and thousands of millionaires among early investors, while also adding to the wealth of a much greater number of shareholders, pension-plan participants and holders of mutual funds. That makes for a great deal of optimism.

Titans New and Old

Every principle of the ruling orthodoxy is defended by citing the success of the New Titans. Free trade, or more precisely the continuing effort by the United States to further unify the world economy by negotiating away trade, investment and licensing barriers of all kinds, is justified above all by citing the success of American high-technology exports, notably including the hardware and software of the New Titans. By contrast, the net loss of some two million jobs – by the lowest current estimate – caused by the chronic excess of US merchandise imports over exports, is held to be of small account because those jobs are said to be in low-skill occupations, in declining industries.

Deregulation, most recently of telecommunications, is likewise justified by the wonderful opportunities it opens up for the New Titans, as also for the new-style 'lean and mean' telephone and cable television companies which are opening up the electronic super-highway, including the Internet. In the process, the existing regional telephone companies, 'the Baby Bells', are in danger of being swept away unless they become drastically more efficient by cutting their employee rolls, as Pacific Bell has done. So long as they remained monopolies with their tariffs and service options strictly regulated by local boards, the Baby Bells were sufficiently protected from competition to be steady, well-paying employers, and generous supporters of all manner of local community activities – to please the local regulators, of course. Now they are busily getting rid of as many employees as they can, and of all other dispensable expenses, to become lean and mean with the best of them. A good employer is a badly managed business according to the ruling orthodoxy, which sees no merit in anything that might impede efficiency.

Even when political leaders criticize some specific consequence of turbo-capitalism, itself a very rare event, they never challenge its principles, make no attempt to resist its workings, and indeed actively promote its further advance. Thus in 1995, President Clinton bitterly complained in public speeches about the current crop of mass-firings announced by major corporations in general, and by AT&T in particular − of 40,000 employees initially, later reduced to 18,000. At the same time, however, the Clinton administration was enthusiastically advocating Congressional approval of the Telecommunications Deregulation and Competition Act of 1995. This breaks down long-established regulatory barriers to allow regional telephone companies, long-distance carriers (AT&T, MCI, Sprint and more), and cable-television companies to compete in each other's markets by offering whatever services they care to provide: local, long-distance, television and data.

It will take some time for interested long-distance carriers to run wires into homes and offices, but the networks of the cable-television companies are already in place, and have plenty of band-width capacity to carry telephone and fax signals as well. With all this new competition bearing down upon them, the regional telephone companies must therefore do exactly what AT&T was criticized for doing, i.e. dismiss tens of thousands of employees to become more automated and more efficient. It is a classic case of false consciousness: President Clinton was deploring the very consequences his administration was bringing about.

Most important, the success of the New Titans is regularly invoked to argue that no real harm is being inflicted by drastic reductions in the number of administrative and clerical employees, whose work is to be replaced by more computerized processing. The latter, it is pointed out, generates its own employment, in writing software, developing customized applications, and in the manufacture and maintenance of computers and their ancillaries. According to the ruling orthodoxy, so readily echoed by almost all and sundry in the United States and beyond, downsizing simply means that some Americans are being forced to move to better jobs: General Motors may throw you out, but Microsoft will hire you, and Microsoft jobs are better.

It is enough to look at the employment rolls of the New Titans of the information age, as opposed to their share values, to see the fundamental error of these expectations. Microsoft and Intel have become huge on Wall Street. The combined value of their shares is much greater than that of General Motors, though the latter remains the world's largest manufacturing enterprise by far. As employers, however, Microsoft and Intel were by no means so huge, with their combined total of 48,100 employees in 1995, as opposed to 721,000 for General Motors, more than half of them in the United States. In fact *all* the New Titans listed above, Apple, Novell, Cisco, Oracle, Bay Net, Sun Microsystems, Sybase, Adobe Systems, Amgen, Cirrus, Informix, Intuit, Cordis, Am.Online, Autodesk, MBC Soft, Picturetel and Peoplesoft as well as Intel and Microsoft, had a combined grand total of some 128,420 employees, less than one-fifth of the number employed by General Motors alone.

The information technology 'New Titans': employee rolls, 1995

Intel	32,600	Microsoft	15,500
Novell	6,165	Cisco	2,262
Oracle	19,000	Bay Net	3,840
Sun Micro	13,300	Sybase	4,016
Amgen	2,200	Peoplesoft	651
Cirrus	1,809	Informix	2,212
Intuit	1,228	Am.Online	527
MBC Soft	987	Autodesk	1,788
Picturetel	1,000	Cordis	3,370
Apple	14,400	Adobe	1,565

Grand total: 128,420 (General Motors: 721,000)

Source: Allan W. Spearman, personal communication, 15 February 1996.

To be sure, General Motors is continuing to reduce employee rolls in both its offices and its factories, while Intel, Microsoft and other software companies are adding to theirs. Thus by 1997 Microsoft was already up to some 25,000, although Apple was down to less than 10,000. And every other month information-technology New Titans climb from obscurity to stock-market prominence. Still, at current rates of change on both sides, it would take decades for General Motors alone to be matched as an employer. One implication is obvious: there are relatively few jobs where there is the most capital value, and vice versa.

There are, however, many other New Titans outside the computer-chip and software industry that have also risen from nothing, such as Southwest Airlines, Nike shoes, Charles Schwab the mega-broker, and Genentech, the premier biotechnology company. Still, they too employ very few people for all their success.

Other 'New Titans': employee rolls, 1994

	Year founded	Employees
Southwest Airlines	1971	15,200
Nike	1972	9,000
Charles Schwab	1974	6,500
Genentech	1976	2,600

Source: Robert J. Samuelson, 'Reinventing Corporate America', *Washington Post*, 29 June 1994, p. A23.

The unimpressive employment figures of very impressive corporate success stories may be compared to the employee rolls of the companies that we should presumably label the Old Titans, the great names of US manufacturing.

The old industrial Titans: employee rolls, 1995

General Motors	721,000
Ford	325,300
Boeing	143,200
Dupont	125,000
Kodak	132,600

Source: Spearman.

If the US economy consisted only of Old Titans with a very large but diminishing number of employees, and of New Titans that employ very few, unemployment would be rising to phenomenal levels. Of course, this is not so because of the vast and diverse array of services, everything from local, State and Federal government to dry-cleaners, with the huge and growing health-care industry in between. Within it, there are the retail trade and fast-food giants, very large corporations that can perhaps be described as non-Titans, which have added greatly to the number of their employees. But there is a catch: they offer neither the superlative jobs that abound in the information technology sector, not the plain but well-paid industrial jobs of the Old Titans. In large-scale retailing and in the fast-food chains, many employees work at the minimum wage, many others earn not much more, and only a few at the top are very well paid, for there is not much of a management pyramid in the outlets themselves, and head offices are also quite small.

Retail and fast-food chains: employee rolls, 1995

Home Depot	62,000
Wal-Mart	434,000
K-mart	358,000
Sears	403,000
McDonald's	177,000

Source: Spearman.

Much Capital, Few Jobs

The wider implications of these simple numbers are enormous. US policy across the board is focused on the promotion of high-technology industries, while the fate of low- and medium-technology industries is viewed with indifference. Certainly in foreign trade negotiations, successive US administrators have striven mightily to open new export markets for high-technology goods and high-value financial and professional services, offering in exchange increasingly free access to the US market; in the process, US low- and medium-technology industries are left to decline as they are increasingly exposed to cheaper imports. From a global perspective, this makes perfect sense as nations trade up, each according to its comparative advantages, world resources are better employed to increase the sum total of world prosperity. These priorities do, however, imply a future in which high-technology industries and high-value services flourish, while low- and medium-technology industries disappear.

What would happen to the United States as a country if the vision of an all 'high-tech' industrial economy were to be realized? With a dozen high-flying Microsofts and lots of successful Peoplesofts, the total capital value of the stock market would soar, perhaps raising the Dow-Jones Index to 20,000 or more, creating billionaires by the dozen and great numbers of millionaires. In the meantime, with the replacement of GM, Ford, Kodak, Dupont and all the other old-style, slow-growing, 'medium-tech' Old Titan manufacturers by New Titans, the total number of well-paid jobs in the American economy would decline to a fraction of present levels.

So long as US industry consisted of the likes of GM and Kodak, this equation simply could not equate. Corporations that sell high-price durables and discretionary consumer goods by the million within the domestic market cannot hope to prosper, or even survive, if the mass of their prospective consumers is employed in retail or other service jobs that pay low wages, instead of working for other well-paying industrial corporations.

In 1914 Henry Ford paid his workers a spectacular daily wage of $5 (*The Wall Street Journal* called it an 'economic crime') to assemble model Ts that sold for $360. It was axiomatic for Ford that his workers be able to buy the cars they made, as indeed they did easily enough if possessed of working-age sons, by saving up just twelve weeks' worth of their wages. If Ford and the rest of the automobile industry had found a way to produce millions of cars with no more than a few thousand workers, their technological success would have been futile, for they would not have been able to sell them. But Ford's axiom is no more. The New Titans can and do prosper by supplying only the world's elites and near elites – the buyers and users of computers, software and peripheral ancillaries – with very-high-margin products in relatively small volumes. Their mass production no longer requires mass consumption to remain in balance – just ask the Mexicans who assemble $20,000 Ford cars in Hermosillo at wages of less than $200 per week, for whom owning one of the cars they assemble is not a realistic aim, but an impossible dream.

It follows that the happy-equilibrium interpretation of structural change is simply wrong: if GM no longer needs you because of more computerization, Microsoft will *not* hire you. First, you are not professionally trained, and Microsoft has no use for uneducated blue-collar workers spoilt by too much pay for brainless assembly-line jobs. In his day, Henry Ford's assembly line was itself a magnificent training device, which transformed illiterate peasants from the villages of Eastern Europe, raw farmboys from the countryside and urban slum kids into disciplined industrial workers, ready to become householders and car owners. They learned to arrive on time by the clock instead of rising with the sun in the changing seasons, they learned what was left and what was right, and then they became at least minimally numerate. Microsoft, by contrast, recruits the ready-made products of expensive educations in the best universities for its software-writing teams, and has little need of anyone else.

Second, if you *are* well educated, Microsoft will probably not hire you anyway — it is just not a labor-intensive business to produce and mail out pre-packaged software, conceptualized and written by a few thousand people and their helpers. As of 1997, Microsoft reportedly hired only 2 per cent of all applicants for software-writing positions, finally offering jobs to only one-quarter of the fortunate few, presumably with all needed qualifications, who were invited to its headquarters for face-to-face interviews.[1]

What this means in a larger perspective is that information technology is not a job-creator in the way electric motors (the last big leap) certainly were, displacing some manual workers along with steam engines, while giving birth to several new industries that offered much employment and still do. Instead, as chance would have it, information technology is a job 'sink' as physicists would say: it destroys clerical and, increasingly, administrative jobs by the million, while providing relatively few jobs of its own, most of them in the United States. Elsewhere, in unfortunate lands with weak software industries, it mostly destroys jobs while producing very few sales and promotion jobs of its own.

Moreover, there is conclusive evidence that what is true of Microsoft and software engineers is also true of high technology in general. It is above all engineers of various kinds that all such industries need, and yet between 1968 and 1995 the median annual salary, including fringe benefits, of engineers with four years of college education and ten years of experience *declined* by 13 per cent in constant dollars, to descend to the far from impressive level of $52,900.[2]

Evidently there is a general oversupply of engineers, even though there may be shortages from time to time in particular specialties; as of now, for example, software-*application* specialists are much in demand. By contrast, even at the height of the boom in 1997, there was still an oversupply of software engineers in general, so much so that employers could pick and choose among job applicants, specifically picking the young who cost less, while rejecting mid-career applicants — not something they could afford to do if there were a

[1] Norman Matloff, 'Now hiring! If you're young', *New York Times*, 26 January 1998, p. A23.

[2] Michael S. Teitelbaum, 'Too many engineers, too few jobs', *New York Times*, 19 March 1996, p. A23.

shortage. The result is that even the highly qualified in a hyper-successful trade are forced to look elsewhere for their livelihood, once they get a little older and are no longer the cheapest labor around: only some 19 per cent of computer science graduates still had jobs in the field twenty years after graduation, according to a recent survey.[3] In spite of all the celebration of their glory, it turns out that the New Titans, which do not employ uneducated slobs, do not employ all that many qualified people either.

The expansion of high-tech education is therefore far from being a sovereign remedy, as political leaders worldwide seem to believe. Countries sadly bereft of qualified technical cadres can certainly benefit from acquiring more of them. In advanced economies, however, to turn out more engineers would only add to their oversupply. For as it happens, the profession is especially exposed to the job-sink effect. Many design engineers are being replaced by a few, now aided by computer-assisted design in three dimensions; many developmental engineers are being replaced by a few, aided by computerized mechanical, hydraulic and thermal dynamic-analysis software; many production engineers are being replaced by a few, aided by integrated systems that convert design data into final tool or process instructions, so as to provide automated linkages to equally automated production. The happy-equilibrium theory would have all that software writing and software application employ as many people as 'manual' engineering used to do, and employ them better. In practice, information technology eliminates many engineer positions while providing jobs for relatively few. This is hardly surprising. On the one hand, firms invest their money to buy software and hardware for 3-D computer-assisted design, dynamic analysis and integrated systems precisely to save much more in engineering hours. On the other, the information technology industry is so profitable precisely because the one-off development work of its software engineers can be sold many times over.

It is true, of course, that even if information technology jobs are few, they do generate many other jobs because they provide high incomes, as well as very high capital gains from retained or expected profits for owner-managers, outside investors and shareholders at large. Though the highest earners do all the saving in the United States, which has the world's only non-saving middle class, much of the income is spent. All that money employs many in construction –

<hr />

[3] Id., citing a National Science Foundation/Bureau of the Census study.

Silicon Valley magnates have acquired a taste for mansions and ski lodges of late – in distribution and retailing, in health care and in all manner of professional and personal services that occupy all manner of people, from architects to house servants, with lots of lawyers in between. The same is true of the other industries especially favored by turbo-capitalism, beginning with financial services, ranging from the spectacular summits of investment banking to the lower depths of extortionate money lending ('sub-prime second mortgage home-equity loans').

The Return of the Servants

Long in decline from its Victorian heights, domestic service has much revived in recent years. There are few under-parlor maids or butlers to be found in Silicon Valley, and only the most ostentatious beneficiaries of investment banking retain the services of a butler, preferably English or at least with a passably British accent. But the reversion to Victorian patterns of income distribution brought about by turbo-capitalism has produced both a large supply of willing servants and employers who can afford them.

Under-parlor maids are still mostly absent, but the new wave of high achievers married to other high achievers employs a great profusion of maids, baby-sitters, cooks, drivers and gardeners. Instead of being the servants of the leisured class, as in Victorian times and all previous eras, they serve an almost-no-leisure class. Only thus can demanding jobs, parenthood, tennis, cocktail parties, the theater and more be combined; behind every woman-who-can-do-it-all success story, there are other women and men who do only one thing.

It was not supposed to work out that way. When domestic servants became less abundant, because expanding industry, commerce and public services provided more dignified and frequently better-paid employment, their disappearance was confidently projected before the Second World War, and almost achieved by the 1960s even in the United Kingdom and certainly in the United States. Since then, the wheel has turned again, and turned back.

Domestic servants complement the profusion of marginal service jobs that have already been noted, a symptom of the cheapening of less skilled labor. More than skill is involved, however, as the declining earnings of engineers in the United States clearly show. By accelerating structural change, turbo-capitalism rewards agility as much as competence. It offers an expanded stream of new opportunities to those who can smartly position themselves to exploit them, while penalizing ordinary people who fail to jump to something better when their jobs are eliminated or downgraded by technically induced change, deregulation or imports. When all must run faster than before if only to stay in place, a few will run ahead and do very well, but many more will fall behind. Until the advent of turbo-capitalism, there was a definite compression of income differentials; it was an increasingly compact pack that was doing the running. Now the runners are increasingly stretched out, with a lengthening interval between the fortunate few far ahead, and an increasing number of stragglers.

To get at the economy's own distribution of income under turbo-capitalism, before the government's income taxes, pensions and welfare payments obscure the situation, one can look at US statistics for the percentage share of aggregate income received by the bottom fifth of all households, and the top fifth, and the other three fifths in between, as in the table below. (In the table, income is defined as including capital gains and employee health benefits, while excluding both income taxes and government cash payments.)

Aggregate income of US households (before government transfers), 1995 (%)

Lowest-earning 20% of all households	0.9
Second 20% of all households	7.2
Third 20% of all households	14.7
Fourth 20% of all households	24.2
Top-earning 20% of all households	52.9

Source: US Bureau of the Census, http://www.census.gov/hhes/income95/ in95agg1.html. TABLE E.

In other words, out of the one hundred million or so American households, twenty million received more than half (52.9 per cent) of the total income of all households, while the other eighty million received the balance of 47.1%, before government transfers intervened to tax at the top, and pay out at the bottom. In other words, left alone, turbo-capitalism generates a phenomenally unequal distribution of income. Moreover, the roughly forty million households in the two lowest quintile slices would have received just 8.1 per cent of all the income earned by all households without the government's intervention, with the bottom fifth receiving less than 1 per cent. What we have here is a precise statistical depiction of the strung-out line of runners, with the top twenty million households well ahead, and the bottom twenty million left far, far behind.

In reality, of course, the government does tax incomes and does provide both generic and means-tested payments under various headings: pensions and survivor benefits ('social security') for the aged, poor or not, who worked and contributed before retiring; public assistance for the aged poor who did not contribute; health care for the aged ('Medicare') and for the poor ('Medicaid'); and disability payments for poor invalids, and for non-working women with dependent children (AFDC) – though the latter has been greatly restricted by the 1997 Welfare Reform law, one of the clearest expressions of Calvinism in modern times.

Moreover, it is a peculiarity of American life that, in addition to the retired, a great many others who earn little or nothing and survive on government assistance may nevertheless own their own homes. This yields no cash unless boarders are taken in, but does generate an implicit income, in effect a return on their investment, inasmuch as they pay no rent. And, of course, Medicare and Medicaid also amount to implicit income, because their beneficiaries receive health-care services that presumably they would otherwise pay for (an admittedly large presumption, considering habitual overmedication on the one hand, and the inability of the poor to pay for it on the other). Once all these additional sources of actual and virtual income are added in, and income and capital-gains taxes are subtracted, the pattern of distribution certainly changes, but less than one might think.

Aggregate income of US households after government transfers, 1995 (%)

Lowest-earning 20% of all households	5.2
Second 20% of all households	11.0
Third 20% of all households	16.3
Fourth 20% of all households	23.4
Top-earning 20% of all households	44.1

Source: US Bureau of the Census, http://www.census.gov/hhes/income95/in95agg1.html. TABLE E.

With the fivefold increase achieved by government redistribution and imputed rent, the income share of the bottom twenty million or so households comes to just over one-tenth of that of the top quintile, while sixty million American households receive much less (32.5%) than the twenty million at the top.

Even that greatly understates what is going on, because the top quintile embraces too many households – some twenty million at present – while the concentration of income and wealth is most notable at the very top of the income pyramid. To isolate this phenomenon it is useful to examine how the top 5 per cent of all households have fared since the Second World War.

Between 1947 and 1956, immediate post-war years of rapid growth, the share of the aggregate pre-tax income of all households received by the most fortunate top 5 per cent fluctuated considerably between 15.7 and 17.5 per cent; and, of course, with marginal income tax rates as high as 90 per cent, the post-tax income share was much less. Between 1957 and 1966, years of social advancement for both the rural and urban poor in an economy that enjoyed very fast growth by present standards (some 4 per cent per year on average), the share of the aggregate pre-tax income of all households received by the top 5 per cent continued to fluctuate, but within a much narrower range from 15.4 to 15.9 per cent. In other words, the top 5 per cent lost ground in a society that was broadly advancing, allowing those at the bottom to catch up.

Next, between 1967 and 1976, when inflation compounded by the first oil-supply crisis intervened to disturb the situation, the range broadened somewhat to give the top 5 per cent between 15.5 and 16.4 per cent of all household income, though the latter figure was registered only in 1967, and if that year is excluded, the range narrows considerably from 15.5 to 15.9 per cent. Finally, between 1977 and 1994, the years in which the broad deregulation that engendered American turbo-capitalism was started, the top 5 per cent of all households did very much better, while the bottom 20 per cent and the next 20 per cent lost ground, as they continue to do.

What these figures show explicitly is the slow upward creep in the share of total income received by the top 5 per cent of all households, the leading beneficiaries of turbo-capitalist change. They also show, just as explicitly, the downward drift in the income of the bottom 40 per cent of all households. By 1994, the latest available year in this series, the roughly forty million households at the base of the income pyramid received not much more than half of what was received by

Aggregate income of US households, 1977–1994 (%)

Year	Bottom 20%	Next 20%	Top 5%
1977	4.2	10.2	16.8
1979	4.1	10.2	16.9
1981	4.1	10.1	16.5
1983	4.0	9.9	17.1
1985	3.9	9.8	17.6
1987	3.8	9.6	18.2
1989	3.8	9.8	18.9
1990	3.9	9.6	18.6
1991	3.8	9.6	18.1
1992	3.8	9.4	18.6
1993	3.6	9.1	20.0
1994	3.6	8.9	21.2

Source: US Bureau of the Census, *Special Study: Inequality of Distribution*, Table 1. http://www.census.gov/hhes2.

the top five million, a phenomenally unequal distribution. In 1977 the same percentage had been 85.7 per cent: in other words, the bottom 40 per cent of households received not much less income than the top 5 per cent. In 1967, however, when inflation was lower and deregulation had barely started, the bottom 40 per cent actually earned more than the top 5 per cent, at 107 per cent, and in the pervasively regulated and non-inflationary US economy of 1957 that percentage had been 114 per cent: that is, the bottom 40 per cent of all households received almost one-sixth more income than the top 5 per cent.

What the numbers reveal only implicitly is the squeezing of the middle classes in between. They, the remaining 55 per cent of all households, have obviously been losing ground: the combined shares of both the top 5 per cent and the bottom 40 per cent have been increasing, from 31.2 per cent in 1977, to 33.7 per cent by 1994. This is not a dramatic difference, but the increase in top-to-bottom inequality and the squeezing of middle-class incomes has been relentless.

Long strings of numbers may tire the eye, but they have their own dramatic import. The United States was never especially egalitarian in its distribution of income, yet it was not until the advent of turbo-capitalism that the present extremes of inequality were reached.

FIVE

The Return of Poverty

As other countries around the world embark on their own paths towards turbo-capitalism, the American experience stands before them as an exemplary model and as a grim warning. It does not help to clarify matters that the perceptions of Americans of how things are in their own country are suffused with an intense historical optimism. True, Americans have never been complacent gloaters, as the English were often accused of being at the height of their imperial glories. On the contrary, Americans have always been critical of their country's condition, and often anxious about its prospects unless this or that menace was successfully confronted. Few years have passed without urgent calls to save America from some grave internal dysfunction or external threat.

The apparent contradiction in these attitudes, which combine in a most peculiar optimistic pessimism, is easily resolved: Americans are so ready to criticize how things stand in their country because they are so optimistic that matters can be put right in short order – often enough just by enacting well-written laws to charter specific government actions, or stop them, or redirect them. The entire 'war on drugs' is propelled by this conjunction: anxiety over the effects of drug use, which are pessimistically viewed as devastating; optimism that drug use can be drastically reduced by sufficiently vigorous anti-drug efforts.

The notion that some evils are predicaments that must be lived with, that not all problems have desirable solutions, that matters cannot always be improved by one-thing-at-a-time measures, is decidedly un-American. But however pleasing this attitude might be on a human plane, it is not of much help when confronting a *systemic* phenomenon such as turbo-capitalism. Moreover, because they vividly remember earlier warnings that turned out to be greatly exaggerated, experienced observers of the American scene tend to be properly skeptical when new alarms are sounded. This time around, it is the turn of the academic economists of theoretical bent to be skeptical when confronted by the contention that turbo-capitalism fractures societies even as it strengthens economies. They dismiss all complaints over the long-term drift towards sharper inequality and the remarkable persistence of poverty as 'non-problems', mere optical illusions caused by misleading statistics. If they do acknowledge any problems in this regard, they blame them on cultural factors beyond the reach of any possible economic policy, or else they insist that, if there are problems, they are well on the way to a solution. This has been true of poverty in recent years.

The official poverty count in the United States, 1995 and 1996

Year	Number of poor	Percentage of the total population
1995	36,425,000	13.8
1996	36,529,000	13.7

Year	Number of poor under 18 years of age	Percentage of the under-18 population
1995	14,399,000	20.2
1996	14,172,000	19.8

Source: US Census Bureau. Poverty annual income thresholds: one person under 65: $7,995; four-person households: $16,036. Data from www. Tables 'Poverty 1996' and 'Poverty 1994'.

Although the incidence of poverty, as officially measured, was declining during the boom years 1995–96, the total number of the poor actually rose in an increasing population. What the statistics also show, however, is that even in 1996 one child in five was growing up in poverty in the United States. Now that adult careers depend so critically on the level of higher education attained, which itself largely depends on the pre-university and indeed pre-school home environment, this high proportion of poor children has nasty implications for the future.

The American poor of any one year's statistics are of many kinds, from graduate students working part-time, who may be destined for affluence in the near future, and the retired living in their own comfortable homes with not much need of cash, to those entrapped in a lifetime of poverty, all the more bitterly felt for being surrounded by the wealth of the richest country in the world. This is the species of poverty that persists, only being reduced for a short while at the peak of each boom, and which is now made more hopeless by the stiff demands of turbo-capitalism, by way of skills, motivation and professional mobility.

It was the great achievement of controlled capitalism, in North America, Europe and Japan alike, both to generate rapid growth and to redistribute incomes so well that by the 1960s poverty itself was transformed from an ancient, inevitable curse to a warning residue of the past, soon destined to disappear. In the United States, characteristically, a 'war on poverty' was officially declared, in full expectation of a rapid and total victory. In the United Kingdom no such declarations were made, but the UK's own brand of controlled capitalism was highly effective in extinguishing poverty, compensating for a slower growth rate by more generous redistribution. In Western Europe, extensive poverty prevalent in entire regions survived only in southern Italy, Spain and Portugal, having utterly disappeared elsewhere, as in Japan. With traditional expressions of the charitable spirit made doubly redundant in northern Europe, by both state welfare programs and the waning of domestic needs, they were redirected abroad, to help the foreign poor. In Scandinavia, then elsewhere in Western Europe, and later in Japan, foreign-aid programs were started and enlarged with strong popular support.

The spread of turbo-capitalism and the upsurge in south–north flows of migration have radically altered the situation. Poverty is back. In the United States, poverty duly declined through the 1960s and the early 1970s, only to increase again – to rise and fall with the business cycle, but always from a high base. In the United Kingdom, the return of poverty has been vigorous enough to conquer entire neighbourhoods. Elsewhere, from Scandinavia to Italy, with controlled capitalism not yet dismantled, poverty is knocking at the door, waiting to re-enter as safeguards and limits are removed. The derelict beggars who had virtually disappeared from Western European cities by the late 1960s are back in force in London as in Paris, in Rome as in Berlin. Naturally, the foreign-aid programs launched in better days have lost much of their popularity, and now survive largely on elite support alone.

Underclass Myths

The link between turbo-capitalism and the persistence of American poverty – and thus the warning it contains – is obscured by the prominence of Blacks among the American poor. Outside the United States, in countries which have not yet abandoned their local versions of controlled capitalism, it may be thought that the advantages of turbo-capitalism can be enjoyed without also having to endure its peculiar kind of poverty as well. But the hopeful equation NO BLACKS = NO POVERTY is false, because the poverty that coexists with a highly dynamic economy is merely a manifestation of increasing inequality: exploding incomes at the top, outright exclusion at the bottom. In the United Kingdom, even more turbo-capitalist than the United States by some reckonings,[1] that lesson has been learned in full, as the unemployable children of the unemployed enter into adulthood in a hundred largely White, public housing 'estates' with incongruously bucolic or elegant names, filled with drink and drugs, habitual vandalism, frequent crime.

Notwithstanding all the cinematic imagery that equates American poverty with color, the figures tell a different story. As of 1996, there were 24,650,000 Whites out of the total of 36,529,000 officially counted as poor in the United States, including 16,267,000 'non-Hispanic' Whites, as compared to 9,694,000 Blacks. True, the proportions were very different: 28.4 per cent of Blacks were counted among the poor, as opposed to 11.2 per cent of Whites and 8.5 per cent of non-Hispanic Whites.[2] Even that lowest of percentages, however, encompasses much more poverty than is known in the countries of northern Europe and Japan, which have both highly advanced economies and the safeguards of controlled capitalism.

It is at this point that one more source of confusion intervenes: the very concept of the 'underclass'. One might think that a plain lack of money would be enough to make anyone poor. According to con-

[1] See Appendix; Heritage Foundation indices.
[2] Ibid.

ventional wisdom in the United States, however, there is an exception: what makes the underclass poor, and especially its children, is not a lack of money, we are told, but rather 'intersecting pathologies' – elusive fathers, apathetic or errant mothers, pervasive drug addiction and an amoral readiness to engage in crime – which together result in chronic unemployment, and therefore in poverty. In other words, a lack of money is not the cause but the result of what amounts to a distinct underclass way of life.

This is what liberals and conservatives alike believe in the United States, only diverging when it comes to the remedies they recommend. Liberals place their faith in welfare payments, social workers, counselling and rehabilitation, while conservatives stress the morally beneficial impact of welfare cutoffs, the inculcation of discipline by home, school and church, as well as strict policing. (Unsurprisingly, given the nature of their politics, both Clinton in the United States and Blair in the United Kingdom have continued to use some liberal prose to wrap their conservative remedies.)

The cultural explanation was once more or less persuasive in one way or another. It no longer is, for it can now be recognized as the product of an optical illusion. It is not that the underclass pathologies do not exist. But the vivid drama of suicidal addiction, endemic crime and chaotic families conceals a much simpler and in a way an even more brutal reality: as the total economy becomes deregulated, computerized and globalized, it has less and less need for non-creative, routine labor of any sort, blue collar or white collar, no matter how sober, stable or hard working.

Why Wages Fall

That much is proved beyond doubt by the long downward slide of pay rates for the less than highly skilled in the United States. When supply exceeds demand, for labor as for any other commodity, prices fall to bring a return to equilibrium at a lower market-clearing price. Measured in constant 1982 dollars, the average earnings of all 'non-supervisory' American employees working in all industries and all services, other than agriculture or government, peaked in 1978 at $8.40 per hour, only to decline to $7.78 in 1980, $7.77 in 1985 and $7.52 in 1990, finally increasing again during the post-1993 boom, but even then only by very little and very slowly, from $7.50 in 1996 to $7.66 in 1997.[3] It is true that over those years there was an increase in the health-care and retirement benefits provided by employers, but that cannot be reckoned completely as added virtual income because there was also a great deal of health-cost inflation, over and above overall inflation rates. That aside, by the broadest measure of average hourly earnings, which includes more than six out of ten of all working Americans, from chief executive officers to part-time maids, the pattern of decline is evident. A reversal may now be underway, but if real wages continue to increase at present rates, it would take a decade of further boom years to revert to the peak of 1978; the current level is that of 1966.

Average hourly earnings of non-supervisory employees in private, non-farm employment, 1950–1997 (constant 1982 US$)

The years of controlled (regulated) capitalism

1950	5.34
1955	6.15
1960	6.79
1965	7.52
1970	8.03
1975	8.12

The years of deregulation and turbo-capitalism

1980	7.78
1985	7.77
1990	7.52
1992	7.41
1994	7.41
1996	7.50
1997	7.66

The much-admired American success in keeping unemployment much lower than in Europe (though higher than Japan) thus conceals a less pleasing reality. By the ordinary workings of supply and demand in a 'flexible' labor market, jobs can be created in all sorts of low-cost services, from fast-food eateries to telephone sales, if the cost of labor is low enough.

[3] 1996 and 1997 rates for the month of December. US Department of Labor, Bureau of Labor Statistics, *Employment, Hours and Earnings, United States, 1909–90*, Vol. I, pp. 3–4; www. Table: hourly and weekly wages.

It is most instructive to look at it from the other way around, concentrating on employment rather than *un*employment. It is very much cheaper for an American firm to hire and pay 95 employees out of 100 available (leaving a 5 per cent unemployment rate, so to speak) at $7.66 per hour, making a total weekly wage bill of $29,108, than for a German firm to pay for 90 employees (leaving 10 per cent unemployed) at $20 per hour, making a total wage bill of $72,000. If German firms could find labor at $7.66 an hour, they too would no doubt hire 95 out of a 100; indeed, they might take all of them in a gesture of cheap generosity.

With American labor so cheap, incidentally, it is easy to see why US corporations and their shareholders have done so exceedingly well since the late 1970s, fuelling successive stock-market booms, the latest of which still continues at the time of writing. US corporate chiefs have done even better, with more than 800 of them earning in excess of a million dollars a year by 1992 – they too being slim pickings as compared to what the chief executives of the 365 largest companies received in 1996, when their average salary and bonus had risen to $2.3 million – without counting retirement benefits, incentive plans and stock-option gains (see table on page 98). Including these, the average take of the 365 during 1996 increased to $5,781,300.[4] That amounted to a 54 per cent increase over the previous year, as compared to a 3 per cent increase in average factory wages, and a 3.2 per cent increase in white-collar salaries. Moreover, since the latter increases were in current dollars, the real increase after inflation was just about zero.

Jobs in big corporations, whether blue collar or white collar, are always much in demand for they pay much better than the 'non-supervisory' averages cited above. At a time of chronically weak demand for all but the cheapest and the most highly skilled labor, those who have corporate jobs have learned not to ask for more.

---

[4] Jennifer Reingold, 'Executive pay' (annual survey), *Business Week*, 21 April 1997. There were also consolation prices for those who failed to make it to the top, in the shape of accumulated stock options whose current value was not exactly insignificant. Henry Silverman of HFS was only no. 17 in the *Business Week* list, with a modest total of $23 million and change for 1996, but he can always exercise his $544 million worth of stock options to pay his bills if hard pressed; Michael Eisner of Walt Disney did not make it to the top twenty at all in 1996 (Disney had a poor year) but his accumulated stock options were worth $364 million, also enough to buy a few groceries. Andrew Grove of Intel, the second best-paid of 1996, also has $72 million, much less than no. 15, John Welch of General Electric at $107 million. And so it goes on.

During the recession of 1990–2, many white-collar and industrial employees kept their jobs by foregoing wage increases in spite of inflation, or by accepting outright reductions – trade union 'give-backs' became common. With the recession over and recovery well underway in 1993 and 1994, the largest corporations nevertheless inaugurated the practice of mass-firings to achieve quick improvements in their balance sheets. Those who kept their jobs did not ask for pay

The best-paid US chief executives, 1996 ($000)

		1996 Salary and bonus	Long-term compen- sation	Total pay
1	Lawrence Coss, Green Tree Financial	102,449	none	102,449
2	Andrew Grove, Intel	3,003	94,587	97,590
3	Sanford Weill, Travelers Group	6,330	87,828	94,157
4	Theodore Waitt, Gateway 2000	965	80,361	81,326
5	Anthony O'Reilly, H. J. Heinz	2,736	61,500	64,236
6	Sterling Williams, Sterling Software	1,448	56,801	58,249
7	John Reed, Citicorp	3,467	40,143	43,610
8	Stephen Hilbert, Conseco	13,962	23,450	37,412
9	Casey Cowell, U.S. Robotics	3,430	30,522	33,952
10	James Moffett, Freeport-McMoran C & G	6,956	26,776	33,732
11	John Chambers, Cisco Systems	619	32,594	33,213
12	Stephen Wiggins, Oxford Health Plans	1,738	27,270	29,008
13	Eckhard Pfeiffer, Compaq Computer	4,250	23,546	27,796
14	Stephen Case, America Online	200	27,439	27,639
15	John Welch, General Electric	6,300	21,321	27,621
16	Richard Scrushy, Healthsouth	11,380	16,197	27,577
17	Henry Silverman, HFS	3,752	19,990	23,742
18	Norman Augustine, Lockheed Martin	2,781	20,324	23,105
19	John Amerman, Mattel	3,732	18,923	22,655
20	Drew Lewis, Union Pacific	3,131	18,320	21,452

Source: *Business Week*, 21 April 1997.

increases, even to match inflation. Many others, however, failed to keep their jobs. Some of them found corporate employment elsewhere in a favorable economy. But for the rest, the only way of avoiding unemployment was to accept whatever jobs they could find, at whatever pay was to be had. It is called 'downward mobility'.

This is an important dimension of the famous 'flexibility' of the American labor market, which the United Kingdom has fully emulated, and which employers all over continental Europe are so eager to import. Former factory workers used to relatively high industrial wages, and former white-collar employees used to corporate salaries, become telemarketers, janitors, waiters, cleaners, pizza delivery drivers, commission salesmen, driving instructors, or manual laborers if fit enough, even if they have a college education.

The Rational Criminal

It is at this point that the underclass comes back into the picture. Ever since the end of the 1970s, the downwardly mobile have been taking away many of the jobs that were once left entirely to the uneducated. Those minimum-wage jobs once formed the lowest rung of the economic ladder, which allowed at least some members of the underclass to climb upwards. In American cities, even the casual visitor can observe the phenomenon with the naked eye: waiters and waitresses, janitors and so on used to be Blacks with little formal education, but are now mostly White high-school or even college graduates. As the less than highly skilled are driven downwards by the transformation of the economy, they poach away the jobs of the unskilled, who are excluded from work altogether.

What this means for the so-called underclass is that its 'pathologies', however real, are also irrelevant, and that the classic liberal and conservative remedies are both equally unavailing. No amount of psychological counselling, social work, drug and crime rehabilitation schemes can make any difference, any more than welfare cutoffs, preachings of discipline and moral values, or tough policing. That all such efforts have a poor success record in their own terms is also beside the point. For even if they were totally successful, they could only at best produce sober, stable and hard-working routine labor for an economy that has less and less need for it. Actually, every addict or otherwise dysfunctional character who is rescued and rehabilitated adds to the excess supply of unskilled labor twice over, by becoming employable, and by reducing the need to employ social workers and policemen.

Once this truth is accepted, it can be seen that the famous underclass pathologies are not so pathological after all. It is surely less painful to be chronically unemployed if one is *not* sober, drug-free and filled with a desire to work at a satisfying job. As for families, they can best be understood unsentimentally, as human clusterings around reliable breadwinners. Given that there is less and less job security even for the highly skilled at a time of dynamic structural change, the less skilled are necessarily worse off, while the unskilled of the underclass have good job opportunities only at the peak of each successive boom. They therefore cannot be reliable breadwinners capable of holding families together. Family breakdown may be favored by cultural factors, but it is in any case pre-ordained by the shortage of jobs for the unskilled.

Even crime turns out to be functional in this setting, not a species of madness, but a rational choice. A full-scale study of drug dealing in Washington DC, based on the analysis of all relevant court records, utterly refuted the conventional wisdom.[5] Its sensational results revealed the huge dimensions of the trade as a source of job and business opportunities; they also demonstrated that its entrepreneurs and employees were perfectly rational in their choices. More than 11,000 regular drug-dealers and almost 13,000 occasional dealers were counted. Their combined net earnings, after expenses, amounted to some $300 million. Even after setting an insurance-type monetary value on the the real risk of injury or death from violent competitors, and also on the minor risk of arrest and conviction, it turned out that drug dealing at an average income of $12,500 per annum in 1987 was profitable enough to be the best career option for its universally uneducated participants. In other words, those who entered the drug trade were making a rational choice based on correct information, and could not have been otherwise directed by any competent management consultant. They were certainly better off than their equals who preferred the alternatives of unemployment or casual labor at the minimum wage. And drug-users who are reasonably efficient thieves are also perfectly rational, for their habit allows them at least intermittent holidays from a world that does not need their honest labor.

Once upon a time, Western Europeans could still comfortably

---

[5] Peter Reuter *et al.*, *Money from Crime: A Study of the Economies of Drug-dealing in Washington DC*, RAND report R-3894-RF (Santa Monica, Calif.: Rand, 1990), p. 92. Based on 1987 court records.

believe that concentrations of the criminalized poor were an exclusively American disease or, even better, a Black/Puerto Rican/Chicano disease. In reality, every advanced country is destined to acquire its own substantial underclass of the non-employable, just as fast as public institutions are sold off to private owners or simply lose their funding, as commercial regulations are abolished along with every other kind of obstacle to the free market – today's computerized and globalized free market. As factories and offices become more efficient and as routine work is automated, sober, stable and hard-working but less than highly skilled employees are forced out and pushed down, forcing the unskilled below them into the chronically unemployed underclass, augmented by unskilled immigrants in many cases. Because the phenomenon has just started and is still so new in Western Europe, many can still believe in the false remedies of rehabilitation, moral values, policing and the rest. Even in the United States, after all, there is still much talk of educating the underclass out of its condition, by providing it with 'the basic skills needed by the economy'. Advanced *and* turbo-capitalist economies do not need basic skills, however, or more precisely, they need them less and less. Thus the optical illusion persists – inevitably if one keeps focusing on the underclass itself, rather than the slide of everyone else.

Are there any remedies? There certainly are – but many people would consider them worse than the disease. Once it is accepted that the underclass is the human residue left behind by the progress of a highly dynamic economy open to the world, it follows that it can be diminished by reducing the pace of economic change. This would certainly reduce social disruption – but also growth. If, for example, assembly-line jobs were protected from foreign competition, thereby stopping the downward poaching of underclass jobs, firms would become less efficient, making the country as a whole poorer, but the poorest richer.

SIX

The Era of Unemployment

Unemployment is the global problem of our times, and more than that: it is a protracted tragedy at the personal level, and destabilizing at the social level. All over continental Europe and far beyond, governments are under enormous pressure to reduce unemployment. Everywhere they are failing, often resorting to costly and ephemeral expedients, including public works programs that may even cause more unemployment.[1] Everywhere their critics accuse governments of passivity or incompetence. In reality, today's global unemployment is an inevitable consequence of the present phase of the world-demand/technology cycle. We happen to be in the surplus-of-everything and thus deflationary phase, which started during the 1980s and which will probably last until well after the year 2000. During this phase, there is excess supply of raw materials and finished goods alike, and therefore unemployment.

The World Demand/Technology Cycle

The workings of the world-demand/technology cycle are best understood by looking backwards before looking forwards. A generation ago, in the 1960s, we were in the opposite scarcity-of-everything and

---

[1] By reducing demand, if funded by current taxation; by causing higher interest rates, if funded by increasing the public debt.

therefore inflationary phase of the cycle. With demand exceeding supply, markets were cleared by rising prices, as exemplified by the upsurge in oil and grain. It was then that the eminent and prominent members of the Club of Rome issued their predictions of catastrophic food and energy shortages to come. Now universally ridiculed, these predictions were nothing more than linear extrapolations of then existing realities. There *was* scarcity, and world commodity markets duly reflected it in their rising prices. With the world's population steadily increasing, it was a matter of simple arithmetic to predict that scarcities would increase, eventually causing great dislocations because of energy shortages, and also widespread famine as more and more people were priced out of the grain market.

What the Club of Rome experts did not appreciate was that the scarcities of food and energy that they correctly observed and merely extrapolated were not the result of anything as fixed and eternal as the world's stock of arable land, or the planet's ultimate store of oil and gas reserves. They were, rather, the result of technological and organizational limitations in exploiting those resources.

Specifically, the agricultural techniques of the time, applied to the world's stock of arable land, could produce X amount of food; because X was then already insufficient as compared to effective demand for food (as shown by rising real prices), it seemed inevitable that X would become even less sufficient in the future, given the world's continuing population increase. Actually the situation would deteriorate even more than that, because the world's stock of arable land was diminishing quite significantly owing to desertification in both Africa and China, and the growth of human settlements everywhere.

Yet, instead of declining, food production started increasing rather rapidly from the 1970s. It was the progress of agricultural technology, stimulated precisely by current and imminent shortages, that intervened to falsify the Club of Rome prediction. New 'green revolution' seeds for rice wheat and maize; more selective pesticides; new fertilizer production and better fertilizer distribution; and new food storage and delivery techniques were all applied. Even with a diminishing stock of arable land, output increased so much that by the late 1980s even overpopulated India became a wheat exporter in good years, prices tumbled and surpluses mounted.

Likewise, the energy production and utilization technologies of the 1960s, applied to the world's known oil and gas reserves, could produce Y amount of applied energy. Y being already insufficient (as shown by rising prices for oil and all other primary energy sources), it seemed inevitable that Y would become even less sufficient in the future. Again, rising prices greatly stimulated both technological progress and conservation, thus overturning the Club of Rome prediction. New offshore oil-drilling techniques opened up additional oil and gas reserves for exploitation; secondary and tertiary recovery methods obtained more output from old fields; better transport reduced the cost of coal; new higher-efficiency processes reduced conversion losses; and many new energy-saving practices were introduced because of higher prices. The overall result was such an abundance of energy that real prices continued to decline. Oil-production capacity, which was strained to the limit by 1973, had risen much beyond current demand by the early 1980s. And what has been true of food and energy has also been true of manufactured goods and most other things produced and consumed in the global economy.[2]

The long-term world-demand/technology cycle

Phase I: scarcity and inflation
Current technologies applied to the known stock of natural resources, plus an increasing world population, cause scarcities and rising prices, i.e. inflation.

Phase II: the technology reaction
Scarcity stimulates the development of new technologies, while prices are still rising, i.e. inflation persists.

Phase III: surpluses and deflation
New technologies applied to the known stock of natural resources result in excess supply and thus falling prices, i.e. deflation.

Phase IV: demand rises to outrun supply
Economic growth and rising incomes increase effective demand, especially in less developed regions. Eventually, given the current technologies of the day, scarcities emerge. As a result, the world-demand/technology cycle rotates back to Phase I.

During Phase I and Phase II, unemployment is low. Only more labor inputs can extract more output with existing techniques, so their

---

[2] The exceptions are extractive rather than productive (e.g. ocean fishing) and cases of rigidly localized production (e.g. truffles), especially when those localities have experienced severe environmental damage (e.g. caviar).

marginal product is high, causing high demand for labor, and therefore rising wages as well as low unemployment. During Phase III, on the other hand, unemployment is high because the new techniques produce abundance without need to maximize the use of labor.

The present Phase III of the cycle is painfully afflicted by unemployment. Some 800 million people of working age throughout the world are officially listed as unemployed. That figure does not include the many millions who simply do not bother to have themselves listed ('hidden unemployment'), having lost all hope of finding a job by those means. It is further estimated that another 700 million people of working age are employed at such low wages that their income is below the official poverty thresholds of their respective countries.[3] Finally, the 800 + 700 million of official estimates does not include the under-employed, who work fewer hours than they would like to ('involuntary part-timers'), or else work at jobs that are undemanding given their skills, such as Tokyo department store greeters, Indian office 'peons' or college-graduate taxi drivers.

In the advanced industrialized countries of North America, Western Europe and Japan, some 36 million were listed as unemployed in 1994, and that number had not declined by 1997. It averages out at a 9 per cent unemployment rate across all three economic regions – almost twice as much as the typical Phase I/Phase II unemployment rate of the 1960s and early 1970s. Again that 9 per cent does not include hidden unemployment, poverty-wage employment and involuntary under-employment.

It would now seem that the predicament of the global unemployed will not be relieved until a reversion to Phase I of the cycle is fully achieved, and Phase II well underway. This is because Phase III technological progress has left behind a large amount of 'structural unemployment', i.e. labor made unnecessary by new machines and new techniques which cannot find alternative employment. Incidentally, youth unemployment, which ranges up to 30 per cent in some regions of Western Europe, is not fully counted within the overall 9 per cent, because much of it is not officially registered as such. Instead, regional authorities, as in Italy, or the central government, as in France, employ large numbers of unemployed youths in make-

---

[3] In 1992, 18 per cent of all working Americans did not earn enough to keep a family of four above the official poverty line even when working 40 hours a week, 50 weeks a year. US Bureau of the Census, 'Workers with low earnings, 1964–90', Series P-60, Number 178, Washington DC, 1992, pp. 3, 4.

work pretend jobs in government offices, schools and hospitals.

Without a 'flexible' turbo-capitalist labor market, in which falling wages induce job creation, there is a very real danger in Western Europe that Phase III structural unemployment will persist, even becoming a permanent, lifetime condition. In parts of Italy, as in parts of France and Spain, the number of unemployed who have never had a real job in their entire life, and who have no current prospect of finding one in the foreseeable future, is frighteningly large.

As we have seen, thanks to both relatively rapid growth and the willingness of unions and individuals to accept declining real wages, US and British unemployment levels are persistently well below the prevailing levels in Western Europe. In Japan, partly because of the pervasive integration of the under-employed, the unemployment rate remains around 4 per cent at the time of writing, in spite of a persistent recession. In Western Europe, by contrast, unemployment levels currently average out at roughly 10 per cent, with Spain's Andalucia as well as certain parts of southern Italy experiencing as much as 20 per cent.

In addition to less rapid growth rates and extreme wage rigidity by American standards, there are two further explanations for the higher unemployment of Western Europe as compared to the United States: first, the great obstacles to the firing of employees, which inhibit employers from hiring them in the first place; and second, tax and insurance payments that increase the cost of labor well above the pay they actually receive. In the United States, those payments add roughly 20 per cent to direct labor costs, while in most of Western Europe they add 40 per cent or more. The very measures that protect those already employed act as a high barrier for those seeking jobs.

The gap between the United States and Western Europe is very much wider when it comes to long-term unemployment (defined as having persisted for one year or more at the data point). In the United States, long-term unemployment only increased from 0.2 to 0.4 per cent between the Phase II year 1979 and the Phase III year 1991, while in Germany the increase was from 0.8 to 1.6 per cent, in the United Kingdom from 1.3 to 3.1 per cent, in France from 1.8 to 3.5 per cent, and most disastrously, in Italy from 4 to over 5 per cent, one in twenty of the potential labor force. That 5 per cent would, of course, be a rather serious unemployment rate in itself, not to speak of long-term unemployment.

It is true that many of those officially listed as long-term unemployed actually work in the illegal 'black economy'. But that is a much smaller consolation than some seem to think. Few jobs in the black economy offer reasonable incomes, and hardly any offer realistic career prospects. For every millionaire gangster in Naples or Frankfurt, for every well-paid journeyman plumber in Berlin or Milano, for every off-the-books house painter in Provence, dozens eke out a poor living from part-time jobs on the fringes of the economy, or petty crime.

The dramatic and persistent difference between Western Europe and the United States in the prevalence of *long-term* unemployment has several explanations, including both the higher US rate of economic growth and the much weaker family ties of Americans, which often make it impossible for them to survive without a job. In contrast to the average German or Italian youth, who will wait within the comfort of the family home until he or she finds a desirable job in the right trade, at the right level, at the right pay *and* close to home, their American counterparts will often accept any job they can find even if poorly paid, and even if it requires moving to a different part of the country.

Prevailing attitudes to work itself are also important. In the United States, it is very common for children of even the richest families and high social status to start working part time while still in school. They deliver newspapers on their bicycles within their own neighborhoods while still very young; they work in restaurants, as pool attendants, as shop assistants and in other such weekend or evening jobs as teenagers, and later as university students during vacations. At that point, their mothers might work as part-time sales assistants in boutiques or elegant department stores to pass the time – the very same places where their friends shop, and indeed they themselves. American adults who lose their jobs are likewise far more willing than Europeans to accept work of lower status. At any one time, depending on how each industry is faring, one can find ex-insurance company middle-managers delivering pizza to the door in New Jersey, or aerospace engineers driving taxis in Los Angeles – it helps that few occupations are foreclosed by licensing or permits.

But the most important explanation for the rarity of long-term unemployment in the United States is far simpler: the absence of long-term government assistance. In the Netherlands, where unemployment payments last for twenty-four months, even in 1990 (the proportion is now higher) 48.4 per cent of the unemployed had not had a job for more than twelve months. In France and the United Kingdom, where the payments last for twelve months, those unemployed for more than twelve months were 38.3 and 36.1 per cent respectively of all listed unemployed. Germany does not conform, because with a twelve-month limit its proportion was virtually as high as that of the Netherlands at 46.3 per cent. In none of these countries, moreover, was there a time-limit on welfare payments subject to proof of need after unemployment insurance runs out, and in some countries, such as Germany and the Netherlands, welfare payments are notoriously generous.

This is the 'moral hazard' that Tony Blair's New Labour government set out to remove, exploiting its presumptive social-concern credentials to do what the Tories could not have dared to suggest: cut off public assistance to the long-term unemployed. The result will no doubt be to induce many people to accept work of any kind for any wage, while adding the rest to the number of derelict beggars on British streets. In the United States, by contrast, where in 1990 only 5.6 per cent of all the unemployed had not had a job for twelve months or more, unemployment insurance payments last for only six months, and there are no welfare payments at all for able-bodied adults, except for mothers with dependent children.

As everyone knows, the very conditions that in Western Europe protect and enrich the jobs of those already employed – high wages assured by strong trade unions, severe restrictions on or even outright prohibitions of dismissals – make it that much harder for young people to find jobs in the first place. There has been stiff resistance (including violent riots in France) against any attempt to introduce flexibility, even by such limited measures as the legislation of 'youth wages' below the official minimum wage. It is not surprising, therefore, that for youths between the ages of fifteen and twenty-four, unemployment greatly increased in almost all Western European countries from the Phase I year 1973 to the Phase III year 1992, reaching levels as high as 30 per cent by 1992, as compared to under 13 per cent in 1973.

In the United States, much crime and drug abuse is attributed to a youth unemployment rate of roughly 9 per cent nationally, with 'inner-city' (i.e. Black) peaks of 20 per cent or more. In Western Europe, the correlation between youth unemployment and crime is much weaker, but there too it is not absent. That aside, the sadness, demoralization, even desperation of youth unemployment has been acutely felt, extending to their entire families and communities.

Growth Without Jobs

What makes the situation so grave is that, in an increasingly turbo-capitalist global economy, even fairly rapid growth need not reduce unemployment by much. Computer-driven efficiency increases continue during recessions as well. When recoveries do come, increasing demand and therefore output, more can be produced without hiring more labor. In the past, more productivity did not mean more unemployment. So why should it be so different now? A retrospective look provides the answer. Taking Western Europe as a whole, half the labor force had been employed in agriculture at the beginning of the century; by 1997 it was less than 5 per cent.

What happened to the other 45 per cent who had worked in agriculture was not unemployment but rather a shift to industry, which accounted for some 35 per cent of the total labor force; to government services of all kinds (some 30 per cent); and to private services, i.e. wholesale and retail trade, crafts and repair, the professions and health care, which jointly accounted for the remaining 30 per cent. It is enough to project current trends in a linear fashion – thereby predicting the future if nothing is done to change it – to see the trouble that lies ahead for Western Europe. Over the next twenty years or so:

- Agricultural employment cannot increase above the level of some 5 per cent of the labor force; in fact, it will almost certainly decline towards 3 per cent or even 2 per cent.
- Because of automation, other forms of technical and organizational progress, and also imports from newly industrialized countries,[4] the current level of roughly 35 per cent of the labor force employed in industry and related services cannot increase; in fact, it will almost certainly decline towards 20 per cent or even 15 per cent.
- Because of the need to reduce excessive accumulations of public debt in many countries, the efficiencies of privatization and also the computerization of government bureaucracies, the current level of

[4] There is a clear correlation between imports of manufactured goods from developing countries and the loss of industrial jobs; Belgium, whose industrial employment as a percentage of total employment has declined more than in any other Western European country (−14 per cent) over the twenty years 1970–90, also imports more manufactured goods from developing countries as a fraction of its GDP than any other Western European country. Japan, which imports the least, has also lost the smallest share (2 per cent) of industrial employment.

roughly 30 per cent of the labor force employed in public services of all kinds cannot increase; in fact, it will almost certainly decline towards 25 per cent or even 20 per cent.

Adding up these totals, in place of the current total of 70 per cent of the labor force employed in agriculture, industry and public services, only 48 per cent or even 37 per cent will be so occupied, leaving a net of 52 per cent or even 63 per cent to be otherwise employed.

To be sure, employment in private services of all kinds can continue to increase, and may account for as much as 45 per cent of the labor force by 2010 or so, a huge 50 per cent increase over the present 30 per cent level on average. Even so, however – if nothing is done to avert the linear prediction – *structural*, long-term unemployment would increase to a minimum of 7 per cent or as much as 12 per cent of the total labor force; adding transitional and cyclical unemployment, this implies unemployment levels in excess of 12 per cent in good times, and of 17 per cent in times of recession. This in turn implies an even greater waste of human talent, a wider sphere of personal and family misery, and more acute social tensions than present unemployment levels already cause. Political upheavals cannot be excluded.

Why structural unemployment has already increased is obvious enough: turbo-capitalist change overlaid on Phase III technological progress, prompted by Phase I shortages. The examples are many: automobile assembly plants required an average of seventy hours of labor to assemble a car until the early 1980s; that has already been more than halved to roughly thirty-five hours, but an average of only fifteen hours is imminent. In heavy engineering, labor saving has been even greater, so that to fabricate a diesel-electric locomotive, for example, the number of labor hours has declined from 12,000 in the early 1980s to only 4,000. The US long-distance telephone company AT&T now handles more phone calls than in 1984, but because of automated systems it employs only 12,000 operators instead of 44,000. Again, because of the industrialization of office work and specifically the introduction of computer tellers, the number of US commercial bank employees declined from roughly 480,000 in 1984 to less than 300,000 by 1997.

Likewise, the entire reason for privatizing state-owned enterprises is to achieve increased efficiency – obtained precisely by eliminating overstaffing, and replacing many employees who do work with more and better machines. In the United Kingdom, the privatization of the state-owned telephone, gas and electricity utilities, of the steel industry, British Airways and British Rail has resulted in a combined loss of more than 300,000 jobs. In the rest of Western Europe, railways are still state-owned, and they employ almost twice as many staff as privatized railways would. The same is true of the remaining state-owned telephone, electrical-power, airline and plain industrial companies. In France and Italy, where the state-owned sector of the economy is very much larger than in other Western European countries, a vigorous privatization program can yield efficiency increases just as large for their economies, with a proportionate increase in their gross national products, and also even more unemployment.

How to Eliminate Unemployment in Five Easy Steps: a French Parable

For France as for any Western European country afflicted by high unemployment, the American cure is ready. First, a comparison is in order. During 1996, employment in private service trades was as follows in the United States and in France, which along with Italy and Japan is the least turbo-capitalist of major countries.[5]

Employment in selected service trades, USA and France, 1996 (as % of total employment)

	USA	France
Wholesale and retail sales	17.5	13.6
Finance, banking, property	6.4	4.7
Hotel and food services	6.6	3.5
Personal and domestic services	1.9	2.5
Health care and social services	11.3	10.5
Total	43.7	34.8

It will be noted that in 1996 there was just about a 10 per cent

[5] INSEE data, cited in Sophie Gherardi, 'Mines d'emplois', *Le Monde*, 25 November 1997 (Economie, p. 1).

difference in the proportion of the labor force employed in these service trades as between the two countries.

During 1996 the declining US unemployment rate averaged 6 per cent, while French unemployment was remaining stubbornly constant at some 12 per cent. Multiplying those employed by 0.94 (USA) and 0.88 (France) respectively, the occupations of each country's labor force were therefore as follows.

Occupations of labor force, USA and France, 1996 (as % of total labor force)

	USA	France
Employed in selected services	41.1	30.6
All other employment	52.9	57.4
Unemployed	6.0	12.0
Total	100	100

If in France, too, the service trades could employ 41 per cent of the total labor force instead of only 30.6 per cent, the country's unemployment would be reduced to zero – an impossible number, of course, but nice to look at.

The American cure for the French disease is therefore rather simple: persuade firms in the service trades to provide more service by employing more people. At present, France is a country of undermanned hotels, long waits at restaurant tables because waiters are so few, automatic gas stations, and sprawling hypermarkets with hardly any employees; most revealingly, the American Toys-R-Us chain employs one-third more people per square meter of shop floor in its US stores than in French ones. In France, as elsewhere, firms in the service trades can best compete by providing more service. Hence they would employ more people – if they could do so cheaply enough to increase their profits.

All it would take to transform the situation, eliminating unemployment in one fell swoop, would be to change the French labor market along American lines:

• *Step 1:* set the minimum wage well below the average wage for unqualified employees.

At the end of 1997, the average US wage for non-supervisors was

$7.66 per hour as we have seen, while the minimum wage was $5.15. In France, by contrast, the minimum wage is close to the average wage for the unskilled. Another version of Step 1 is simpler: allow wages to fall.

- *Step 2:* cut total employment costs by reducing add-on social-welfare contributions.

French employers are indeed very heavily burdened as compared to their American or, indeed, British counterparts. On top of a £1,000 wage, the latter must add £100 for health, retirement and unemployment benefits. The equivalent French charge is £256, but in addition employers face five more payments: family allowance fund (£54), workers' injury compensation (£9.60), general surtax (£11.60), social tax (£2.40) and pension fund (£37.50). As against the British employer's total of £1,100, the French employer pays £1,371. True, French social services are far better, but Step 2 means that they must be cut drastically – for the difference cannot possibly be made up by employee contributions: *their* deductions already take away £213.30 from the £1,000, as opposed to £80 for British employees.

- *Step 3:* abrogate most labor laws.

In France, as in Italy and indeed most of Western Europe, employers have excellent reasons not to engage even labor that is cheap enough on an hourly basis to be hired profitably: laws that require four weeks of paid vacation per year plus lots of sick leave, that set a 35-hour working week limit, that severely restrict overtime, and that make it impossibly costly, or simply impossible, to dismiss employees, while requiring at least one month of severance pay ('liquidation') for each year worked when employees retire or resign voluntarily (negotiated payoffs for involuntary dismissals are far higher).

For French employees, as for those in most of Western Europe, the labor laws are a guarantee not only of economic security, but also of personal dignity. Most work hard enough, but they need not fear abrupt dismissal if they momentarily displease the boss. Indeed, there is no all-powerful boss in the American sense; instead there are two parties to a contractual relationship, one with all the economic power, and the other with many rights protected by law.

For French employers, on the other hand, the labor laws mean that each new employee hired represents an inflexible commitment.

Most trades have their multi-year cycles of high and low demand, while quite a few have seasonal cycles too. Because none can be dismissed, as few as possible are hired.

Thus Step 3 requires the rewriting of most job-protection laws, to allow any employee to be dismissed with one month's notice, and to limit severance pay, paid vacations, overtime bonuses, etc. to whatever contractual obligations employers choose to accept, if any at all. In other words, negotiations would replace legislation, removing its counterweight to the economic power of employers.

At this point, all would be set to induce employers to hire more people. In France, however, there is a shortage of employers, because many trades and even simple shops require licenses that are costly or unobtainable. Moreover, new banks, investment houses and financial services of all kinds cannot be established without obtaining permits subject to very strict restrictions. In conformity with the turbo-capitalist American model that excludes all such obstacles, a further step is needed:

- *Step 4:* abolish all commercial licensing restrictions on hotels, restaurants, cafés, bars, fast-food outlets, and retail shops of all descriptions and categories. With only local zoning laws, hygiene requirements, etc. left in place, a proliferation of new employers would rapidly emerge in those trades. Issue permits freely to new banks and financial enterprises, subject only to fiduciary requirements and inspections. This alone would rapidly close the 50 per cent gap between American and French employment in the sector.

At that point, only one minor obstacle would remain. The French state not only taxes employers rather heavily, but also treats them as extensions of its bureaucracy. French wineries produce wine and paperwork for the state; French spark-plug factories produce spark-plugs and paperwork for the state. Forms of all kinds and all lengths must be filled in and sent in on time to ministries, departments, bureaus and local bodies, each month, each quarter and each year to avoid stiff penalties. There is an ocean of forms, to report purchases and sales and stocks, shipments in and out, every manner of detail on employees in hand, and more besides, quite aside from the income and expense data needed to report taxes.

For the only purpose at hand, the reduction of unemployment, the government's own internal paperwork cannot be cut. To do so would diminish the only French advantage, the great number of government jobs:

Government employment, 1996 (as % of total labor force)

	USA	France
Percentage of the labor force employed by central, regional and local government	4.6	8.2

The paperwork now inflicted on employers, on the other hand, can certainly be cut, or at least drastically simplified, or just computerized. If the French state must continue to satisfy its insatiable hunger for information, each bureaucracy can establish an Internet Web site, into which employers could simply feed their computer data raw, letting hungry bureaucrats wash it and cook it as they please. At present, many a potential entrepreneur, ready to face all the risks of the market, is deterred from going into business by the terrors of form filling and fines. That brings us to the final change:

• *Step 5:* abolish all non-tax paperwork for firms with fewer than fifty employees (the American cutoff number for most bureaucratic purposes); receive data from the rest from computer to computer, or verbally by voice mail (the usual US practice at the State level).

Once all these things were done, nobody in France would be forced to remain unemployed – there would be plenty of jobs for people of all skills and none. All it would take to ensure that nobody but the rich or the intensely ascetic remained with idle hands to do the Devil's work, would be to cut off unemployment benefits and all public assistance to those who refused offered jobs, as in the United States. There would be no more loitering in the slums of northern Paris, no crowds of idle men among the low-rent estates (HLMs) all over France, more customers for cafés, but fewer who would linger during working hours – except that they too would be abolished, for all factories and shops would be free to operate twenty-four hours a day, seven days a week, including Christmas, Easter and the New Year, as in the United States.

With labor costs drastically reduced, and their life made much easier by the removal of almost all restrictions and the abolition of almost all form filling, French entrepreneurs and French companies large and small would greatly prosper, and so would their shareholders and the managers of the largest companies, who could look forward to pay levels some 200 times higher than those of their lowest-paid employees, as in the United States. The French stock market would celebrate a second *libération* by years of ever-rising share values that would raise the CAC index to the skies. Sales of private jets would soar, the ice-cold market for Côte d'Azur mega-villas would become red hot, and the French fashion and luxury-goods trades, now bereft of buyers, might have to impose rationing.

All would be exceedingly happy except for one particular group: French employees who already have a job, who are among the 88 per cent who are not unemployed. They would have lost not only today's relatively high pay, their paid vacations and sick leave, their severance pay guarantees and part of their health and pension benefits, as well as their current security of employment, but also their entire power to resist the will and whims of their employers, and much of their dignity with it. This particular group happens to account for many more people than the unemployed, or senior executives, or large-scale shareholders, or the small band of disinterested free-market enthusiasts. Because France is an elective democracy, in 1996 a net majority advisedly said *non* to a 'flexible' labor market and a turbo-capitalist France – and it is unlikely to ever say *oui* except to the most limited of changes.

Japan: Full Employment as the National Goal

Until 1990, the Japanese were widely admired and sometimes feared for the phenomenal success of their export industries, and their country's swift rise to colossal financial power. After 1985, when the newly upvalued yen seemed to be conquering all before it, the accelerating rise in the price of Japanese buildings and land, and the accelerating rise in share values on the Tokyo Stock Exchange generated fabulous capital gains that spilled out into the rest of the world. Financiers everywhere learned to spell and even pronounce Dai-Ichi-Kangyo, Sumitomo, Fuji, Mitsubishi, Sanwa, Norinchukin and more easily IBJ, each of them banks with more assets by 1988 than Citicorp, the largest of all American banks at $208 billion: the Japanese top seven had $1,700 billion in assets, i.e. $1.7 million a million times over.[6] On Wall Street and in the City of London, as in every financial center, large and small, all over the world, Japanese banks and investment houses, with the giant Nomura in the lead, became prime underwriters and buyers of new bond issues, a prime source of corporate loans and of direct investments.

With all the shares and bonds quoted on the Tokyo stock market valued at a combined total of $5,200 billion by the end of 1989 – as compared to $4,300 billion for all three New York stock exchanges, and $1,300 billion for the London Stock Exchange[7] and an even greater explosion of Japanese real-estate values, the global buying potential was enormous. The Japanese could have purchased entire cities, and much of American industry.

In the event they bought very little, considering. True, individual Japanese tycoons became famous for picking up vineyards in France, hotels in Hawaii, Impressionist paintings at London auctions, office blocks in Hong Kong, and golf clubs everywhere during the briefest stop-over visits, before hurrying back to see how much their holdings had risen in the meanwhile. Also true, insurance companies, banks, real-estate companies and plain industrial firms made a great splash by buying 'name' properties such as the Rockefeller Center in the heart of Manhattan and the famed Pebble Beach resort in California, while quietly spending much more to accumulate several hundred billion dollars' worth of US Treasury bonds, as well as shares in many US high-technology companies. Much more of the unrealized capital gains, however, were used to raise bank loans, with which other speculators could be outbid to buy Japanese real estate and Japanese stocks, thus driving up their prices still further, thus inducing banks to lend yet more against those upvalued assets, thus winding the spiral ever upward, with more outbidding and more loans. The banks themselves could lend ever more because their reserve assets of real estate and shares were being upvalued with each turn of the spiral.

When the government's Bank of Japan finally intervened at the end of 1989 to stop commercial banks from fuelling speculation with their loans, the 'bubble economy' started to sag immediately. As real-estate prices and share values started to drop, there were some

[6] Keizai Koho Center, *Japan 1990: An International Comparison* (Tokyo, 1990), Table 3–18, p. 30.
[7] Keizai Koho Center, *Japan 1992: An International Comparison* (Tokyo, 1992), Table 9–7, p. 76.

immediate bankruptcies among the most daring and foolhardy bit players, but no massive liquidation took place. While individual speculators were wiped out, the large commercial banks protected friendly corporations by rolling over their loans even if no interest was being paid, and the Ministry of Finance protected the banks. This harmonious collaboration turned out to be a great mistake. Because the decks were not energetically cleared of non-performing loans, because asset values did not crash to make them attractive purchases once again, instead of a quick and devastating bust that would have allowed a quick recovery, there was a slow decline covered up by more rollovers, and more loans. It was not until 1997 that the most badly over-extended commercial banks and investment houses were finally shut down, seven years too late – seven years of persistent stringency and recession.

Once the bubble economy collapsed, the Japanese ceased to be admired, or feared. Their export industries continued to thrive, indeed reaching new heights – the 1998 contest for the top-selling car in the US market featured Honda versus Toyota, the 1997 winner. The Japanese as a whole continued to earn and save in huge amounts, still buying billions of US Treasury bonds at each auction, still funding investments all over the world. When the South-East Asian and Korean economies suffered their catastrophic financial crash of 1997, the largest share of the rescue loans sent in directly or through the International Monetary Fund came from Japan: the United States did all the talking, the Japanese did much of the funding.

None of that seemed to matter. All of a sudden the 'Japanese model' no longer seemed impressive, or even interesting. All along, however, it had not been its goal to maximize financial accumulation, let alone to allow frivolous rich men to buy French vineyards, Hawaii golf clubs, Van Goghs or English mansions. The American model *is* tycoon-driven, the Japanese is not. There was and is a true Japanese model, but its goal could not be further removed from any of the above. That goal was, and still is, to ensure a place in the economy for every Japanese citizen who wants to work. Thus the true character of the Japanese model ironically emerged only during the long post-1989 recession that followed the collapse of the bubble economy.

Once taken for granted, fast growth came to an end – though the Japanese economy continued to grow at a rather higher rate than that of the United States until 1995 or so. This scarcely helped the many banks paralyzed by the double blow of the collapse in land prices and Japanese shares: while their own capital base lost just about half its value, many of their assets (i.e. loans outstanding) also became valueless when clients who had borrowed to buy land and shares at the top of the market could neither repay their loans nor even keep up interest payments. Only the liabilities of the banks (i.e. deposits) did not decline. The banks therefore had to cut their lending, especially to smaller firms. As the lack of credit started to strangle the economy, consumer demand collapsed and many firms and shops saw their sales decline by a third or more between 1990 and 1997.

Yet unemployment did not exceed 4 per cent until 1998, amidst ominous talk of an outright depression, or even imminent economic collapse. The banks were in trouble – so much so that in early 1998 even mighty Sumitomo Bank had to offer a 10 per cent coupon to sell its dollar-denominated preferred shares on the New York market, implying an almost Mexican risk rating. Many corporations were in trouble, especially if they had borrowed money to buy real estate or other corporate shares during the boom years. Nevertheless, virtually all Japanese who wanted to work still could, in spite of economic circumstances that would have resulted in 20 per cent unemployment in the United States, perhaps 30 per cent in Europe. It was in a perfect symmetry of opposites that in June 1998 the official unemployment rate happened to be exactly the same, 4.1 per cent, in both the United States and Japan. For Japan, mired in a deep recession with the stock market at 37 per cent of the 1989 peak, and Tokyo real estate on offer for one-third of 1989 prices, that 4.1 per cent was the highest rate since 1956, a most alarming sign of economic crisis. For the United States in high boom times, it was the cause of much celebration, as the lowest rate since 1973, further evidence of the amplitude of American prosperity.

Full employment was always the overriding purpose of Japan's very particular version of controlled capitalism. Though best known for its protracted resistance to the globalization of Japan's own economy – while exporting hugely – its core was always a pervasive system of *internal* controls. While Japanese politicians engaged in intra-party and inter-party politics, the framing of policy was left almost entirely to the bureaucracy – an allocation of roles quite unknown in the United States, and rare in Western Europe as elsewhere. The senior bureaucrats of the Ministry of Finance, the Ministry of International Trade and Industry, and the other ministries and bureaus with an economic role, rarely issued formal orders or prohibitions. They relied mostly on informal 'administrative guidance' rather than on laws or regulations. Their power was chiefly manifest through the consensual acceptance of their informal suggestions, which could amount to no more than casual remarks made at a dinner with leading businessmen, or a few oblique comments reported in the press.

Though not as strong as it once was, the influence of the senior bureaucrats over the Japanese economy is still strongly felt. Everyone remembers their historic achievement in guiding Japan's rise from poverty – a reputation badly dented but not destroyed by the post-1990 recession. Moreover, they derived much prestige from their educational status: the top-ranking ministries attracted the best graduates of the best universities, in a country where education is the only true religion.[8] While politicians are a western innovation in Japanese society – and no one is surprised by their corruption – the top bureaucrats have been viewed as the successors of the Samurai officials of old Japan, and thus are expected to be stoic, incorruptible and totally devoted to the national interest. That is why when a few low-level Ministry of Finance officials were arrested in January 1998 by a posse of a hundred prosecutors for accepting dinners and golf outings, the blow to its prestige was devastating.

As things used to be, when high officials spoke, top corporate managers, industrial associations, much of the press, and public opinion at large would listen and obey. Now the press is routinely critical, and some top corporate managers do not hesitate to challenge specific policies, or indeed the entire authority, of the top bureaucrats, which ultimately subverts democracy. Yet nobody should expect Japan's bureaucratic elite to lose its special position of power in Japanese life, no matter how much its prestige may be further diminished. Japanese politicians remain focused on their intense factional and party politics. Few are able and willing to frame policies and impose them on their nominal subordinates. Ultimately, however, the power of the bureaucracy is sustained by many of the little people of Japan, for it is the bureaucracy that shields them from market forces in one way or another.

American trade negotiators, along with their European colleagues nowadays, constantly preach the advantages of free markets, free trade and free competition to the Japanese. But the overall purpose of Japan's remaining trade barriers and many commercial regulations is precisely to protect Japanese society from the disruptive effects of

[8] To this day, most Japanese cannot understand why Europeans have only one religion; they, on the other hand, will have a Shinto wedding and a Buddhist funeral, and they enjoy Christmas too.

any competition, foreign or domestic – only thus can a job be ensured in the economy for every Japanese citizen who wants to work.

What is most striking about the Japanese model from a Western, or perhaps one should say turbo-capitalist, perspective is its tendency to protect the economically weak against the economically strong. For in contrast to the Western macroeconomic approach, which emphasizes broad policies to increase or suppress demand, so as to achieve broad results, whether to stimulate employment or control inflation, the Japanese model safeguards occupations and jobs category by category.

Small shopkeepers are protected by a Large-Scale Retail Law, which severely restricts the spread of discount chains, supermarkets and department stores – there are only some 2,000 in the whole of Japan, mostly confined to the central areas of the larger cities. Because Japanese shops are physically so small and so numerous, in excess of two million at the last count, five million or so Japanese shopkeepers and their employees are protected from more efficient forms of distribution. This, in turn, ensures the livelihood of more than a million subdistributors; one can see them everywhere in their micro-vans, from which they supply tiny shops in tiny quantities. At the last count, there were more than 600,000 food and beverage shops; more than 400,000 shops selling drugs, toiletries, books and stationery; and more than 200,000 dry goods and apparel shops. Another two million Japanese make their living from more than half a million mostly very small eating and drinking establishments, not counting another 200,000 *sushi-yas*, coffee bars, pubs, beer halls, cabarets and nightclubs. In addition, Japan's hotel trade includes a huge number of traditional *ryokan* inns, a few with as many as fifty rooms, most with only four or five.

The above means various things in human terms. To begin with, most of the Japanese who work in the lodging, eating, drinking and fun trades, as well as in retail outlets, are the owners themselves and their families – not employees as in the United States, and mostly poorly paid as we have seen. Not that the income of the Japanese owners is high on average; in fact many shopkeepers earn very little. Still, they have their independence and the dignity that goes with it; moreover, their place of work also provides much of their social life in many cases, for shops often serve as neighbourhood venues, while cafés and bars often function as informal clubs.

To assure the income of the four million or so Japanese primarily engaged in agriculture and fishing, there are many import limits, support programs and product subsidies, the latter often much higher than their European equivalents or the American, which are now being rapidly phased out. The much greater difference, however, is that in both the United States and Europe much of the government's money is intercepted by large-scale agricultural businesses, while in Japan all sorts of regulations ensure that only individual farmers and their cooperatives benefit from subsidies. As for the majority who chiefly grow rice, they have also been protected by an absolute import prohibition, which is only now giving way to very limited quotas.

Villages and small towns are protected as such from the competition of larger cities, through the lavish assistance they receive from the central government – not only for roads and other basic infrastructures, but also to build youth clubs, cultural halls, museums, artistic displays and sports facilities. The aim of the central government is to induce young people to stay, instead of leaving for larger cities.

Craftsmen of every kind are protected from cheaper imports – Korea and China produce many crafts that are considered typically Japanese – by both overt tariffs and unofficial customs-house conspiracies. And there are special barriers against the import of leather goods, to protect the leather workers who mostly belong to the socially despised and especially vulnerable *Eta* minority.[9]

Finally, while many important industries, including the automotive, heavy machinery, electrical and electronic sectors, require no protection at all since they are formidable exporters, processing industries (paper, plywood, glass, petrochemicals, etc.) suffer from high energy or raw material costs – and therefore they each receive effective protection. As for the high-technology computer, biotechnology and aerospace industries, they have been not only protected from imports, but positively assisted as we shall see. In theory, Japanese tariffs are the lowest in the world. In practice, imports that would disrupt the Japanese economy are still being kept out in many cases and in many informal ways – and without violating the letter of trade treaties.

Once all these distinct categories and a few more are added up (fishermen too are assisted, for example), it may be seen that the proportion of Japanese shielded from creative and disruptive competition is very large indeed. The overall result of Japan's version of controlled capitalism is that Japanese consumers routinely receive

---

[9] *Eta* are Japan's ritual outcasts, often descendants of butchers, flayers and tanners, trades despised in mostly Buddhist Japan. *Eta* are excluded from most good jobs, and rarely accepted by others as spouses.

excellent service and routinely pay very high prices. On the other hand, these same Japanese enjoy all the benefits of personal economic security in their role as producers. For unlike American turbo-capitalism, which favors consumers at the expense of producers, or the European practices that protect those already employed at the expense of the unemployed, Japan's controlled capitalism does ensure full employment – in part by institutionalizing under-employment. There is a tacit bargain between the government bureaucracy and the firms, industries and entire sectors of the economy that receive its protection: in exchange for all the help they get, they must provide enough jobs to keep real unemployment very near zero – the pre-crisis unemployment rate of 2–3 per cent was mostly due to the minority of Japanese who change jobs, a rare event in a Japanese life.

Accordingly, even though the continuing post-1989 recession is the most severe since 1945, hardly any of Japan's large 'name' corporations has fired any of its own employees, though their subcontractors did reduce the casual portion of their labor (notably including illegal immigrants). Most of the largest corporations have continued to hire their usual quota of young entrants into the labor force at every level including university graduates, even though their existing personnel are already under-employed in many cases. Other employers have continued to hire their quota of males only, reducing their intake of females – unfair no doubt, but a realistic response to the prevalent tendency of Japanese women to stop working after marriage. Thus all over Japan, highly automated plants which achieve extremely high efficiencies with very little labor coexist with plainly overstaffed offices.

The felt obligation to preserve jobs extends right across the service sector, which of course employs many more Japanese than all of the large industrial corporations. The part-time saleswoman who complemented her husband's salary by working in a tiny camera shop is still there, even though the owner could easily tend to his diminished custom of recession years all by himself. She faithfully worked for him in good times, she needs the money, and those are good enough reasons to ensure her own earnings at the expense of much-reduced profits.

What all this shows is that employment comes first in the Japanese model, before efficiency or profits. Because most shares of most companies are still owned by other companies in a never-ending chain of cross-ownership that is only now being disentangled, the few individual (and foreign) shareholders cannot complain when their dividends are cut to zero to maintain high levels of employment.

Foreign visitors immediately notice the exceptional tranquillity of Japanese crowds. They may attribute all this calm to the homogeneity of Japan's population, to ancestral discipline or oriental impassivity. But they would be wrong. Before its post-1945 version of controlled capitalism stabilized Japan's economy, the country witnessed a great many very violent strikes, any number of political assassinations, and frequent mass demonstrations that often degenerated into outright street fighting.

To be sure, the Japanese model sacrifices economic efficiency at every turn, and the consumer pays the very stiff price every time he or she goes into a shop. As Western economists see it, nothing could possibly justify the waste of resources caused by deliberate inefficiency, and the resulting impact on living standards. It is a fact that the Japanese standard of living is on average much lower than the American in purely material terms, even though average Japanese money incomes are substantially higher. But that is a very incomplete truth, for it overlooks society-wide and personal benefits that may count for much more – *even in purely monetary terms*. The contrast in that regard is, of course, much sharper when one compares not residually statist Europe with Japan, but rather the country that is now at the opposite end of the spectrum, the turbo-capitalist United States of today, my own country.

When I drive into a gasoline station in Japan, three or four clearly under-employed young men leap into action to wash and wipe the headlights and windows as well as the windscreen, check tire pressures and all the different oils, in addition to dispensing the fuel. For all that excellent service, I have to pay a very high price for the gasoline. The Japanese bureaucracy, determined to protect these low-end jobs for youths who lack the talent for better employment, as well as small gasoline stations in rural areas, does not allow self-service pumps; and in any case it forces all gasoline stations to compete by offering lavish service because gasoline prices are fixed by the government, and price cutting is banned.

Back in the United States, I fill my own tank much more cheaply from a self-service pump, but there too three or four young men are waiting – sometimes even in person, but certainly by implication. In practice, I still have to pay for those young men who are *not* employed by the gasoline station. My car insurance rates are higher because of their vandalism and thefts, my taxes must be higher to pay for police, court and prison costs, as well as welfare payments. If I am very unlucky, I may also have to pay in blood.

A seventeen-year-old youth from Washington DC recently killed a Korean immigrant shopkeeper while absent from a psychiatric clinic, where he had been sent for killing a taxi driver at the age of fifteen. An article on the youth noted that more than $100,000 had been spent on his psychiatric treatment;[10] his thirty-year prison term will cost another $750,000 or so. Not counting two deaths and his trial costs, even at very high Japanese prices the cost of *not* employing that one youth would pay for at least 151,108 liters of gasoline. To paraphrase Nicholas of Cusa, it might therefore be said that American free-market gasoline is very expensively cheap, as compared to Japan's employment-generating, cheaply expensive gasoline. There is no assurance, of course, that those young men whom I see loitering would actually accept gasoline station jobs if they were available for them. But what is certain is that in Japan the government acts to ensure that there are job openings for less talented youths who are incapable of more demanding employment.

There is a very good reason why Japan's version of controlled capitalism was not widely imitated even when it seemed to be phenomenally successful (its goal having been misunderstood). It critically depends on the quality of the detailed administrative guidance exercised by very efficient, very hard-working and very honest bureaucrats. It is easy to see that exactly the same model would only result in massive corruption and economic stagnation in the vast majority of countries that lack an abundance of efficient, hard-working and honest bureaucrats.

As it is, many Japanese have now come to believe that their own version of controlled capitalism is also afflicted by corruption, that it also leads to stagnation. Other Japanese simply resent the high prices of virtually all goods and services; a great many travel overseas and can see for themselves how much cheaper almost everything is in the United States if not in Europe, not noticing perhaps the far inferior quality of every form of service. Others do not travel, but Japan is a country of book and newspaper readers, far more literate than Americans or Europeans overall, so even those who stay at home know full well how much better off consumers are abroad.

Propelled by young and not so young thrusters who want all the freedoms of American entrepreneurs, by corporate executives of bold temper who want to emulate their American counterparts, a new

[10] Ruben Castaneda, 'Teen who left NY center admits killing DC clerk', *Washington Post*, 14 July 1994, p. B1.

consensus is forming in Japan. It would abolish most market rules and restrictions, formal and informal, demote the already partly discredited bureaucrats, stop the protection of all weak industries and weak firms, and release competition in all its forms. Riding the spirit of the times, the ambitious and innovative are making rapid progress in persuading their fellow Japanese to accept turbo-capitalist reforms. Even ordinary employees of no particular skill, who are bound to lose more than they gain, can now be heard mouthing the new slogans. Understandably, it may not occur to all of them that a turbo-capitalist Japan would no longer have full employment even in good times, let alone when in a deep recession, and that along with discount stores and supermarkets many prisons would also be built, to house that portion of the economically excluded who would turn to crime to make a living. For that, too, comes with the package.

SEVEN

The Theory and Practice of Geo-Economics

The intensified competitive struggles of turbo-capitalism cut across international borders, but they should not incite national-ist reactions. The contenders, after all, are not in any real sense national, but merely firms out to make a profit, often publicly quoted companies whose owners change as investors around the world buy or sell their shares. And yet as soon as the Cold War ended, economic rivalries visibly intensified. No longer forced into a compulsory solidarity by a common fear of the Soviet Union, Americans, Europeans and Japanese started a whole series of new quarrels over trading rules and industrial leadership in sectors that were revealingly labelled 'strategic' from aerospace to TV serials. Lesser countries stayed out of those fights, but pursued their own industrial aims, to build up favored sectors against the global competition that might otherwise sweep them away. The era of geo-economics was upon us.

In the Balkans, the Persian Gulf and other unfortunate parts of the world, old-fashioned territorial struggles continue as they have throughout history. In those backward zones of violence, actual or threatened, military strength remains as important as it ever was. And so does diplomacy in its classic form, still serving to convert the possible use of military strength into an actual source of power and influence, whether to threaten adversaries or reassure allies. But in the central arena of world affairs, where Americans, Europeans, Japanese and other advancing peoples both collaborate and compete, the situation has drastically changed. War having become almost unthinkable among them, both military power and classic diplomacy lost its ancestral importance in their mutual dealings, remaining of use only to confront troublemakers on the periphery.

But the millennium of peace has not yet arrived. The internal solidarity of peoples still derives from a common national identity, which exists only because it excludes other peoples. To say 'American' is to speak of something that is meaningful only because there are non-Americans. In many cases, it is still a cultural identity that defines the 'we' as against the 'them'. To be French or Italian or even Brazilian is a much more specific 'we' than the multicultural American 'we', and carries a stronger emotional pull. In some cases, as in Japan, this exclusive identity is still widely imagined to be racial, although it is enough to look at a Japanese crowd, ranging in color from pink-white to deep brown, to expose that particular fantasy. Whatever the nature or imagined constituents of national identities, world politics is still dominated by states that are based on their 'we' that excludes a larger 'them'. And states are, of course, *territorial* entities, marked off against each other by precisely defined borders, jealously claimed and closely guarded. Even when there is no thought of any military confrontation, therefore, even when they cooperate most amicably in all sorts of ways, states are inherently adversarial.

States and their governments, however, are not merely adversarial by nature, they do not merely reflect as a mirror might, underlying national identities. Consciously or not, their everyday actions and declarations, meant to protect, promote or advance 'national interests', also tend to stimulate, encourage, accommodate, harness and exploit adversarial popular sentiments that define a 'we' against a hostile 'them'. In the backwaters of world politics, where territorial conflicts persist, wars or threats of war provide an ample outlet for hostile sentiments. But when it comes to the central arena of world politics where Americans, Europeans and Japanese collaborate and contend, it is chiefly by economic means that adversarial attitudes can now be expressed.

Warfare by Other Means: Geo-Economics

This new version of the ancient rivalry of states, I have called 'geo-economics.[1] In it, investment capital for industry provided or guided

---

[1] I.e., the logic of conflict in the grammar of commerce; see 'From geopolitics to geo-economics', *The National Interest*, Summer 1990.

by the state is the equivalent of firepower; product development subsidized by the state is the equivalent of weapon innovation; and market penetration supported by the state replaces military bases and garrisons on foreign soil as well as diplomatic influence. The very same things – investment, research and development, and marketing campaigns – are also done every day by private firms for their own purely commercial reasons. But when the state intervenes to encourage, help or direct these very same activities, it is no longer plain vanilla economics that is going on, but rather geo-economics.

The geo-economic arsenal also includes other weapons, old and new. Tariffs can be merely taxes, imposed with no other aim in mind than to raise revenue; likewise, quota limits and outright import prohibitions may be meant only to cope with an acute shortage of hard currency. But when the purpose of such trade barriers is to protect domestic industry and allow it to grow, it is again geo-economics – the equivalent of the defended frontiers of war and old-style world politics.

Prohibitive tariffs or more simply outright bans can straight-forwardly stop imports, but almost all trading nations were members of the General Agreement on Tariffs and Trade (GATT), and now belong to its yet more restrictive successor, the World Trade Organization (WTO). The GATT treaties already dissuaded the arbitrary imposition of tariffs, quotas or import bans; the WTO adjudicates stronger prohibitions, and can impose penalties on offenders. Thus some countries resort to hidden trade barriers, the geo-economic equivalent of the ambush, that most powerful of tactics in war.

A very common method is deliberately to frame health and safety regulations, or labelling, packaging or recycling requirements, to exclude foreign products. Other ways of ambushing imports are legion, but the most comprehensive on record was the covert South Korean war on car imports that persisted until 1997. Because South Korean automobile companies were themselves vigorous exporters, the South Korean government could not simply forbid car imports, or impose prohibitive tariffs. Instead it relied on a plausibly deniable ambush strategy. First, local companies of any size were tacitly forbidden to become importers and distributors for US, European or Japanese manufacturers. Next, when the latter tried to establish their own showrooms and outlets, the local property owners they approached were quietly ordered to refuse sales or leases. Finally, when foolhardy South Koreans bought one of the few imported cars to be found, the tax authorities immediately summoned them for exceptionally thorough audits of their incomes and past taxes. Word soon got around, and very few·imported cars were ever sold before the 1997 financial crash, which both reduced all car buying to a trickle and promised to open up the market in the future – because the United States and Japan both demanded it before agreeing to grant their rescue loans.

In East Asia especially, unwritten and undeclared obstacles to imports are common. Aside from specific maneuvers meant to keep out specific imports, the normal operating procedure of some 'customs' services can itself be an obstacle to free trade Every single container, every single case, every single box and every single package – including air-express envelopes – is individually opened for inspection, in contrast to US and Western European practices, whereby customs officers rely on the exporter's declaration, only performing some spot checks. This plus the requisite record-keeping guaranteed delays, until recently compounded in the case of Japan by the requirement of a visual image as well. Japanese cameras are sold all over the world, but Japanese customs inspectors did not use them until recently. Instead they sketched the imported article in a free-hand drawing.

Delay may only irritate, but some delays are purposeful. Imports of new products that threaten domestic industries are sometimes defeated by employing the device of compulsory standards. The relevant authority can secretly consult with local industry deliberately to set standards that will exclude imports made by the strongest competitors. And announcements of new standards can be held up until local industry has tooled up for mass production. When that moment arrives and the market is finally opened to all comers, the locals can start to sell right away – while their foreign competitors are just starting to reconfigure their products. It was thus with cellular telephones and high-definition TV in the American-European-Japanese 'war of the HDTV standards'.

In some cases, arbitrary standards can keep out exports indefinitely. For example, Japanese standards require that plywood be made of tropical hardwoods, not pine or other softwoods. There is no reason at all why this should be so, softwood being just as good for the purpose. But the effect has been to protect Japan's plywood industry from American and Scandinavian competitors, which have the unbeatable advantage of much cheaper raw material. And there has also been a side-effect: the irrevocable destruction of the tropical rain forests of the Philippines, Thailand, Indonesia and Malaysia.

Trade barriers mostly serve to preserve the local market for local industry, but sometimes they can help export industries. Countries with scarce natural resources can impose export taxes on raw materials but not on worked products, to encourage local processing. Most African countries, for example, no longer allow the export of raw logs, but only of semi-finished wood. Many in the United States have urged a similar rule, but American national forests are still being cut down – for the sake of lumberjack jobs, it is said, though many saw-mill jobs could be had if the export of raw logs were stopped. Saudi Arabia and other oil producers achieve the same effect by selling crude oil at high prices, while offering refined products and petrochemicals at low prices.

In geo-economics as in war, however, the offensive weapons are more important. Of these, research and development, force-fed with government support and the taxpayers' money, is perhaps the most important. Just as in war the artillery conquers territory by fire, which the infantry can then occupy, the aim here is to conquer the industries of the future by achieving technological superiority. In 1990, for example, the US Advanced Battery Consortium was established to develop a more efficient power source for cars than the old lead-acid battery, which is much too heavy for the scant power it yields. With $130 million from the US Department of Energy and another $130 million jointly provided by General Motors, Ford and Chrysler, the Consortium started to fund innovative battery projects. By 1992 it seemed to have found a promising candidate in the 'ovonic' battery, developed by Stanford R. Ovshinsky and his Energy Conversion Devices Inc. with $18.5 million from the Consortium. By 1998 hopes in that direction had faded, but the brotherly collaboration of all three US automobile companies, which are supposed to be forever competing, was full of meaning: this was not merely a business undertaking, but rather an American geo-economic offensive against the Japanese automobile industry, ironically carried out by a typically Japanese-style government and industry consortium.

The artillery of state-encouraged research and development is crucial, but the infantry of production may also need assistance. Airbus Industrie, maker of passenger airliners, received many operating subsidies in the past, and so do other favored companies or entire industries.

Usually there is no need of embarrassing all concerned by overt payments: government purchasing on generous terms achieves the same effect much more discreetly. Japan, for example, had no computer industry to speak of in 1960 when the Ministry of International Trade and Industry (MITI) launched a five-year program to develop *national* computers.[2] IBM had already established a factory in Japan, but its computers were not considered 'national' enough: only those who bought Japanese computers received cheap loans from the government's Japan Electronic Computer Corporation. Further, MITI offered to allow IBM's competitors, General Electric, RCA and Xerox, to sell their computers on the Japanese market, but only if they agreed to share their technology with Japanese production partners. When IBM introduced its revolutionary System 360 in 1964, making joint-venture Japanese computers virtually obsolete, MITI's response was the Super High Performance Electronic Computer Program, which pooled the resources of government and industry laboratories to catch up. In the meantime, the government helped local industry more directly, by purchasing its computers even if they were both inferior and more costly than IBM's.

In the early 1970s there was another upheaval: Japanese companies that were sharing the technology of General Electric, RCA and Xerox were left bereft when all three abandoned the field after IBM unveiled its innovative System 370. MITI's response was another injection of cash for research and development, and it also forced Japan's six companies to combine into three for greater strength. Counter-attacking more directly, MITI helped to fund the new US Amdahl company, headed by the noted ex-IBM designer of that name, by way of a Fujitsu–Hitachi partnership. Amdahl unveiled the secrets of IBM's computer architecture for an undisclosed amount, but certainly much too little for such premier industrial jewels. And so it went on, year after year, by one means or another. Although MITI's research programs were overtaken each time by fresh American innovations (workstations, parallel computing, fault-tolerant logic, local-area networks, windows software, etc.), Japan's computer industry was helped very effectively nonetheless.

The final offensive weapon is predatory finance. If the artillery of research and development cannot conquer markets by sheer technological superiority; if operating subsidies are not enough, export sales may still be won against strong competitors by offering loans at below-market interest rates. The United States has its Export–Import 'Exim' bank that provides loan guarantees to finance exports, and all

[2] Kenneth Flamm, *Targeting the Computer: Government Support and International Competition*, The Brookings Institution, Washington DC, 1987.

major industrial countries have their own equivalents. Thus foreigners routinely pay lower interest rates than local borrowers, whose taxes pay for the very concessions that foreigners receive. This already amounts to hunting for exports with low-interest ammunition, but the accusation of predatory finance is reserved for cases where interest rates are suddenly reduced in the course of a fought-over sale. Naturally, the chief trading states have promised each other that they will do no such thing. Naturally, they frequently break that promise.

In traditional world politics, the goals are to secure and extend the physical control of territory, and to gain diplomatic influence over foreign governments. The corresponding geo-economic goal is not to achieve the highest possible standard of living, but rather the conquest or protection of desirable roles in the world economy. Who will develop the next generation of jet airliners, computers, biotechnology products, advanced materials, financial services and all other high-value output in industries large and small? Will the designers, technologists, managers and financiers be Americans, Europeans or East Asians? The winners will have those highly rewarding and controlling roles, while the losers will have only assembly lines – if their home markets are large enough. When 'transplants', i.e. foreign-owned factories, replace domestic production, the local employment of manual and semi-skilled labor continues in full, but finance and all higher management functions are transferred back to the owner's home base, or possibly to regional headquarters in some third country.

A New Role for Elite Bureaucrats

Geo-economics is therefore a very appropriate projection on the world scene of classless meritocratic ambitions, just as war and diplomacy once satisfied aristocratic ambitions, offering desirable roles for military officers and diplomats who were aristocrats, or acted as if they were. Today's meritocracy of senior technologists and managers is not much less modest. They do not desire bemedalled uniforms or sumptuous balls, but they do want to be in command on the world scene, as the developers of technology, not mere producers under license; as the designers of new products, not mere assemblers; as industrialists not mere importers.

From Power-politics to 'Geo-economics'

Traditional Power-politics
Means: (1) Military strength; (2) Diplomacy; (3) Propaganda; (4) Weapon development.

Goals: (1) Territorial security; (2) Expansion; (3) Influence over other states; (4) Prestige.

It was the main action in the main arena of world affairs. Now marginalized to backward zones of armed conflict (Middle East, Yugoslavia, etc.). The main action in the main arena is now:

Geo-economics
Means I: By state-assisted/directed private entities: (1) High-risk research and development; (2) Market-penetration investments (incl. 'dumping'); (3) Production over-investment for market-share forcing. (Also performed by private entities for purely economic reasons.)

Means II: By the state only: (1) Tariffs, quotas (the equivalent of defended frontiers); (2) Regulatory and covert impediments to imports (= ambushes); (3) Discounted export financing (= raids); (4) National technology programs (= theater campaigns); (5) Economic and technical intelligence.

Goal: The conquest (or defense) of important roles in high-added-value, 'strategic' industries (telecommunications, information technology, biotechnology, aerospace, and high-tech automotive components). Winners have financial, creative and higher management functions and control. Losers may only have assembly lines if their domestic market is large enough.

Implications
Economic

(1) Severe comparative disadvantage for firms in targeted industries if unprotected or poorly protected by ineffective or uncooperative state bureaucracies and governments.

(2) Chronic overcapacity in sectors in which state-assisted firms compete for market shares beyond profitability limits, e.g. aerospace, super-computing, automotive.

(3) Chronic waste of generic resources by over-investment, and of research and development human resources by national technology programs.

Political

(1) Geo-economics is power-enhancing for governing elites, which cannot control plain business.

(2) If others practice geo-economics, abstention may mean economic defeat.

(3) Geo-economic struggles may replace power-politics in stimulating national cohesion.

(4) Geo-economic struggles can erode residual power-politics alliances.

134

Not all states are equally inclined or equally capable of participating in geo-economic struggles. Just as there is no successful warfare without effective armed forces, so there can be no successful geo-economic action without ambitious industrialists and effective economic bureaucrats. But even in advanced countries where both are to be found, indeed especially in advanced countries, the central role of state officials in any geo-economic action is bound to distort it. Perfectly honest and well-meaning bureaucrats, who happen to serve in ministries of commerce and industry, will inevitably pursue the normal ambition of bureaucrats – to serve the state well, and to gain recognition and power in the process – by furthering their own geo-economic schemes of industrial defense or industrial conquest. Equally honest bureaucrats serving in foreign affairs ministries may concurrently pursue their own equally normal ambitions by furthering schemes of tariff reduction and international economic cooperation.

For European and Japanese bureaucrats especially, but increasingly for American bureaucrats as well, geo-economics offers the only possible substitute for the military and diplomatic roles of the past. Only by invoking geo-economic imperatives can they claim authority over mere business people and the citizenry at large. Obviously the urge is much more powerful in countries such as France and Japan, which have traditionally powerful and proud bureaucratic elites. Highly educated and carefully selected – and also greatly respected until each country's moment of crisis in the late 1990s – they are especially unwilling to surrender their privileged position by allowing unfettered free enterprise to have its way.

Those ambitious enough to seek career advancement in the great institutions of the state will not want to devote their lives to such petty war and petty diplomacy as will continue in backward regions of the world even in a fully achieved geo-economic era. Unless they embrace geo-economics, they must allow mere commerce alone to reign on the main stage of international life, under the undisputed control of business people and corporations. By embracing it, state bureaucrats can assert their authority anew, not in the name of strategy and security this time, but rather to protect 'vital economic interests' by geo-economic defenses, and geo-economic offensives, geo-economic diplomacy and geo-economic intelligence. In 1990, with the Cold War not quite ended, both the Central Intelligence Agency and the National Security Agency were already conducting in-house studies of their potential role as suppliers of economic, industrial and commercial intelligence. Nothing is more natural than the attempt of bureaucrats to find new justifications to keep their bureaucracies well funded, but of course official intelligence is only of value if there is an official user which can use it, an activist economic bureaucracy similar to Japan's MITI rather than the US Department of Commerce. In the event there were eager users aplenty:

- The Office of the US Trade Representative, in effect a ministry of foreign commerce, for intelligence on hidden trade barriers – indeed a subtle business – and also for the bargaining strategies of other countries; it is far easier to negotiate successfully if one knows just how much the other side has been authorized to give up, and what concessions it must have.
- The US Department of Commerce, for foreign export violations, such as the relabelling of products made in third countries – a chronic problem for China-made exports subject to tariffs when they are routed through tariff-exempt countries – and also for the overseas end of domestic export violations, chiefly the sale of controlled equipment and technologies to countries under US embargoes.
- The US Department of Energy, for oil and gas information world-wide, as well as for non-military advanced technologies of US interest, chiefly new battery concepts and other ways of producing automotive energy.
- The US Department of Agriculture, for violations of import or export regulations, and of fishing restrictions meant to protect endangered species.

And more besides, with the one exclusion that official intelligence is not to serve private commercial purposes, for no government organization can help one corporation rather than another – unless there is an officially sponsored consortium that helps all of them. Other countries may have lesser intelligence capabilities, but also fewer restraints on their use, so that economic intelligence broadly defined has become a crowded field.

Actually much more is happening in the central arena of world affairs than the pursuit of bureaucratic aims by under-employed bureaucracies. States as a whole are impelled by the urge to acquire geo-economic substitutes for their decaying security roles. Thus countries that are not ideologically inhibited are likely to be pushed further along the geo-economic path than the balance of costs and benefits would warrant.

The overall results of bureaucratic and political impulses to find new geo-economic roles vary greatly from country to country, and from industry to industry. But fundamentally states tend to act geo-economically simply because of what they are: territorially defined entities which exist precisely to outdo each other on the world scene in one way or another. In spite of all the other functions that modern states have acquired as providers of assorted services, varied infrastructures and individual welfare benefits, their reason for being still derives from their historical function as providers of security from external foes as well as from outlaws within. In the past, these were enemies in arms who had to be fought; today they are competitors in the marketplace with whom free competition is for some reason a losing game.

The winners in each sector of industry naturally favor unlimited free trade. The losers may accept defeat and leave the field. But geo-economics offers the alternative of a state-supported second round, and every instinct of states and their bureaucracies is to try to do just that, if only to remain in center stage, almost as in war.

Only a few of the independent states now in existence have fought a war in living memory, and yet the governing structures of almost all states are still heavily marked by warlike purposes. In how many countries does the Minister for Telecommunications, or Energy, or Foreign Trade outrank the Defense Minister? Only in one as a matter of fact – fittingly enough that country is Japan, where the Defense bureaucracy (*Boecho*) is a *cho* (translated as 'agency'), a unit inferior to a *sho* or ministry, as in *Gaimusho*, the Ministry of Foreign Affairs. And the *Boecho*'s head is a Director-General, equivalent to a US under-secretary or a British 'minister of state' rather than a full minister.

In the train of history, the last wagons, the poorest countries with the most inefficient and most corrupt state bureaucracies, cannot yet wage wars because their armies are incapable of operating beyond their frontiers, being only fit to pillage and oppress their own citizens at home (some of the West African units sent to Liberia as peace-keepers in the civil war of 1991 fell apart into looting bands, while the more disciplined Nigerians saved the day). For the same reason, those states cannot yet act geo-economically either, or indeed do anything at all to their own economies that is better than doing nothing at all. For them, the free market and free enterprise are indeed the only salvation.

The wagons in the middle, countries with partly developed economies – some much poorer on a per capita basis, such as India, and some rather richer, such as Turkey – are all capable of war, against each other at least, but are usually much too absorbed in territorial conflicts to pursue geo-economic policies seriously. Their governments do try to protect and develop local industries in various ways, but except for military industries their efforts are usually weak and inconsistent. And those that are free of warlike entanglements, such as Brazil, attempt geo-economic action at their peril, for their bureaucracies are not up to the task of doing better than free enterprise would do quite unassisted. Often they do much worse.

The wagons at the head of history's train, the United States, the countries of Europe, Japan and others like them, are all materially capable of waging war effectively, but their societies and cultures are allergic to war. Certainly their populations and governing elites are now convinced that they cannot usefully fight one another virtually for any reason. Yet each has a state structure still organized for warlike rivalry, all too easily tempted to pursue the aims of war by geo-economic means.

Is Geo-Economics New?

Some might dismiss all of the above as new verbiage for old themes. It is certainly true that rulers and states have always pursued economic aims, and have never lacked for economic quarrels with other rulers and states. Sometimes special tolls and high duties, trade prohibitions or outright blockades were sufficient, but sometimes marketplace rivalries were finally fought out with blood and iron. In the past, however, the outdoing of others in commerce and industry was overshadowed by the more pressing priorities of war and diplomacy, chiefly the quest for security – a sufficient reason for many wars – but also the pursuit of glory or internal political advantage by single rulers or ruling groups, by ambitious individuals or entire castes. Then commerce and its needs were utterly subordinated, as profitable trade links were cut by warring armies, and as wars were fought alongside trading rivals against trading partners. Thus in 1914, France went to war against its chief trading partner, Germany, in alliance with Britain, its chief rival in the colonial trades. If security needs dictated an alliance against a common enemy, even while there was a head-to-head economic competition with that very ally, the preservation of the alliance had absolute priority, for its aim was survival not merely prosperity.

This, indeed, is how and why all the commercial quarrels between the United States and Western Europe – over frozen chickens, microchips, beef and others – and between the United States and Japan – over everything from textiles in the 1960s to supercomputers in the 1980s – were so easily contained during the decades of the Cold War. As soon as a trade dispute became noisy enough to attract the attention of political leaders on both sides, it was promptly settled, often by paying off the loudest complainers. Trade quarrels were not allowed to damage political relations, which would in turn threaten alliance solidarity before a menacing Soviet Union.

As the importance of military threats and military alliances continues to wane for the countries in the peaceful central arena of world affairs, economic priorities are no longer suppressed, but can instead emerge and even become dominant. Trade quarrels may still be contained by the fear of their purely economic consequences, but not by political interventions motivated by strategic imperatives. And if the internal cohesion of nations must still be preserved by a unifying external threat, that threat must now be economic, or rather geo-economic.

Exactly this recasting of public attitudes is manifest in the strictly economic fears that many other Europeans express before the industrial and financial might of undivided Germany, and in American attitudes towards Japan until its post-1990 financial downfall. Gorbachev's redirection of Soviet foreign policy away from Cold War hostility had barely started when Japan was abruptly promoted into the role of America's chief enemy, judging by the evidence of opinion polls, media coverage and countless Congressional pronouncements. To place anti-Japanese full-page advertisements in the daily press, decorated with rising-sun flags or even menacing sumo wrestlers, became standard operating procedure for trade associations lobbying for government protection. It was as if a country long united internally by a common fear of the Soviet Union had moved as one to find a geo-economic substitute in Japan, to preserve its unity. In the late 1950s, it was the shock of the Soviet launch of the first orbiting Sputnik satellite, and of the apparent Soviet lead in ballistic missiles, that persuaded the US Congress to pour money into higher education, to win the military-technological race. In the late 1980s, educational reformers across America likewise cited the Japanese lead in public education to solicit money for their schemes. Enemies, real or imagined, can be useful.

Is geo-economics a regression to the age of mercantilism? Is 'geo-economics' nothing more than an unnecessary new word for that ancient practice? There are parallels, of course, for in both cases state authorities act against each other in commerce or industry, instead of allowing private interests to trade with each other as they see fit for their own private interests. But the central aim of mercantilism was to acquire gold – not a foolish purpose for kings in need of gold coin to pay their troops. With gold, regiments could be raised to win wars; without it, defeat was inevitable. Gold was thus military strength at only one remove. And unlike illiquid agricultural land or buildings, even private gold holdings could readily be taxed. Hence mercantilism was purposeful for kings even if harmful for their countries: by encouraging shipping and export trades while discouraging imports, taxable gold would accumulate within the ruler's reach. Mercantilism was an economic phenomenon, but its purposes were strictly political, indeed strategic.

Because the purpose of geo-economics is so very different – to maximize not gold holdings, but rather high-skill jobs in advanced industries and sophisticated services – all is different within it: the means, from research and development to export finance; the immediate aims of technological and market superiority; and the consequences. Even the vigorous pursuit of geo-economics need not lead to 'beggar-thy-neighbour' competitive devaluations, import bans, high tariffs or any impediments at all, although there might well be export subsidies. Certainly it is not a quest for gold, or indeed for wealth as such, that drives the new form of international rivalry.

The greatest difference, however, was that mercantilism was always overshadowed by war. When commercial quarrels became sufficiently inflamed to degenerate into political quarrels, they in turn could easily lead to war, and often did. Sixteenth-century Spain decreed that all trade to and from its American colonies must travel in Spanish bottoms through Spanish ports, but British and Dutch armed merchantmen conveying profitable cargoes to disloyal colonists defied Spanish sloops, readily turning into privateers once war was declared to seize the rich silver cargoes bound for Spain. A century later, the Dutch replied to the mercantilist laws of the British Parliament that prohibited their coast-wise English trade by sending their frigates to sink British shipping, in 1667 memorably sailing up the River Thames itself to sink British warships. Earlier the Portuguese had won the India trade not by outcompeting Arab traders, but by sinking their more efficient but much smaller ships. Sailing all the way from the Atlantic, Portuguese ships were hopelessly disadvantaged as transports, but their much heavier gun batteries settled the outcome.

Geo-economics, by contrast, is a game that is played by countries that have already ruled out warfare among themselves. Super-computers kept out by import barriers cannot be forcibly delivered by airborne assault to the banks or universities that might buy them; nor can competition in the world automobile market be pursued by sinking the car ferries of competitors on the high seas. Armed force has thus entirely lost the dominant role it once had in the age of mercantilism – as an admissible, indeed almost routine, adjunct to economic rivalry. Instead, in the new geo-economic era, not only the causes but also the instruments of rivalry must be strictly economic. If commercial quarrels do lead to political clashes, as they are now doing with some regularity with the waning of alliance imperatives, these political clashes will have to be fought out with the weapons of commerce: the more or less disguised restriction of imports, the more or less concealed subsidization of exports, the funding of competitive technology projects, the provision of competitive infrastructures, and so on.

Not all states are equally capable of implementing geo-economic policies, as we have seen. But beyond that, not all states are equally inclined to try. For all sorts of reasons, historical, institutional, ideo-logical or political, some states are much more active than others in the new form of international rivalry, with some even refusing to act at all, just as states as varied as Burma and Switzerland desired only neutrality during the Cold War. Elsewhere, in the most advanced countries, nothing has been finally determined as yet. Instead, the desirable extent of geo-economic activity has itself become an issue of political debate and partisan controversy. In the United States, Republicans firmly oppose any sort of 'industrial policy' – that being the current jargon for any measures meant to promote the growth of promising industries – while Democrats have wavered back and forth. In France, by contrast, the governing elites who long pursued vast military and diplomatic ambitions have shifted their attention to the pursuit of equally vast geo-economic ambitions – Airbus Industrie is just one of their endeavours. In most European countries, the public debate continues between the US and French extremes, while in East

Asia the wisdom of geo-economic activism was not seriously questioned until the financial crash of 1997.

Of the different forms of coexistence between geo-economically active states and private enterprise, there is no end. Small, localized businesses, the myriad of retailers, workshops, cafés, dry-cleaners and such, expect nothing from the state, and nothing is expected of them – except for taxes. At the opposite extreme, major corporations and prominent tycoons routinely try to manipulate bureaucrats, politicians and public opinion to obtain favors from public authorities. In the past, they might have pressed their case for tariff protection, say, with strategic self-sufficiency arguments. Nowadays, private companies in aerospace, telecommunications, data processing, biotechnology, amorphous materials, ceramics, etc. invoke geo-economic arguments to ask for research grants, co-investments or cheap credit. At the same time, going the other way, bureaucrats and politicians try to enlist private corporations to pursue their own geo-economic aims, or even select a specific firm as the country's 'chosen instrument' in a given industry.

Even more common, no doubt, are cases of reciprocal manipulation, as in the dealings of the largest international oil companies – American, British, French, Italian – with their respective state authorities and political leaders. Top oil company executives and senior foreign policy officials, oil company representatives overseas and diplomats in place, oil company country-experts and intelligence officers, often collaborate so closely that they might as well be interchangeable, and sometimes are – oil companies are often generous employers of ex-officials.

In the past, unfriendly dealings between governments and private enterprise usually featured underdeveloped countries on one side, and foreign companies on the other. Over the years, especially from the 1930s until the 1960s, many foreign-owned companies were expelled, nationalized with or without compensation, or heavily fined in the wake of every imaginable accusation, from the standard claim of tax avoidance and the over-exploitation of natural resources, to the mistreatment of local employees, the sale of contaminated products and, of course, interference in domestic politics. Often the accusations were justified.

Now, however, it is increasingly the public authorities of more advanced countries that are coming into conflict with foreign business enterprises. Geo-economically active states, striving to promote their country's industry, must obviously oppose foreign companies that are the chosen instruments of their rivals, as well as those that simply have the misfortune of standing in the way. Thus the US government must confront Airbus Industrie to protect Boeing from predatory practices, while IBM was under attack from the Japanese government for more than thirty years, simply because Japan's MITI was striving to conquer a market share in the mainframe-computer sector – ironically, by the time its chosen instrument, Fujitsu, achieved significant success, mainframes were being increasingly displaced by local-area networks and smaller machines.

Geo-economic rivalries entail unprecedented risks for private enterprise in high-technology sectors. Firms that invest vast funds of their own in the hopes of achieving a major breakthrough can find themselves suddenly overtaken by another country's 'national technology program', which might come up with the better mouse-trap first, by using taxpayers' money in abundance. To be sure, state-sponsored research and development programs can fail, as Japan's once-celebrated 'Fifth Generation' computing project failed in the 1980s – expenditure of some $400 million did not yield a single marketable product. Yet even those most confident of the inherent superiority of 100 per cent private brains in the service of 100 per cent private enterprise must now hesitate before investing in the better car battery, for example, in competition with the US Advanced Battery Consortium, which already has $130 million in public money and might get another $130 million, or $1.3 billion for that matter.

Private companies can also find themselves competing with foreign companies that resort to systematic underpricing, with the resulting losses covered by sponsoring state authorities. This was the fate of Boeing for years on end until long-subsidized Airbus became a profitable concern; but also of many other purely private companies in high-technology sectors, in which there are any number of subsidized 'chosen instruments'. When public funding is concealed, as it often is, a victim-company may even enter a new market quite unaware of its fatal disadvantage.

A World of Rival Trading Blocs?

Most people take it for granted that the global market can only become more open in the future, with ever-fewer barriers to trade. The possibility that commercial quarrels between Americans and Europeans, the United States and Japan, and the European Union and Japan might instead lead to the emergence of rival trading blocs, each with barriers against the other's exports, seems outlandish. After all, except for agricultural products, the European Union is jointly more open to external trade than its individual members ever were; and as a practical matter, it is much easier for outsiders to sell in the EU-wide market than in separate national markets. This is just as true of the US-Canadian-Mexican NAFTA common market. Finally, there is no 'yen zone' and there never was, except in journalistic imaginings. If rival European Union and North American trading blocs did emerge, Japan would be strictly on its own, for neither Korea nor Taiwan let alone China would ever accept its economic tutelage, and throughout South-East Asia only Malaysia and Thailand would welcome any form of exclusive association with Japan. Thus, so far, one cannot even speak of trading blocs, still less of rival trading blocs.

Above all, the semi-open global market of today seems so *natural*. Yet it did not come into existence naturally, or even because the theory of free trade persuaded all concerned on its intellectual merits alone. It is very much a man-made object, in fact a US-made object, the result of more than fifty years of American diplomacy, American pressure and American willingness to open the US market first and most.

Starting on 1 January 1948, when the original General Agreement on Tariffs and Trade came into effect under US sponsorship, all sorts of trade barriers were reduced or eliminated step by step, sometimes item by item in an endless series of negotiations. It was GATT that introduced the 'most favored nation' principle, under which any barrier-reducing bargain between any pair of members automatically applies to all. The GATT 'Kennedy Round', negotiated from 1964 to 1967, was especially important: today's liberalized international economy owes much to its unprecedented tariff reductions.

The United States and most other countries had purely economic reasons for wanting the expansion of trade that GATT promised, and has continued to deliver. But it was no coincidence that the original GATT treaty was vigorously promoted by the United States at the very outset of the Cold War (no country under Soviet influence joined), and that the Kennedy Round was concluded as the Cold War was approaching its climax. For the strongest motive for trade liberalization – stronger than purely economic advantages, against which there were always disadvantages to be reckoned – was always political and strategic. GATT was clearly meant to be the commercial counterpart to the pan-Western strategic alliance against the Soviet Union.

Its history would suggest that, if the Soviet threat ever disappeared, GATT and the further progress of trade liberalization would be endangered. And that is exactly what happened. Following the collapse of Soviet power, instead of the almost routine advances of the past, the successful negotiation of the final GATT 'Uruguay Round' launched in 1986 was long and difficult indeed, with the outcome an uncertain cliff-hanger till the very end almost ten years later. Since then, liberalization has continued to advance under the sponsorship of GATT's successor, the World Trade Organization, but only by dint of the most strenuous efforts. Instead of quiet progress, it is open disputes and cliff-hanger finales that have become the routine, most recently over the liberalization of financial and insurance services.

In the meantime, there has been a proliferation of unilateral trade measures: non-tariff barriers have been increasing in recent years, instead of being gradually eliminated as in the past. When the US Congress inserted the '301' provision in the Trade Act of 1974, its drafters were careful to ensure that both its wording and intent would clearly be consistent with GATT and now WTO rules.[3] Under 301, the President is given broad authority to act against foreign import barriers. First the US Trade Representative is empowered to investigate suspect foreign trade practices to detect unfairness; if found, they are to be formally defined as such. At that point, the President must alert the foreign country in question that specified retaliatory measures will be enforced by a certain date unless the barriers are removed. No public announcements or threats were called for – all could be handled by quiet diplomacy.

When, however, the US Congress legislated 'Super 301' in 1988, it was less respectful of GATT/WTO rules. The US Trade Representative is no longer merely authorized to act, but is formally required to act. The office must publish for public use an annual list of improper trade barriers, identifying the countries responsible for each; it must identify 'priority' barriers and priority countries; and it must set firm deadlines for remedies, with retaliation also mandatory if the barriers are not removed. ('Special 301' is the equivalent, for copyright and other intellectual property rights.) Thus the President can no longer act discreetly, but must instead issue overt threats,

[3] Section 301 of the Trade Act of 1974 (codified as amended in 19 U.S.C. SS 2411–2416) was compatible with GATT's Articles XXII and XXIII.

which can no longer be quietly withdrawn at his discretion. This, of course, was the very purpose of Super 301, for it was the prevailing view in Congress that the original 301 was not being implemented energetically enough.

The paradox of a worsening atmosphere amidst the prosperous growth of ever more liberalized world commerce should not surprise. Commerce leads to interdependence, which does not guarantee harmony as its celebrants forever claim; on the contrary, it is an irritant. In 1997–98, for example, a completely new quarrel was underway between the US and Japanese governments over Japanese taxes – not Japanese taxes on US firms, mind you, but taxes on Japanese firms and, indeed, individuals above all. US government officials from President Clinton down to mere under-secretaries felt entitled to tell the Japanese government how to conduct its own fiscal policy, indeed to demand cuts in specific Japanese taxes, because it held that they were depressing consumer demand, thus inducing Japanese companies to export more, while at the same time making it harder for American companies to sell in Japan.

The quarrel became much more heated and much more public – with new fiscal lectures delivered on television – following the cascading financial crashes of Thailand, Malaysia, Indonesia and South Korea. All would need to export more while importing less to reduce their mountains of foreign debt, and unless Japanese consumers did their bit, those exports would mostly flow into the United States, increasing the trade deficit, which was already at record levels. The Japanese counter-argument, that a high budget deficit and higher public debt called for tax increases rather than tax cuts, was largely ignored on the American side, because US officials were focused on the immediate crisis rather than on the long-term balance of Japanese public finance. In the event, the Japanese government abruptly changed its policies once Japanese corporations added their voice to American (and European) pressures, cutting some taxes while at the same time increasing public spending. It remains to be seen whether the Japanese government will have occasion to return the favor by telling the US government how to run its affairs.

Beyond the irritants of interdependence, the international economy is inevitably affected by the calculations and the fears that come from that fraction of it that is 'geo-economic', rather than simply economic. In the past, the doings of a handful of warlike countries affected many other countries, and indeed militarized world politics as a whole. Today, likewise, geo-economic struggles between Americans, Europeans and Japanese are eroding their old alliance solidarity, and the resulting ill-feelings are beginning to affect all other trading countries of any importance. They fear, understandably, that they will be caught in the crossfire. The Airbus Industrie/Boeing struggle already has all the characteristics of a full-bore commercial war, in which the gains of one side really do require losses on the other. This alone shows the falsity of the oft-cited distinction between war and commercial relations, in which both sides should gain and usually do. Obviously, most commercial dealings are not warlike, but some are.

War is, indeed, fundamentally different from commerce. The logic of conflict is, loosely speaking, 'zero-sum' because the gain of one side is in itself a loss for the other, and vice versa. This is so in war, in warlike diplomacy and in oligopolistic competition, but not in many-sided ('perfect') competition, wherein any two sides can both gain (or lose) concurrently. Moreover, the logic of conflict is paradoxical: it is governed by the coincidence of opposites, because all actions unfold in the presence of an adversary that tries to defeat whatever is being done. This is why the worst of approach roads for an attack may be the best, if it confers the advantage of surprise – making the bad road paradoxically good, and the good road paradoxically bad. And that is why victorious armies that advance too far can bring about their own defeat by over-extension, just as weapons that are too effective are the most likely to be made ineffectual by the enemy coun-termeasures that their very effectiveness evokes. In the logic of conflict there is always a culminating point, beyond which action turns into its opposite. And the same logic operates at every level of strategy: for example, the Soviet Union's accumulation of military strength eventually resulted in its military impotence, once enough states were frightened into forming a blocking coalition against it. In the linear logic of everyday life and of plain commerce, by contrast, good is good and bad is bad, and success can facilitate further success without any culminating point leading to a downfall.[4]

War is thus truly different from commerce, but evidently not different enough. In particular, an action–reaction cycle of trade restrictions that evoke retaliation has a distinct resemblance to crisis escalation that can lead to outright war. And if a commercial conflict does break out between any major trading powers, the classic mechanisms of world politics would extend its reach: one can visualize

---

[4] For a systematic overview, see my *Strategy: The Logic of War and Peace* (Harvard University Press, 1987).

how a future European Union Ambassador to Egypt might patiently explain that Egyptian exports to the EU would inevitably suffer, if the country were to purchase a Japanese power-station, as 'rumored in the press'; and then his Japanese colleague would arrive to demand the contract, also threatening retaliation, while the Americans would try to persuade the Egyptians that their only way out is to award the contract to an American company. And if states do join to form larger economic blocs, as is now happening in North America with the US–Canada–Mexico free-trade zone, and as happened long ago with the European Union, the adversarial logic is driven outwards but still persists, and on a much larger scale. Alliances, after all, are formed against a common enemy, even if only geo-economic rather than strategic. And if no enemy is manifest, one can always be found.

What should reliably deter a trade war is its cost to all concerned, and eventually to the entire world economy. If it were a matter of costs and benefits, then surely no trade war could possibly start, for it could not be profitable to any side in the long run, or even the short. But when there is no strategic confrontation at the center of world affairs that can absorb the adversarial feelings of nations, there is the danger that they may be diverted onto their economic dealings. If that happens, all bets are off. For when hostile sentiments are unleashed, there is no more prudent cost accounting, but only the desire to punish – even if the punisher is thereby also punished.

To be sure, many confidently believe that the economies of the major trading states are simply too interdependent to allow geo-economic adventures. Now that automobiles are often assembled in one country with engines from another and dashboard electronics from a third, now that both chemical and electronics industries so greatly rely on the ceaseless international exchange of countless intermediate products to make their finished products, and now that both public and private borrowers so often require loans from abroad, it is perfectly true that adversarial economic maneuvers – and the retaliation they would evoke – could easily have disastrous effects on employment and output, as well as the financial stability of firms and entire states. Alas, the interdependence that grew so easily in the late Cold War era, when economic cooperation within each camp was the natural adjunct of strategic confrontation between them, guarantees nothing at all.

No two economies were more interdependent than the French and German in August 1914, or the German and Soviet in June 1941. In both cases, each side imported large quantities of essential raw materials and industrial products from the other, and in both cases there was indeed much economic disruption, yet they went to war nonetheless, uncaring of even greater losses. If humans acted in accordance with sober calculations of their economic interests, the history of the species would not be the record of its crimes and follies. Hence it is widely optimistic to believe that a commercial war between rival trading blocs can be reliably dissuaded merely because it would impoverish all concerned. War itself did that quite effectively as well as kill and destroy, yet it was common enough and still is.

The very emergence of geo-economic phenomena shows how weak that inhibition actually is. Any geo-economic activity whatever must be unprofitable from a global viewpoint, as compared to plain, free-market economics. But that is true only in strictly economic terms, and those terms may simply be irrelevant: the bureaucrats, politicians and industrialists who favor geo-economic activities are not doing so in the hope of immediate profits, and will not stop doing so for fear of suffering losses. Airbus Industrie continued to lose money for more than twenty years without seriously displeasing the French, German and British governments that paid for the ride, for it did create an entire airliner industry that directly employs thousands of scientists, engineers and managers – that being its task all along, not to earn profits. Likewise, it is no use pointing out that all economic activity is inherently transnational, so that it can only be deformed by attempts to force it into the territorial boundaries of geo-economics. For that is exactly what has been happening, with 'local content' requirements, followed by inquisitions to uncover the percentage of imported components. Not untypical was India's version, unveiled in December 1997: foreign automobile manufacturers that want to establish assembly-lines in India must achieve a 50 per cent local-production ratio by the third year of operation, and 70 per cent by the fifth year; moreover, by the fourth year they must offset all their imports of parts or finished vehicles with exports of equal value. Moreover, just because geo-economics must be inefficient from a global viewpoint, it does not mean that it cannot be efficient for any one country or trading bloc. War too has always been a losing game: all states would have been better off if none had played it. Yet so long as war and diplomacy dominated world affairs, participation was compulsory to avoid subjection, occupation, defeat, even annihilation.

The end of the 'Free World' strategic solidarity that once suppressed all commercial quarrels is inevitable. But the advent of geo-economic conflicts between rival North American, East Asian and European trading blocs is not at all inevitable. True, emotional pressures triggered by temporary economic difficulties can start action–reaction cycles. Resentments aroused by severe trade imbalances, by per-emptory market-opening demands or by particularly intrusive foreign actions do not cause only momentary outbursts of criticism. Each episode leaves a durable residue of hostility, sharpening unfriendly feelings against whichever country is at the other side of such transactions. Thus cold-blooded calculations of profit and loss need not suffice to avert the outbreak of unrestrained geo-economic rivalries.

Yet we also know that arms races can be stopped, and that antagonistic emotions can be diverted – against the common human enemy of ecological disruption, for example. But for that to happen, some sort of super-WTO treaty would be needed to achieve a consensus on a 'general and comprehensive geo-economic dis-armament'. The step-by-step approach to trade liberalization, followed for decades, can no longer keep pace with the proliferation of commercial quarrels over subjects old and new. In the past, it certainly failed to prevent the US Congress from enacting the 301 and Super 301 trade retaliation measures, or the sweeping and discriminatory import bans on Japanese consumer goods imposed by Korea and Taiwan. In any case, the seemingly more conservative step-by-step approach is actually full of risks, for it can be overtaken at any time by the outbreak of trade or finance quarrels, or even geo-economic arms races. As far as the United States is concerned, Fujitsu's very direct attack on IBM provoked no particular reaction, no doubt because of IBM's diminishing importance and political status. But one may wonder what reactions a similar threat to Boeing might evoke. As it is, US presidents have already acted as salesmen for Boeing against Airbus – over the phone with the King of Saudi Arabia in the case of President Clinton in 1996, in hot pursuit of orders from the Saudi government-owned airline.

Certainly a general and comprehensive economic disarmament plan would be a drastic remedy indeed, for it would prohibit all subsidies, direct and indirect, all forms of state-supported technology development or export promotion, and all barriers to the import of financial, insurance and professional services. Considering the diffi-culties of ordinary trade negotiations over much narrower issues, success is not highly probable.

In the meantime, however, the priorities of the geopolitical era still condition the outlook of most Western political leaders, certainly in both Europe and the United States, less conclusively in Japan. What they learned during the Cold War was that the Alliance had to be preserved at all costs, even if it meant tolerating import-caused unemployment, one-sided barriers to exports, uneven financial restrictions, high interest rates caused by irresponsible budgets, and imperious demands for exceptions to free-trade rules. The presidents and prime ministers, the finance ministers and central bankers, the corporate executives and entrepreneurs, the experts and publicists who have long congratulated one another and themselves for the miracles of the international economy, meaning the pan-Western economy, have rarely paused to consider how great was Moscow's assistance to their successful economic cooperation over the years.

With all due respect for the achievements of two generations of experts, bankers, international civil servants, diplomats and politicians, their remarkable economic collaboration was largely a by-product of the geopolitical confrontation with the Soviet Union. The Cold War had only freshly ended when the first indications emerged of how sorely it might be missed. The challenge now is to preserve what is in fact a global alliance without the powerful solidarity evoked by a common enemy.

EIGHT

The Industrial Policy Debate

The huge shift of power from government to private business that is both the essential cause and leading consequence of turbo-capitalism, is only loosely related to globalization, the opening of national economies to one another. Each country is dismantling its own version of controlled capitalism in its own way, at its own pace, according to its own internal politics. When that happens, one of the results is more globalization, but other consequences are usually more important.

Yet there is a good reason why the advance of turbo-capitalism is accompanied by so much talk about globalization. For business interests, talk of globalization is the best way of enlisting national solidarity in their struggle against the laws and institutions they find most restrictive. French corporations now demanding an end to employment-protection laws, for example, naturally prefer that attention be focused on their battle against foreign competitors, rather than on the conflict with their own country's trade unions.

It is the same all over the world, always with the same contradiction: globalization implies that nationality no longer matters, what with mobile corporations owned by anonymous shareholders all over the world. Yet those who most insist on its importance keep invoking the national interest. Perhaps it is true that consistency is only the curse of small minds. Certainly it does not prevent business interests as well as disinterested experts, and otherwise interested government officials, from invoking national solidarity for another purpose that contradicts the logic of globalization: 'industrial policy'.

For many years now, industrial policy has been a hotly debated subject in Western Europe and even in the United States among the experts, while attracting very little attention from mass media anywhere. Proponents argue that the government could and should assist the progress of high-added-value advanced industries, notably computers and software, telecommunications, biotechnology, energy production and storage, and a few more; often the argument is cast in defensive form to emphasize the danger of losing an entire sector of industry to foreign competitors that are helped by their own governments. Opponents insist that any government interference with the free workings of market forces can only be wasteful and ultimately counterproductive.

The tools of industrial policy have been many and varied. Most basic is the funding of research and development to provide advancing industries with innovative new products and production techniques. The US computer industry was a leading beneficiary until the 1970s, Airbus Industrie and aerospace in general were European favorites, as we have seen, while in Japan many industries were assisted at one time or another.

Another type of industrial policy is the supply of long-term investment capital at concessionary interest rates, specifically to allow efficient large-scale plants to be built from the outset. Hence, new products can find their market without being held back by the high initial costs of small pilot plants. This was something of a Japanese specialty for process industries, but not unknown elsewhere.

Tax concessions can also be granted to allow higher profits to accumulate in favored sectors, subject to the obligation of using the extra money for investment, rather than high executive salaries or dividends. The same purpose can also be achieved by restricting imports in various ways, assuring high profit margins on domestic sales to allow firms to subsidize their own exports. This is a better alternative to 'dumping', i.e. selling abroad below cost, and it need not even be a violation of international trade treaties.

Further measures on behalf of particular industries have included preferential government purchases, almost regardless of price or performance – a method still much used to sustain European military industries, and which was critical to the growth of Japan's mainframe computer industry. A far more aggressive tool of industrial policy is the manipulation of import restrictions to force foreign companies to hand over technology to local would-be competitors, in exchange for access to the local market – a standard Chinese method ever since the country's post-Mao turn to market economics. The subsidy of loans to foreign buyers of expensive capital equipment is so widely employed that even the United States fully participates in the practice. A more indirect method is the encouragement of mergers, to consolidate industries considered too fragmented to compete effectively on world markets – a common measure very widely applied, which often backfires by creating monopolies. Only in Japan did the bureaucracy ensure very consistently that consolidation would not go too far – it was a key principle that in industries which were collectively protected, the different firms should remain fiercely competitive with each other, lest they become sluggish and self-indulgent.

Just as war did not begin with nineteenth-century Prussia, although systematic war mobilization and war planning certainly did, so also industrial policy is far from new, except in the consistency and breadth of its methods. Peter the Great is famous for having sponsored the creation of a Russian sea-going shipbuilding industry from nothing at the start of the eighteenth century, on occasion turning his own highly skilled hands to good use. By then, the government sponsorship of new industries was already a well-established practice in France, where industrial policy is still associated with the name of Jean Baptiste Colbert, Louis XIV's great minister, who sponsored, subsidized and protected shipyards, foundries, textile mills and long-range commerce with the Indies, with very mixed results. Many European governments did the same, starting with cannon foundries and powder mills in the eighteenth century, and continuing through the railway age till now, as did Ottoman Turkey, nineteenth-century Siam, which imported Western technicians and tutors, and the yet more exotic government of pre-colonial Madagascar, which tried and failed to avoid colonization by acquiring Western skills.

It remained to the post-1868 restored Imperial Japanese government to do it faster and better than any had done before it, by establishing iron works, foundries, shipyards and textile mills, starting a tradition that was to continue all the way up to today's residual support of nanotechnology, robotics and advanced materials. It was the Japanese also who invented *two-sided* industrial policy in the 1970s, combining the systematic promotion of new industries with the equally systematic phasing out of decaying industries, notably textiles in the 1970s and shipyards in the 1980s. Once the country's postwar economic success was widely recognized in the 1960s, Japan's example rekindled interest in industrial policy in Europe, and in the United States too for a while. It was, however, in South Korea, Taiwan and Singapore that it found its closest imitators, the Koreans being especially slavish in copying specific institutions, as with their KOTRA, a straight copy of the Japan Export Trade Organization.

The Bureaucratic Trap

The case against industrial policy can be summarized in one word: bureaucracy. More specifically, the argument is that even highly efficient, perfectly honest and supremely wise government officials cannot outperform the free market in shaping the development of industry. Their unitary decisions will lack the blind wisdom contained in the sum total of competing firms and entrepreneurs, from whom one or a few can emerge to run ahead of the pack by finding just the right technological and marketing paths to elusive success. And, of course, efficiency and honesty, let alone wisdom, cannot be taken for granted.

On the contrary, very few countries have bureaucracies that can be entrusted with anything so delicate and so replete with loose money as industrial policy. Even in ordinary state functions, from the issue of personal documents to the operation of schools, hospitals, prisons or the armed forces incompetence is common all over the world, corruption not rare. Only in government purchasing are the highest bidders routinely successful – that is, the ones who can best include margins for bribes or spotlessly legal political contributions in their bids. It follows that virtually any form of industrial policy can easily become a further way of looting the public treasury, or exploiting hapless consumers, or both.

Thus state funding for industrial investment can end up in sham enterprises, better supplied with false or inflated plant and equipment invoices than with any actual plant or actual equipment. This was often the case with Italy's *Cassa del Mezzogiorno* and other programs to build industry in the South, until the big clean-up of the 1990s. Their grants littered the southern countryside with empty factory buildings, built by firms whose peak earnings came just before they opened for business, when they collected the grants paid against phoney invoices.

Likewise, in Latin American countries especially, Japanese-style tariffs that were meant to raise the prices, and therefore the profits, and therefore the capital, and therefore the investments of local import-substitution industries would merely spawn one-screwdriver façade plants. Local consumers would end up subsidizing the re-assembly of imported breakdown kits (sometimes more costly than complete units), or mere repackaging, or even just relabelling, paying for the privilege by sky-high prices.

In eastern Europe, great efforts were made to establish export industries after the 1960s, importing much costly US, European and Japanese machinery for the purpose – the resulting debts are still now being repaid. As it turned out, their products proved mostly unexportable, because the technology bought was already outdated by the time it was installed, and because of bad quality control. Real costs, however, were high owing to the inefficiency of bureaucratic management.

In extreme cases – for example, in West Africa – even seemingly foolproof measures have a way of being positively damaging. Thus industrial-policy prohibitions on the export of raw hardwood logs, meant to induce the growth of local sawmills, have merely reduced hard-currency earnings from timber exports. Few sawmills have been built to cut wood for export, simply because political insecurity and government corruption inhibit all forms of investment. At the same time, however, raw-log exports are reduced to the levels that bribery permits notwithstanding the prohibition. When raw logs are smuggled out to adjacent free-export countries, the illegal proceeds cannot be remitted to local bank accounts, flowing instead into equally illegal foreign accounts.

Western European bureaucracies are not supposed to be corrupt, and some, most notably the French, are even considered very efficient. Opponents of industrial policy accordingly emphasize its vulnerability to political exploitation on behalf of vested interests who are generous with their political contributions; or else on behalf of local constituency interests – or those of other politicians when favors are being swapped. As the opponents see it, investment funds provided or channeled by the government would go not to promising but needy start-up sectors, but rather to industries already well represented politically by way of employee votes, contributions and lobbying. By definition, these would be well-established industries, the ones that have the least need of government help, and which are much more likely to have glorious pasts than promising futures.

Equally, import restrictions would not lead to the capital enrichment of industries poised to become champion exporters, but would rather end up supporting the weakest industries, least fitted to compete on world markets. The same is true of all other industrial-policy measures, they claim, including preferential government purchasing: it too would be captured politically to fatten the fattest cows, while doing little to help new industries that lack the money and the connections to extract favors from political elites.

Free-market true believers are not content with such merely pragmatic arguments. They insist on the blind wisdom thesis, noting that in times of accelerated technological change product markets evolve in unpredictable ways. That is why IBM was caught utterly unprepared by the personal computer revolution, GM missed the boat on mini-vans and sport-utility vehicles, and the totality of America's electronics industry completely misunderstood video-recorders and facsimile machines as low-volume $20,000 professional machinery, of interest to only a handful of highly specialized users. No group of government officials is likely to do any better in picking future winners and losers – yet that is the essential starting point of any industrial policy. As the opponents see it, if an activist bureaucracy had set out in the 1950s to encourage and finance the growth of the most promising new industries, the money would have been wasted on manufacturing plants for nylon shirts, mimeograph copiers, eight-track tape players and analog calculators.

Nor would that necessarily imply incompetence. Indeed, competence in any ordinary sense has nothing to do with it, the opponents claim, because even the best analysis of *present* information cannot anticipate scientific advances, which always require the rejection of present information as to what can and cannot be done. And it is scientific advances that in turn determine the configuration of future products and the evolution of production technologies. Only the broadly varied strivings of many different competitors can yield the handful of triumphant successes, the Xerox, Apple and Microsoft of the hour, while all other competing initiatives miserably fail. As always, free-market enthusiasts rejoice in the cruel discipline of commercial Darwinism, which evokes the workings of nature at its most profligate: the successful fertilization of each human egg by just one lucky spermatozoon out of many, the successful growth of just one adult frog from a myriad of tadpoles.

Compelling though it is, the theoretical argument against industrial policy – that is, the impossibility of scientific forecasting – immediately evokes a practical counter-argument: the recorded success of Japan and other countries in forcing the development of new industries that would not have grown spontaneously. In most cases, of course, there was no need to predict the unpredictable, for industries can be new to one country when they are not new to the world. The French officials who lead the European Arianespace consortium, which now has two-thirds of the lucrative global market for the launch of satellites into orbit, have simply been more efficient than Americans or Russians in applying booster and guidance technologies that were originally developed by Americans and Russians. Aside from emulation and imitation, however, government officials have often been able to do the theoretically impossible by coming up with winning technological breakthroughs: as far back as Napoleon, French industrial policy transformed sugar from a costly tropical luxury into a cheap food, by sponsoring the first successful beet-extraction process. And it was the Pentagon that funded the entire new craft of large-scale software programming from the late 1950s, to come up with semi-automatic air defenses, thus opening the way for the full use of electronic computers, themselves originally developed under government sponsorship for code breaking.

Nor does the stream of globally successful new Japanese product configurations and industrial techniques derive from any visible process of natural selection. Low-cost consumer quartz watches, video-recorders, facsimile machines, copiers, headset stereos and solar-powered calculators, just like transistor radios before them and 'lean manufacturing' generally, have come not from lucky tadpole start-ups, but from the same cast of full-grown frogs: Hitachi, Toshiba, Canon, Matsushita, Sony, Toyota.

In response, opponents of industrial policy challenge the evidence. They argue that such things as software programming, computers and even sugar-beet extraction had all been invented by individual scientists before government officials ever got into the act. As sure-fire winners, they were much too obvious to miss. The government's money merely subsidized developmental work that private enterprise would have paid for anyway.

When it comes to Japan's record, they insist that the Samurai of Tsusho Sangyo-Sho (MITI) actually failed miserably – except in claiming much of the credit for the achievements of Japanese private enterprise. They explain Japan's postwar industrial success as the result of plain hard work, a good system of mass education, the abundance of capital supplied by very high savings rates, and the exceptional loyalty of corporate employees – all derived from deep-seated cultural propensities, not bureaucratic wisdom. To that end, the opponents of industrial policy keep reciting the list of MITI's greatest errors: its failure to forecast, or support, the growth of Japan's automobile industry (Honda was famously advised to stick to motor-cycles); its over-investment in steel during the 1960s and in aluminium during the 1970s; and the failure of the 'Fifth Generation' computing program. As for the absence of start-up tadpoles from the Japanese scene, the explanation is that natural selection and the finding of developmental paths through trial and error also work in Japan – but *within* the large Japanese companies. They function, in effect, as conglomerates of many different enterprises, many of which fail and wither, while a few succeed and grow.

These are persuasive arguments, but it is revealing that they are least persuasive to those who know the most about Japan and its economy. Thus Chalmers Johnson, the noted Japanologist who wrote the standard work on MITI,[1] remains not coincidentally a fervent advocate of industrial policy. While recognizing that MITI has failed at times, Johnson insists that it is eminently worthwhile to have a government department staffed with elite officials to promote industrial development. Only they can coordinate the use of government funding, regulatory powers, research activities and foreign-trade policies for the greater benefit of favored industries. Without a central coordinating body, different ministries and departments can only pursue their own goals, often on divergent tracks.

A MITI-type body can also ensure the commercial development of inventions originally sponsored by the government. Johnson notes that all major Western governments do in fact use the taxpayers' money to finance research and initial development in many areas of science and technology respectively. So why not ensure that the marketable results, if any, are also developed and marketed for the benefit of those same taxpayers?

Having a Policy Without Knowing It

At present the United States government spends some $5 billion each year on medical research – more than three times as much as Japan. In the American case, however, the commercial exploitation of the results is neither guided nor assisted by the government. Instead, when individual scientists on the government payroll, working in government-funded laboratories, complete 90 per cent of the develop-

[1] *MITI and the Japanese Miracle: The Growth of Industrial Policy 1925–1975* (Stanford University Press, 1982).

ment of a promising new diagnostic test, medicine or technique, they join with venture capitalists to set up private biotechnology companies, which then fund the final 10 per cent of the work.

More often than not, when one of these tadpoles comes up with a valuable product, it does not in fact grow up into a frog to manufacture and market it, providing rewarding employment, dividends or just revenues for the taxpayers. Scientists are mostly disinclined to go into business for life, while venture capitalists generally want to collect their winnings, not pour more capital into production companies. Hence new inventions are sold to established pharmaceutical companies, often enough one of the large Japanese or European mass-production 'fermenters'. Lucky scientists and venture capitalists become personally very rich, the taxpayers who have paid for 90 per cent of the research get nothing, and the manufacturing, marketing and management jobs generated by the new product often end up abroad.

The same is largely true of British, French and German government-funded medical research. The one difference is that even fewer of the rewards are kept at home, because of the shortage of local venture capitalists, and the less businesslike attitude of European scientists. In the spirit of disinterested scholarship at its best, the results of taxpayer-funded research are often simply published, leaving it to others, both foreign and domestic, to reap any commercial gains. An activist MITI could certainly be of use in this setting, to assert control over valuable inventions originally funded by local taxpayers, and to ensure that local pharmaceutical companies produce and market the goods, to generate jobs and tax revenues.

The strongest argument for industrial policy, therefore, is that the government of almost every advanced country already has one, even if like the *Bourgeois Gentilhomme* it speaks prose without knowing it, or in this case has policies that impact on industry in fragmented instead of purposeful ways. Even with the Cold War ended, much money is spent on military research and development, which could generate 'spin-off' inventions and production techniques of commercial value. This is not the goal, however, hence no systematic efforts are made to promote spin-offs, unless the contractors themselves do so for their own benefit rather than that of the taxpayers. Nor is medical research the only field of civilian scientific endeavor, though routinely it attracts the most funding. In any case, all sorts of government ministries and departments act every day in ways that impact on industry, through the regulations they issue and the equipment and services they purchase. It would only require an effort of conscious coordination to extract valuable benefits. Finally, in all major countries including the United States, for all its free-market rhetoric, there are isolated examples of out-and-out industrial policy, as we have seen. Undeterred by the phenomenal fluidity of the sector, the US government even sponsored a semi-conductor research consortium, Sematech.

Moreover, Sematech is not the only American example. Even while the Bush administration (1988–92) was loud in proclaiming its entire devotion to private enterprise and its horror of industrial policy, the US Department of Energy quietly organized the US Advanced Battery Consortium, while the Pentagon funded flat-screen monitor research for laptops. Those typically Japanese-style ventures are, of course, blatantly heretical violations of free-market doctrine. They also offer a promising mechanism for the development of a critically important component, which may yet determine the fate of the American automobile industry. If countries will thus be sinful anyway – and many are, including the resolutely free-market United Kingdom – they might as well sin systematically to obtain the full benefit for their taxpayers.

NINE

Turbo-Capitalism Comes to Russia

How Russia became a market economy is an epic theme worthy of a Homer or a Tolstoy. In August 1991, when Boris Yeltsin climbed on a tank to proclaim the end of the Soviet Union and the rebirth of Russia, the failure of Mikhail Gorbachev's attempts at reform had left a wrecked economy under disintegrating state control. Capital, labor and property were still allocated by thoroughly demoralized central planners; raw materials and a shrinking supply of finished products were increasingly allocated by black marketeers, thieves and smugglers as bureaucratic control collapsed – except for its perverse power to prohibit *legal* commerce.

By 1994 the Russian economy was disorganized in the extreme. Everywhere factories were being shut down for lack of raw materials, or intermediate products, or components, or markets, or operating capital, or all of them. Farm lands poorly tended for sixty years were more neglected than ever before. Coal mining was interrupted by strikes, oil output was diminished by the lack of essential supplies, rail transport and shipping were disrupted. Production and incomes were much lower than in 1991. As rapid inflation consumed pensions and wages, and as unemployment steadily increased, many Russians had less to eat, less to wear, less to consume than in 1987, when the first Gorbachev reforms started, or for that matter less than in 1985, when he came to power. The banned Communist Party was reborn under a new name, and won a majority of parliamentary seats by recalling memories of the good old Soviet days of zero unemployment, zero inflation and old-age pensions sufficient for food, even books, not to speak of the lost glories of an immense empire.

But by 1994 also, Russian capital, labor, property, raw materials and products were already mostly allocated by the free forces of supply and demand in functioning markets.[1] According to Western economic textbooks, this was enough to ensure that the broken pieces of the post-Soviet economy would be re-assembled by profit-seekers into operating firms, which would eventually launch production, employment and incomes on an upward path. And so it was: by 1997 the Russian economy stopped declining and started growing again.

To turn the dilapidated state economy of 1991 into the market economy of 1994 was the stunning achievement of a handful of brave, young liberal ministers under Yegor Gaidar. With Yeltsin's unsteady support, they overcame the fierce resistance of the powerful Soviet-minded barons in command of loss-making industries all over Russia, who extracted government bank loans to pay their bills with the support of legislators elected by their own employees. Workshops, warehouses and shops were rapidly incorporated, their shares in part sold, in part given to employees; tenants in state housing were allowed to buy their apartments very cheaply; gas, oil, electricity, major factories and military industries were privatized, at least nominally, under their Soviet-era managers.

The immense state economy was sold off with brutal speed. There was no possibility of careful valuations or measured disposals; the wealth was often entrapped by well-connected traffickers. Yet it had to be done quickly or not at all, for the state economy was collapsing fast. As the Soviet-era command links between raw material and energy suppliers and factories, and between agriculture and food distributors, continued to disintegrate, the choice was to insert private enterprise buyer–seller market relationships between them, or else face total breakdown. Soon only farmers would have food, only coalminers would be able to heat their homes, only pharmacy stock-keepers would have medicines. Had the world clearly understood what was about to happen, there would have been a great cry of alarm at the coming prospect of a Russia with no functioning state, its soldiers unfed, even perhaps its ballistic-missile installations abandoned by crews turned into foraging parties.

In spite of every form of resistance from ancestral inertia to

---

[1] Anders Åslund, *How Russia Became a Market Economy* (Brookings Institution, Washington DC, 1995).

convinced Stalinism, from parliamentary protests to outright personal intimidation, Gaidar and his men did it, and quickly enough to avert the imminent anarchy. Yet instead of being celebrated by a Homer or a Tolstoy, the heroic deed was only reported by fallible journalists, neither poetical nor trained in basic economics.

A Gangster Economy?

It is these same journalists who have propounded the conventional wisdom that *mafiya* extortion and official corruption are more important than free markets in shaping the Russian economy, preventing its progress. In a widely cited estimate, crooked officials and plain gangsters were said to have sent some $100 billion into their foreign bank accounts since 1990 and 1995, thus depriving the Russian economy of much more hard currency than the sum total of post-1991 Western aid. Countless newspaper articles have profiled the unappealing beneficiaries of the new economic order, from violent thugs with platinum-blonde molls and BMWs, who do their showing off in restaurants, to sleek ex-officials in Armani suits with Vienna bank accounts, Manhattan apartments and good friends in the Kremlin, who show off in *New York Times* interviews.

Far more numerous are the less obviously criminal and much less glamorous 'biznessmen' – thousands of them – who traffick in stolen raw materials diverted for entirely private export, who help thieving managers transfer company properties to personal ownership, who collaborate with foreign adventurers to smuggle consumer goods in and weapons out, or who simply buy, sell and earn without bothering to pay taxes. Most visitors to Russia have encountered specimens of this type in the hotel lobbies that are their favorite places of business; some earn just enough to get by from day to day while waiting for their big hit, but quite a few have become seriously rich very quickly. It is no longer even remarkable to see a Jaguar with a Russian number plate drive into its owner's millionaire villa at the right end of Cap d'Antibes beyond the plage de la Garoupe, to be outbid for a Mayfair apartment by a Russian with green plastic shoes and a briefcase full of banknotes, or to find all the Grand Canal suites at the Gritti or Danieli booked by a Russian wedding party.

There is no doubt that the pervasive criminalization of the Russian economy imposes real costs. The purchasing power of an impoverished population is further reduced because the fees of *mafiya* 'protection' blackmail increase prices. Efficient private-enterprise firms suffer from the unfair competition of less efficient rivals backed by corrupt officials. Other honest firms best their competitors in the market, only to be confronted by their hired guns – not lawyers with briefcases, as the phrase would be read by Americans, but killers with sub-machine guns. And, as anywhere else, tax evasion must ultimately be offset by inflationary money printing, or higher taxes inimical to growth. Moreover, the intense popular resentment of both gangsters and tycoons certainly threatens Russia's economic liberalization very directly: much of the electorate has repeatedly voted for neo-communist legislators, and even for outright Stalinists – though even they could only slow down privatization, not reverse the advance of the market.

The political threat is real enough, but in purely economic terms the conventional wisdom is all wrong. To begin with, it overlooks the natural evolution of the capitalist animal. The fat cows that yield their abundant milk in advanced economies – stable, highly capitalized firms that offer good employment, pay their taxes in full, invest in new plant, develop new products and even contribute to charities – were not born as such. It was as lean and hungry wolves that they originally accumulated capital, by seizing profitable market opportunities in any way they could – sometimes by killing off competitors in ways that today's anti-monopoly commissions and anti-trust divisions would not tolerate; often by cutting costs in every way possible, not excluding all the tax avoidance they could get away with. As their payroll days turn from dramatic cliff-hangers to mere routine, as their financial reserves grow, as their shares prosper, as the original entrepreneurs and investors become rich, the wolf loses its fangs, gains weight and size, grows udders.

When countries and their economies undergo truly drastic transformations, however, as Germany, Italy and Japan all did in the aftermath of the destructions of the Second World War, and as Russia is now doing, conditions are too harsh even for wolves. They, after all, work for their living, hunting for their prey among the opportunities of organized markets. Only ruthless hyenas can survive and prosper in the chaos of thoroughly disrupted economies, by traffficking in whatever can be profitably sold, legal or otherwise, by buying up valuable real estate for pennies from desperate owners or corrupt officials, by the improvised manufacture of substandard products for deprived consumers, or by the simple theft of abandoned, semi-abandoned or just poorly guarded public property.

That is how many of the dynamic industrial firms that now fill the landscape of Emilia-Romagna, most Japanese real-estate fortunes that long ago diversified into industry and finance, and not a few of the businesses that propelled West Germany's rise to prosperity had their start in the immediate post-1945 years. It was by black-marketeering, predatory buying, substandard manufacture and efficient stealing (the polite expression was to 'organize') that the hyena-entrepreneurs of those days accumulated the capital that enabled them to become honest wolves, and eventually highly productive cows.

Legend has it that some of Emilia's leading metal-working and machinery firms were first equipped with tools and equipment looted from a *Wehrmacht* weapon-repair train – in effect, a rolling high-precision factory – abandoned in April 1945. In Japan, old people still vividly recall some of today's tycoons in their original incarnations as gambling masters, GI dance-hall operators, or purveyors of rare nylon, cigarettes and tinned meat luxuries diverted from American military stores – that is why some of the richest people in Japan have never been admitted to polite society.

In Germany's case, the persistence of a large US military market for companionship and sex after 1945 made the ownership of night-clubs and brothels the prelude to many a business career. Others preferred the black-marketeering of PX supplies from alcohol to shirts, becoming millionaires in due course if they used the profits to buy bombed-out sites for the coming property boom. And everywhere hyenas broke the fewest laws by acting as such in the most elemental sense, acquiring wrecks and war-surplus, by seizure or trade, to sell scrap metal to steel mills or uniform cloth to garment workshops, and otherwise convert the thousand leftovers of war into the first supplies of peace.

Had the police forces of each country been effective enough to round up all the hyenas and lock them up, the economic recovery of West Germany, Italy and Japan would have been slower, for many of the successful entrepreneurs of the 1950s and 1960s would never have been able to accumulate capital in any other way for their starting investments.

All this is true of Russia – only more so, because so long as state ownership endured, even simple theft could be highly beneficial for the entire economy, often more so than honest work. To understand how this could be, it is first essential to recall that, for all its organized decrepitude, the Soviet economy was hugely if wastefully productive. The still intact Soviet Union of 1989 produced more electricity per capita than Italy (5,986 kW vs. 3,650), more steel per capita than the United States (557 kg vs. 382), much more mineral fertilizer than Japan (119 kg vs. 12), more tractors per thousand people than West Germany (1.9 vs. 1.3), more cement per capita than France (488 kg vs. 469) and even its meat production at 70 kg per capita was not all that low compared to 32 for Japan, 63 for Italy, 96 for West Germany and 120 for the United States.

Yet the Soviet standard of living was incomparably lower than those of France, Italy, Japan, West Germany and the United States. Statisticians quarreled in trying to come up with exact numerical comparisons, but in truth such comparisons were entirely meaningless. What could conversions into an X-dollar or Y-pound or Z-lire income per capita *mean* when so much patience or ingenuity was needed to buy 100 grams of butter, and it took special connections to be able to buy a decent pair of shoes?

Beneficial Crimes

The too-obvious explanation of the huge gap between impressive production figures and the poverty of everyday life was the huge cost of Soviet military ambitions, by then in the final stage of their baroque excess. It is true that much steel did go into the making of tanks and warships, and cement too was consumed in huge amounts to build gigantic underground command centers, as well as more mundane airfields, missile silos and much else. But that was certainly not true of agricultural tractors and fertilizer, in both of which the Soviet Union outproduced not only West Germany and Japan, but also the United States, France and Italy. Neither were claimed by the armed forces for their own use in any significant quantities, yet all those tractors and all that fertilizer did not finally produce enough grain for home consumption, let alone the export surpluses that France, the United States and even India must regularly dump on world markets.

By the highest estimates, the military used up some 30 per cent of the Soviet Union's gross national product, but the gap between the production of basic inputs and the supply of ready-to-consume outputs that were actually of use to the Soviet population was very much greater than that. So where did all the missing abundance go? The explanation is that by 1989 many parts of the Soviet economy were not just inefficient, in failing to make the most of their resources, but actually destructive. Perfectly good Uzbek cotton was manufactured into shirts so poorly cut and of such ugly colors and patterns that vast stocks remained unsold – not even Soviet consumers would buy them. The raw cotton had real value – it could have been exported for hard currency to finance imports of anything at all; the finished shirts were utterly unexportable and unwanted at home, except as rags. Hence all the spinning, weaving, dyeing, cutting and sewing actually removed value from the raw material, turning valuable virgin cotton into cheap scrap rag of use only to paper-mills.

The same was true of leather, wool and synthetic fibers, which imported Western plants produced in vast quantities by 1989. It was also true of wood, steel plate, polymer plastics, and of many other inputs that went into Soviet light industry as valuable raw materials, only to come out as less valuable finished goods. Likewise, the structural iron and steel and the cement not reserved for military use, which ended up on Soviet building sites, was effectively lost for several years because the pace of construction was so extraordinarily slow: 5–7 years even for standard housing and the simplest factory buildings. Quite a lot of the material was lost for ever, as unsheltered cement bags solidified and iron rods rusted away.

Above all, by the 1980s Soviet agriculture had become a wasteful luxury even more costly than the armed forces. While the Soviet army at least kept its tanks in service for twenty years or so, Soviet state and collective farms ruined tens of thousands of tractors, reapers and combine harvesters of near-Western quality each and every year, because of poor or no maintenance, or simply because they were left to rust in the open all winter long once the last harvest was brought in. Animal feed, often imported with scarce foreign currency, was left to rot in neglected barns, or outside them. Fertilizer produced from valuable petroleum feedstock, or expensively imported, was simply dumped on fields by the truck load, actually reducing crop yields. Pesticides, including costly bromines, were carelessly expended rather than applied, poisoning ground water instead of protecting plants.

Given such a counterproductive system, simple theft can indeed be highly productive – it definitely increased the overall standard of living of the former Soviet Union. Cotton and other raw materials diverted from official channels were used to fashion useful products by domestic or illegal craft work. Construction materials stolen from interminable official projects provided the means to build many houses and dachas with illegally hired or do-it-yourself labor. Gasoline removed from state trucks, which often drove about uselessly, could provide much-needed fuel for private car owners. And it was largely with stolen fertilizer, pesticide, seeds, animal feed and farm tools that the tiny private plots of collective farmers produced a great part of the Soviet Union's food supply, and almost all its more appetizing fresh vegetables.

Inevitably, thieves and final consumers could be brought together only by a functioning illegal market, which in turn could be operated only by criminals sufficiently organized to do the job. Plain thieves and black-marketeers could not do the job alone. Bureaucrats and policemen had to be paid off at every stage of acquisition, transportation and distribution, often in places far away from individual traffickers in the immensity of the Soviet Union. Only widely represented gangs, the Soviet *mafyia*, could do the necessary bribing, naturally collecting 'protection' money to pay for the service. And because not all traffickers were equally eager to pay up, bribery gangs needed to have enforcers in their ranks. It was this crypto-capitalist system that emerged fully ready to function in sector after sector, in place after place, as the liberalization progressed. Many, if not most, of the Russians who bitterly complain about the *mafyia* had greatly relied on its indispensable services during Soviet times.

By the late 1990s much of the economy has been privatized, though enough of it remains in state or quasi-state ownership, as counterproductive as ever, to allow some room for the sort of theft that increases Russian living standards. A large though diminishing number of state firms have been privatized only very nominally – they are still run by their old managers, in the old inefficient ways. That aside, the *mafyia* has lost its primary, largely beneficial role as a collection of theft rings. Its secondary role, street-level extortion, as now widely practiced against restaurants, cafés, bars, shops and stalls, certainly adds no value. It merely redistributes income from many, mostly very poor, consumers to fewer, richer gangsters. They, on the other hand, have become much more violent than they were in Soviet times, not only because a democracy with poorly paid policemen is no match for even a decrepit totalitarian dictatorship in keeping public order, but also because the character of the profession has drastically changed.

The advance of the market, with its ever-increasing opportunities for legal commerce, has acted as a centrifuge, separating out the thieves, traffickers, bribery specialists and enforcers of the original *mafyia* of Soviet days. Many of the bribery specialists and traffickers have moved on to better things, quite a few of them having transformed themselves into local merchants and money-lenders, or even commodity dealers, international traders and bankers. Habitual thieves are caught, keeping Russian prisons as full as they ever were. This has left a much higher density of enforcers in the *mafyia*, which has accordingly become much more violent – though aside from the thugs who enjoy hurting reluctant shopkeepers, there is still an inner core of resolutely criminal, yet commercially minded operators.

It is because of them that Russian organized crime can still remain on occasion a beneficial force: it is the only counterweight to powerful firms backed by corrupt officials, which now engage in ruthless monopolistic practices. At the local level, ex-Soviet officials who now own shops, restaurants, cafés and workshops do not hesitate to use their old Party connections to drive competitors out of business – by contriving the imposition of huge taxes and fines, or hygiene inspections followed by shut-down orders, or by persuading friends in the local government to enact arbitrary administrative rules, damaging or lethal to their competitors. In Gogol's *The Inspector* there is the perfect anticipation of such local cliques of potentates, and of their methods.

In most cases, there is no possibility of obtaining timely redress from the hopelessly overburdened and glacially slow Russian courts, which remain woefully unequipped to deal with commercial and fiscal matters. Only the local *mafyia* may be able and willing to resist the ex-Party clique – if the two are not one and the same – and at a price, of course. That is how the only 'luxury' restaurant in Volgograd (formerly Stalingrad) managed to remain in business in 1995, repelling the fiscal and hygiene attacks engineered by its dingy competitors with *mafyia* counter-intimidation.

One restaurant does not a free yet *mafyia*-protected economy make, but the same phenomenon is widely reproduced from Brest-Litovsk to Valdivostock. In essence, it is a gritty and very provincial version of that eternal prerequisite of freedom: the separation of powers. Instead of Holy Roman Emperor and Pope, instead of Parliament and King, instead of Legislature and Executive, there are the local ex-Party cliques of former bribe-takers, and the local *mafyia* headed by former bribe-givers. In between the two, some freedom of action can exist for those who are neither officially backed nor gangsters. Charles Louis de Secondat, baron de Montesquieu would have approved.

On a much larger scale, genuinely private industrial firms – including joint ventures with foreign partners – are now often confronted by the extortionate pricing of the local headquarters of officially backed suppliers of natural gas, oil, coal and electricity. For the liberalization has created many natural monopolies, yet there is still no functioning anti-monopoly law, or any judicial mechanism to regulate utility prices. The young and capable Boris Nemtzov, appointed deputy prime minister in 1997, secured an anti-monopoly brief for himself from President Boris Yeltsin, only to be blocked and forced to renounce it by prime minister Viktor Chernomyrdin, a close ally and reputed co-owner of the colossal Gazprom gas and oil company.

Again, the only possible counterweight is organized crime. It is a tall order for a bunch of mere gangsters to take on big business, whose friends − or owners − in high places all the way up to the Kremlin can unleash entire regiments of commandos against them. In the more extreme cases, however, the extortionate pricing is set at the local level, by nearby and thus vulnerable officials. In one case, an important industrial firm based on the technology of a globally prestigious foreign partner, but located in a very remote area, was confronted by a sudden 500 per cent increase in gas prices ('that is how it is under capitalism − it's supply and demand, and we control the supply'). With immediate closure as the only possible alternative, the enterprising foreign manager on site, who had once done the same job in Sicily, turned for help to the local *mafyia*, which in turn threatened the local gas-company officials with serious bodily harm, eventually persuading them to accept a tolerable compromise − including a cut for themselves, of course.

Finally, there is the truly extreme case: it is widely rumored in Russia that the entire second war against the Chechens originally started in a struggle over pipeline fees between the Grozny *mafyia* and a large Russian oil company with very strong Kremlin connections. If that is true, the local *mafyia* now has its own semi-state, the Islamic semi-republic of Chechnya, a blow for ethnic independence, if not for anyone's freedom.

Normally without need of much violence − let alone full-scale war − local *mafyias* act in many places and many ways to resist the excessive concentrations of economic power brought about by government corruption, or rather by the prevalence of under-the-table joint ventures between Russian government officials and the new private firms run by ex-officials, including the very highest officials and the very largest firms. *Mafyia* gangs are, in effect, competitors that use physical force, or more often just the threat of force, to offset monopolistic market power in an economy that is still lawless in a commercial sense.

Nor is Russia unique in deriving economic benefits from organized crime. Colombia, Peru and Bolivia all receive much hard currency from the drug trade. Only in Colombia – by far the most prosperous of the three, whose population has the highest entrepreneurial potential – does the accompanying most violent lawlessness inhibit economic growth. Thus the country would be much better off without the drug trade. In tranquil Bolivia, by contrast, where even San Borja and Trinidad, the local mini-versions of Medellin and Cali, remain very peaceful indeed, the drug trade is of great benefit twice over: it provides much income and many jobs locally, and it attracts US drug-suppression funding for the national government of South America's poorest country. Peru is in a middle position. Its population is certainly poor enough to benefit seriously from drug money. But the residual Sendero Luminoso guerrillas, now degraded into the gunmen of the trade, magnify greatly the impact of the associated criminality, dissuading foreign investment, retarding growth and slowing the country's democratization.

By contrast, the *Yakuza* gangsters of Japan have certainly been of great economic benefit to that country in the past. Highly organized, so much so that at least one gang has more than 20,000 registered members, the major gangs have been quietly tolerated by the police, to the point that they have overt street-level offices. Each *Yakuza* gang collects protection money within its territorial boundary from Japan's 'water trade': hostess bars, gambling dens, strip joints, no-pants cafés, porno-shops, massage parlors and brothels. Naturally, the local *Yakuza* carefully monitor what goes on inside these establishments, to ensure that they are getting their proper cut. In the process, they also act to stop whatever would endanger their revenues, from incautious attempts to overcharge the wrong victims (out-of-towners and upstart businessmen are fair game; local notables are not) to drug dealing, which would soon attract the attention of the police.

This is why the formidable Japanese police, numerous, resolute, well paid and highly disciplined, tolerate the *Yakuza*'s control of the water trade: anywhere else in the world, its murky premises would be the primary outlets for drugs, but not in almost drug-free Japan. The police normally come down very hard on *Yakuza* that stray beyond their tolerated sphere, whether by engaging in drug traffic or attempting to extort money from ordinary restaurants, cafés, bars or any normal shop engaged in legal commerce. In other words, the *Yakuza* too have their specific place in Japanese society; they are not truly outlaws, as their Western counterparts always are.

There are, of course, grey areas, in which the police act on a case-by-case basis, or else limits that shift over time and vary from place to place. Street selling by illegal immigrants, all but a few adventurous youngsters financing the next stage of their world tours, everywhere under *Yakuza* control, is tolerated only in specific streets of specific cities, inside some subway stations but not others. An altogether more important grey area is the *Yakuza's* role in the construction industry.

Because of the extreme fragmentation of land ownership into a huge number of tiny house plots, developers often find it impossible legally to buy up sites big enough for apartment houses or office buildings. Only with the help of hired gangs and their colorful repertoire of threats, vandalism and mostly symbolic bodily violence (wounding or killing is utterly beyond the limit) can house-owners be persuaded to sell, even at very high prices. Many of the modern buildings one sees in Japanese cities could never have been built without *Yakuza* help, which is just as essential for the Japanese construction industry as ferro-concrete.

One day, Russia too will acquire a functioning system of commercial and anti-monopoly laws, fair and equitable taxation, and courts that can actually protect citizens from the exactions of arbitrary, corrupt government officials, and local or national monopolies. Only then will it be safe to unleash the police against the *mafiya*, to stop the social and political damage it is certainly inflicting on a large scale. In the meantime, it remains virtually the only force interposed between lawless economic barons and the defenseless consumers and entrepreneurs of Russia.

Will Russia Ever Prosper?

When everyone is convinced that an economy is in splendid shape, all good news is accepted at face value, while all signs that something might be amiss are overlooked – that is why the 1997 East Asian debt crisis came as such a surprise. Highly-paid investment bankers who kept telling their clients to put more money into Indonesia, Malaysia, South Korea and Thailand until their stock markets and currencies both collapsed, simply paid no attention to what they themselves call 'fundamental indicators': trade and overall balance-of-payments accounts, debt burdens for public or private borrowers, foreign-exchange reserves. When everyone believes that an economy is doing poorly, every piece of bad news is given serious attention while even very positive fundamental indicators are ignored – and that is how it has been for the Russian market economy since its inception.

There has certainly been no lack of bad news. It is beyond question that the chaotic transition from the old Soviet planned economy to today's market economy has been costly, so that whatever passes for a gross national product was lower in 1997 than in 1987. For one thing, the disintegration of the Soviet empire also largely shut down its supply chains, leaving factories all over Russia without the raw materials and components that used to come from Eastern Europe or other Soviet republics, while also depriving them of their established markets. The same was true within Russia, as oil, metal ores, cotton, timber, scrap metal and other raw materials were exported for hard currency, legally or otherwise. So the Russian economy suffered a protracted decline of production until 1997 at least, though the actual loss of real value was less severe because much of what had been produced before was almost useless, as we have seen.

The reality was bad, but the news was often worse. From 1991 until the present, the Russian economy has repeatedly been depicted as facing an outright collapse, with the currency worthless, firms large and small forced to close down, famine close behind, electrical power supplies interrupted (fatal in winter), and 'blood in the streets' from infuriated mobs. These waves of panic were not manufactured by ill-informed or perhaps malevolent foreign observers. They originated in Russia itself. Perhaps it is true that Russians have an affinity for high drama.

Except for a few moments of short-lived euphoria, negative perceptions have mostly prevailed, fed by a steady stream of bad news. Aside from the hardy perennials of corruption and crime, each season has yielded its crop. In mid-1998, for example, one more wave of the Asian fever seriously depressed the Moscow stock and bond markets, drawing attention to Russia's debt exposure; a higher-than-expected budget deficit aroused the concern of bond-holders fearful of inflation; strikes disrupted coal production once again; and the Duma, dominated by neo-communists and the anti-government Yabloko party, passed a new law limiting foreign ownership in one more attempt to sabotage the remaining privatizations, further alarming foreign investors. The overall result of these waves of bad news was to obscure far more important positive indicators that every troubled Asian economy would envy: Russia has had a persistently favorable trade balance over the years, and indeed a positive current-account balance overall. And the total debt of the Russian state remains rather low.

It does not help matters that much confusion persists about the most elementary facts and figures of the Russian economy and public finance. This confusion keeps Russian as well as foreign investors in a state of high anxiety, magnifying every problem into a crisis, amplifying every negative indicator. Thus statistical problems become real-life financial problems: only very high interest rates can keep volatile capital invested in Russian treasury bills, and the resulting interest payments arc a heavy burden on the budget.

The East Asian economic and financial crisis that started in 1997 had very little *direct* impact on the Russian economy. Aside from raw materials that have other markets, Russian exports to East Asia were very small to begin with, while Japanese and other East Asian investment in Russia was almost insignificant. All that happened once the debt crisis exploded was that some promised South Korean investments were cancelled. But when perceptions dominate reality, the indirect impact was serious. Successive waves of fear coming from East Asia caused sharp rises in the interest rates demanded by buyers of Russian treasury bills in November 1997, January 1998 and May–June 1998, each time increasing the deficit and driving up interest rates still further, until the catastrophic default of August 1998.

Yet the total Russian state debt was not at all high in 1998: some $130 billion of direct government borrowing plus some $70 billion of outstanding treasury bills, including roughly $20 billion held by foreign investors. The total of $200 billion was only 42 per cent of the Russian-calculated gross domestic product, a lower proportion than in most Western countries including the United States, while both Italy and Japan have almost three times as much state debt. But short-term debt – the $70 billion in treasury bills – was high. With average maturities of less than one year, roughly $6 billion had to be sold each month. When investors were especially nervous and reluctant to buy, as in May/June 1998, interest rates rose to as much as 80 per cent per annum, as compared to less than 5 per cent for US Treasury bills, less than 1 per cent for Japan's.

It was the same with the other bad news of the time: negative perceptions greatly exceeded negative realities. French or American strikes hardly impact on the respective stock markets, but the May 1998 Russian strikes brought down Moscow's. Though not catastrophic, the problem is serious because it is recurring. By 1998 Moscow wages were high enough to attract illegal migrant workers from the Ukraine and beyond. Wages elsewhere in Russia are very low, yet it is not for higher wages that Russians went on strike once again. Many of the remaining state-owned enterprises periodically stop paying wages to their employees, for months on end. Elsewhere, they would have left to seek other jobs. In Russia, however, many still live in free or almost-free employee housing, they still rely on the surviving clinics, crèches, canteens and even resort hostels that state companies have not yet sold off or shut down. In the one-factory towns that still dot the Russian countryside, there are no alternative facilities, nor any other housing. Hence they remain employees even when unpaid, going on strike instead of going away. This problem has no solution so long as state-owned enterprises which are in fact bankrupt continue to survive on inadequate and irregular loans from regional and local authorities – loans they cannot possibly repay.

As for the Duma's latest sabotage of privatization, it was a serious blow but also a much-less-than-catastrophic continuing fact of life. When Yeltsin won the presidency in 1997 with a gigantic media blitz financed by the new Russian tycoons, he did not win the Duma elections as well. The result was a continuing struggle for power between the presidency and the opposition majority in the Duma. The Duma continued to vote against the privatization of agricultural land, the key to any reform of Russia's perpetually troubled rural economy. And it kept trying to resist the remaining industrial privatizations. The special law that contributed to the May/June 1998 panic was an attempt to interfere with the imminent sale of the major state-owned electricity supplier ('Unified Energy System'), due to become the second-largest Russian private company after the oil and gas giant, Gazprom. It is quite certain that this privatization, too, will proceed, and that any legal restriction on foreign ownership will be evaded.

Of all the confusions that obscure Russian economic realities, two are especially damaging: the undercounting of the country's gross domestic product, and the tangled web of its public finance. Even reputable experts continue to confuse the rather small 'Federal' budget with the much bigger 'general budget of the government', which also includes regional and local budgets, the state Pension fund, the Employment fund, and a few more social-welfare funds. Federal tax revenues were running at some 11 per cent of the gross domestic product in 1998 – a very low proportion. General budget revenues, on the other hand, came to more than 30 per cent, a rather high proportion considering the narrow scope and poor quality of public services. This particular confusion played a role in amplifying the supposedly desperate problems of 1998, which the world's newspapers described as a 'tax collection crisis'. Its cause, it was said, was that Russians were not paying their taxes, and the result would be an upsurge in inflation, because the Russian state, unable to collect taxes, would instead print banknotes to pay its way. Remedies were also suggested: more tax officials, tougher laws, more police raids on firms and homes. That evoked the despairing rejoinder that the only result would be to increase extortion and bribery.

Once the two state budgets are separated out, however, it becomes apparent that there was no tax-collection crisis in 1998 but rather an ordinary, familiar public expenditure problem. All interest payments on state debts appear in the Federal budget, whose expenditures amounted to 14.9 per cent of the gross domestic product in early 1998, a very modest level indeed. Given revenues at 11 per cent, the Federal deficit was running at only 3.9 per cent of the gross domestic product, considerably below the conventional safe limit of 5 per cent. General government expenditures, on the other hand, came to 35.9 per cent of the gross domestic product in early 1998 after a series of drastic cuts, so that the overall deficit was roughly 5.9 per cent, scarcely above the safe limit. Yet the financial markets found a reason to panic nonetheless in the *expectation* that the deficit would explode in 1998, largely because it had risen to 8.2 per cent of the gross domestic product by year-end 1997. In reality, Russian government expenditures are eminently controllable: much of the money is actually spent by regional and local authorities to prop up failing state-owned enterprises. As they are privatized or simply shut down one by one, that particularly wasteful use of tax revenues will come to an end.

All of the above is further complicated by the systematic under-counting of the gross domestic product. On the one hand, Russian officials from Yeltsin down bitterly complain that people are evading taxes on a huge scale in a 'black' economy of plain-paper or no invoices, cash payments and unregistered transactions of all sorts. On the other hand, their gross domestic product statistics that are supposed to measure the health of the entire economy, and whose 'percentage of' figures repeatedly frighten investors, only add up the payment accounts of the 'white' economy, with a very small allowance for the black. The experts of the International Monetary Fund, and more important Anders Åslund, whose estimates over the years have been shown to be far more accurate than those of the CIA or IMF, believe that the real Russian gross domestic product is almost 25 per cent larger than officially measured.[2] In other words, the Russian economy has been growing, and its government budget deficit amounts to much less than 5 per cent of the gross domestic product.

Even the clearest of positive indicators – for example, Russia's persistently strong performance in foreign trade, a reflection of its wealth of natural resources – is obscured by the flow of often trivial bad news. Almost all ex-Soviet republics and East European countries were running trade deficits during the 1990s. By contrast, Russia had a very nice surplus in 1996 at $23.1 billion, and even with rising imports and lower oil prices, there was a $17.4 billion trade surplus in 1997. True, the services balance was negative, and so was the investment-income balance, but the country's ability to export oil, gold, timber, diamonds and even some manufactures overcame both to yield an overall current-account surplus of $4.0 billion for 1997. The US economy, by contrast, was running a larger deficit each month.

Globalization and the Information Deficit

Russia has been a beneficiary of the globalization implicit in turbo-capitalism, through trade, investment, and the inflow of technology high and low, from air-traffic computers to bottling plants for soft drinks. But Russia has also repeatedly been damaged by the information deficit that is a feature of our turbo-capitalist, globalizing times. There is much more money about than sound information of sufficient depth, and a far greater willingness to invest at long range than to investigate complicated foreign realities.

Currency and bond traders, investors and investment-bankers, assorted analysts and advisors educated in varying degree to understand the complexities of their own financial markets, and perhaps those of other well-established markets, now trade in Moscow's as well. They know little of its people and institutions, and much of what they think they know is wrong. Understandably, traders who work frantic fourteen-hour days are not likely to be especially well read about Russia, Russian history or its cultural propensities, including the peculiar Russian delight in playing the doomed hero in the third act of a tragedy. Nor do they know Russian, of course. It does not

[2] Anders Åslund, personal communication to author, 25 June 1998.

help that English is the universal language of financial markets, for it means that those who know only English are constantly venturing in Russia as in other countries where essential financial information in the local language is only translated partially and late. The results of this ignorance have been serious, imposing heavy costs on the Russian economy, as well as unwarranted benefits on occasion – there have been some grossly over-optimistic investments too.

Any money coming in from abroad, however volatile, is better than no money. So Russian nationalists who blame foreign bankers and financiers for the country's problems are as foolish as their counterparts in Malaysia. And it goes without saying that financial markets must fluctuate to function at all, that their movements always include speculative anticipations, and that any market is exposed to unwarranted outbreaks of panic as well as purposeful bouts of liquidation. Naturally, the newer the market, the less experienced its operators, the more fragile its institutions, the wilder are likely to be its gyrations. Hence Moscow's financial market, as those of other emerging economies, cannot be expected to be a model of stability – and no financial market at all, not even Wall Street's, can assure ever-rising values. But it is undeniable that the information deficit of global finance does add its own gratuitous contribution to the periodic turmoils of Russia's finance as well as those of many other countries.

Each time that happens, funds that might have been highly productive are abruptly withdrawn, and interest rates are driven up further than they have to be, dislocating the equilibrium of public finance, damaging private borrowers perhaps to the point of bankruptcy. On occasion the effects are more severe, turning small crises into large ones, large ones into bigger ones. Sooner or later a disastrous domino effect – triggered perhaps by sheer misinformation – will bring down Wall Street along with other large and established markets, to briefly frighten investors and pension-claimants at best, or set off a global recession at worst.

There being no end to natural ignorance and markets being inherently unstable, the only possible remedy is some sort of monitoring organization endowed with powers of immediate intervention. Each national financial market is subject to some sort of official supervision, often strict. Each separate stock and commodity exchange has its own controlling authority, empowered among other things to stop trading in moments of sheer bootless panic. Ironically the only financial market that has no official supervision, no controlling authority, is the global financial market which is the most vulnerable to misinformation and hysteria. It cannot long endure without either a major disaster or some effective safeguards – or, more likely, first one, and then the other.

TEN

Free Trade as Ideology

The god of the market-worshippers that celebrate the glories of turbo-capitalism is Adam Smith, but theirs is a devotion that crucially depends on not reading him. Being far wiser than his modern worshippers, Smith filled his work with exceptions, exclusions and reservations to the rule that free markets always allocate most efficiently, maximizing the common welfare. As for the specific worship of free trade between countries – a veritable religion for the American and British ruling elites – it is just as important not to read either Adam Smith or his worthy predecessor, Henry Martyn. A merchant in the East India trade in the early eighteenth century and a pithy writer, Martyn recognized that wealth may point in one direction, welfare in another.

Seventy-five years before Adam Smith published his *Inquiry into the Nature and Causes of the Wealth of Nations,* and seventy-seven years before Adam Smith became a commissioner of customs in Edinburgh (thereby ironically holding, through the influence of the Duke of Buccleuch, a secure post charged with obstructing imports into Scotland), Henry Martyn's *Considerations upon the East India Trade* of 1701, written to oppose the East India Company's monopoly, had already anticipated most of what is right and wrong about the theory of free trade:

Things may be imported from India by fewer hands than as good would be made in England, so that to permit the consumption of

181

Indian manufactures is to permit the loss of few men's labor ... A law to restrain us to use only English manufactures, is to oblige us to make them first, is to oblige us to provide for our consumption by the labor of many, what might as well be done by the labor of few, is to oblige us to consume the labor of many when that of few might be sufficient.

Martyn captures the opportunity-cost essence of the free trade argument lucidly enough:

If nine cannot produce above three bushels of wheat in England, if by equal labor they might procure nine bushels from another country, to employ these in agriculture at home, is to employ nine to do no more work than might be done as well by three.

That is what is right about free trade theory. Import barriers artificially preclude efficiency gains identical to those achieved by better technology, better organization or any other source of domestic productivity. That goods or services originate from a point on the surface of the planet that happens to be classified as foreign at a given time (subject to change by conquest or voluntary union) is an entirely meaningless attribute in purely economic terms. (Until the late 1950s, there were still tariff – *Dazio* – barriers *within* Italy, so that trade-foreigners were as near as the next town.)

Equally, all that is wrong about free trade is already evident in Martyn's pamphlet:

If the same work is done by one, which was done before by three; if the other two are forced to sit still, the Kingdom got nothing before by the labor of the two, and therefore loses nothing by their sitting still.

In other words, what benefits the Kingdom, or the gross national product as we would now say, need not benefit all its subjects, and may indeed turn some into paupers. Of course, the same is true of any other increase in efficiency, such as might ensue from the use of better software. But simply because any change in trade barriers is a matter of presumptively democratic *political* decisions, unlike changes in computer usage done by private firms or individuals for their private reasons with private funds, the employment implications cannot be overlooked.

In poor countries, given favorable circumstances including foreign investment, free trade can drastically alter the total economy, lifting much of the population to a much higher level of income. In affluent countries, however, long on total national wealth but now increasingly afflicted by the return of poverty in the most vulnerable fraction of their populations, it is not necessarily a good idea to enrich the Kingdom by replacing three with one, leaving the other two 'sitting still'.

Most economists would immediately point out that it is much better for all if the many gainers from any given market opening compensate the few losers, rather than to keep protectionist barriers that reduce the total incomes of all. They say that, sometimes offering a quick calculation – and then they leave the scene. That some workers may be protected by some trade barriers, while compensation schemes are *never* implemented, is a political phenomenon outside the scope of the profession as now defined. For they who invoke Adam Smith have mostly abandoned his broad political economy for an abstract economics of 'other things being equal', and purely theoretical compensations for any adversities.

In particular, most contemporary economists simply ignore the possibility that people might actually prefer to live in a country whose economy is somewhat less efficient than it could be, because of protectionism among other impediments. In fact, they implicitly assume that societies exist to serve the needs of their economies, instead of the other way round, thereby attributing no importance to the stability of employment (as opposed to earning levels), the upkeep of traditions (e.g. Japan's rice-farming culture), or the avoidance of gross increases in the inequality of incomes and wealth.

True, many of those who attack the ruling orthodoxy of unrestricted free trade go beyond societal welfare-versus-wealth arguments, intrude into purely economic analyses, and in so doing keep repeating the same elementary errors. They persistently and grossly over-estimate the importance of international trade and investment flows for the national economies of major countries, and most notably for the huge American economy. In this 'turbo-capitalism' critique of mine, by contrast, globalization ranks as a distant fourth after privatization, deregulation and technological change.

Most commonly, the errant opponents of free trade keep confusing competition among goods with wage competition. It is each country's internal labor market that sets wages, so that, say, German workers whose employers are competing head-to-head with, say, Indian exports are not themselves competing with Indian workers, whose own wages are only very indirectly relevant to their own. Only the competition of other German workers matters – so that Indian exports can only affect the wage rates of German workers indirectly, insofar as an unfavorable trade balance causes unemployment and thereby reduces wages (in Germany's case only in theory, because German wages are kept downwardly rigid by trade-union power).

Some opponents of free trade are so overcome by their eagerness to translate Cold War animosities into 'geo-economic' rivalries that they misconstrue them as *national* confrontations. Yet for each Boeing–Airbus Industrie truly zero-sum market war over airframes, there is an American GE–French SNECMA alliance of engine manufacturers. Because for each major country the strongest trading competitors are also routinely the largest export customers, geo-economic rivalries are destined to remain strictly confined to the specific industries involved, without descending into emotional national rivalries. And moreover, most amazingly, even supposedly trained economists tend to reveal an inability to understand the ancient and elementary theory of comparative advantage when arguing against free trade. The advantages in question are *internally* comparative, so that even if Lazo is less efficient than Worko in producing everything, its least-bad industries can still profitably export to Worko, whose own resources are best employed by its better industries, not the weakest industries with which Lazo is competing.

Protectionism as Sin

But most advocates of free trade do not merely oppose trade barriers, they are offended by them. For they know that only the free interplay of supply and demand – the invisible hand – can set market-clearing prices with neither waste nor contrived shortages, thereby signalling to all producers what is the most efficient use of their scarce resources at any one moment in time. And they are frustrated in their knowledge that, if all trade barriers were removed, the planetary income and standard of living would swiftly and greatly increase, because every producer would be free to exploit fully its own particular comparative advantages, eliminating a planet's worth of inefficiencies, large and small. Instead, every state in the world artificially segments the planetary market, by imposing its own obstacles to imports by way of prohibitions, quota limits or tariffs – and sometimes to exports as well, often by pretending that only processed and not raw materials must be sold abroad. Each state thus distorts not only its own internal market but, by successive displacements of supply and demand, all markets, everywhere. By so doing, the entire world's efficiency in using scarce resources is diminished, leaving the planet much poorer than it need be.

Because all competent academic economists know these things to be true, and because so little else in their inventory of theories remains unrefuted, most economists are greatly irritated by any and all arguments for trade barriers. In addition to proving them costly for the standard of living, they are eager to expose them as the spurious excuses of domestic producers, out to exploit the consumer by raising prices behind the shelter of import barriers.

- When it could be argued that grain self-sufficiency was a strategic necessity, most economists asked why the agricultural interest should be allowed to levy its own permanent tax on all consumers, given that a one-off accumulation of reserve stocks of imported grain would be far cheaper, even including storage costs.
- When it is argued that a particular industry could eventually become competitive if it can first grow to strength behind barriers, most economists assert that long-term lenders can finance the infancy of any industry far more efficiently than captive consumers. Nor would they ask for the indefinite continuation of enervatingly profitable import barriers, as protected industries always do.
- When it is pointed out that import barriers can preserve employment, most economists trot out the compensation counter-argument, as if that theoretical construct were a practical remedy.

The emotional intensity of the free traders is particularly evident when they are confronted by important defectors from their own ranks. In 1865 Richard Cobden lamented on his deathbed not his own imminent death, but rather John Stuart Mill's apostasy in formulating the infant-industry argument:

> I believe that the harm which Mill has done to the world by the passage in his book on *Political Economy* in which he favours the principle of protection in young communities has outweighed all the good which may have been caused by his other writings.[1]

[1] George Armitage-Smith, *The Free Trade Movement and Its Results* (London, 1898), p. 53, cited in Douglas A. Irwin, *Against the Tide: An Intellectual History of Free Trade* (Princeton University Press, 1996), p. 128.

Alfred Marshall as late as 1890 was no less mournful over Mill's defection:

> When John Stuart Mill ventured to tell the English people that some arguments for protection in new countries were scientifically valid, his friends spoke of it in anger – but more in sorrow than in anger – as his one sad departure from the sound principles of economic rectitude.[2]

This is not so harsh as Cobden's condemnation, but equally replete with sentiment.

It was just the same with Keynes. Originally he was the purest of the pure:

> We must hold to Free Trade, in its widest interpretation, as an inflexible dogma, to which no exception is admitted ... even in those rare cases where by infringing it we could in fact obtain a direct economic advantage.[3]

But Keynes, too, was to deviate from the path of economic rectitude. Reacting to the UK's very high unemployment rate, knowing that the government would not devalue sterling and that the unions would not accept wage reductions, in 1930 Keynes 'reluctantly' proposed tariffs as the only remaining method of increasing employment, through import substitution.[4] The government of the day had asked for some remedy in a grim situation. Keynes offered the only possible remedy. But it dismayed his erstwhile friends, colleagues and admirers, some of whom reacted with outright hostility. The well-known economist Lord Robbins (my own teacher) spoke of Keynes's 'extraordinary naiveté' in believing that import duties could easily be removed *once they had served their purpose*.[5] At the time, millions were living on the dole, eating bread and jam for breakfast, lunch and dinner, but Keynes's opponents worried about the economic distortions that might linger in the aftermath, perhaps years later.

After accepting in full every possible objection, including the marginality of all foreign trade and investment in very large economies, Keynes has the last word: one should do what one can, even at the expense of sacrificing abstract principle for mere flesh and blood.

[2] Alfred Marshall, 'Some Aspects of Competition', 1890, cited in Irwin, op. cit., p. 129.
[3] *The Collected Writings of John Maynard Keynes* (London, 1971–1989), vol. XVII, p. 451.
[4] Keynes, op. cit., vol. XX, p. 378.
[5] Irwin, op. cit., p. 196, emphasis added.

ELEVEN

Money as Religion

What distinguishes turbo-capitalism is accelerated structural change, producing more creation and more destruction, more efficiency and more inequality. Its political essence, however, is the shift of power from public authorities to both private and institutional economic interests. Inevitably, this reduces the sphere of democratic control, a process much applauded by libertarians who believe that the economy is or should be entirely private, and that the public has no right to control private property in any way, for any reason. Needless to say, others disagree, arguing that only a degree of political control can safeguard the public interest by limiting capitalism's more traumatic effects on the lives of individuals, families, neighbourhoods, cities and entire countries.

Yet that is increasingly a pious hope, or futile threat, if one prefers. While the natural environment is increasingly safeguarded by severe limits on business as well as personal activities, the social environment is increasingly left to be the free-fire zone of private business. This reflects the most striking feature of our turbo-capitalist times, the hollowing-out of democratic governance over the economy. But that is not the result of turbo-capitalism alone, for it has had a coincidental fellow-traveller ever since the 1980s: the doctrine of orthodox monetarism, which seeks to deprive governments and those they represent of all power to regulate money.

Like all religions, orthodox monetarism has both a supreme god – hard money – and a devil, inflation. Mere common sense suffices to oppose *high* inflation, and to fear hyper-inflation as the deadly disease of currencies. But it takes the absolute faith of religion to refuse even very moderate inflation at the cost of immoderate unemployment and stagnation, as the Europeans have done, or to accept unnecessarily slow economic growth for years on end, as in the United States.

To be sure, the American version of monetarism is much more pliant to popular desires than European orthodoxy – the same is true of the other religions practiced on both continents. Just as the Catholic Church is forced to allow more latitude in pragmatic America, where even devoted Jews drive on the Sabbath, the local version of orthodox monetarism has restraint imposed upon it. Certainly the US Congress would legislate the Federal Reserve right out of existence rather than tolerate the horrendous levels of unemployment long prevalent in Europe. The essential doctrine, however, is identical. In the United States too, orthodox monetarism devalues labor rather than money, but instead of unemployment there are falling real wages – more than half of all jobs throughout the US economy now pay less than they did twenty years ago, in constant dollars. No wonder that millions of new jobs keep being created, as US presidents are happy to boast: American labor is cheap.

Like many religions, orthodox monetarism also has its chief priests, constantly striving to assert their independence from secular parliaments, politicians and public opinion. Central bankers assert the right to ignore the public will by invoking their duty to a higher authority, the sublime sanctity of hard money. Central bankers in office – invariably for terms of papal length, often prematurely renewed to reassure the financial markets – are surrounded by an aura of sovereign power very properly denied to mere government ministers or even prime ministers and presidents, common mortals voted in and out of office by the ignorant masses. And when central bankers do at length retire, they are not uncommonly elevated to financial sainthood, their every fleeting opinion reverentially treasured, their candidacy for any position of special trust eagerly accepted, their very names talismanic, as with Paul Volcker in Wall Street and far beyond it, and Guido Carli in Italy, where by contrast the names of most past prime ministers evoke only opprobrium.

Because their power largely derives from their supreme command of the crusade against the devil inflation, central bankers naturally see its insidious presence everywhere. Very often, they detect 'disturbing signs of incipient inflation' or even 'alarming warnings of mounting inflationary pressure' in output, employment and wage statistics that many respected economists view with equanimity, or even find positively reassuring. Every time new statistical indicators are published, there are calls for slightly lower interest rates for a bit more growth, but these minor outbreaks of heresy are easily squashed.

There is a simple proof of the doctrinal supremacy of orthodox monetarism: any policy initiative that is branded as 'inflationary' hardly has a chance to be evaluated and discussed, and is, indeed, usually rejected out of hand. By contrast, the term 'deflationary' has no resonance at all. It is heard as a merely technical expression, not as a powerful condemnation of over-restrictive fiscal and monetary policies that strangle growth, and which in the 1930s brought about the Great Depression, political chaos, dictatorships and war.

It is perfectly true, of course, that real incomes and real wealth cannot be created by printing money, and that inflation hurts the poor disproportionately, and certainly all who live on fixed incomes, as well as wealthy rentiers who live on bond incomes. By contrast, inflation enriches all who own real estate and other marketable assets, and thus the already rich in proportion, while disproportionately enriching smart speculators (as does deflation, however). It is also true that, if unchecked, inflation naturally accelerates into hyper-inflation, which not only destroys currencies, but also degrades economic efficiency as people run to spend their suitcases of banknotes instead of working, and may even wreck the entire financial structure of societies. That being the very worst manifestation of the devil, the ultimate Satan-Beelzebub, it is not surprising that the German Bundesbank still invokes the explosive German hyper-inflation of the early 1920s 'that led to Hitler' (it was followed by ten years of democracy, but never mind) when refusing to cut interest rates.

Thus inflation is bad and hyper-inflation terrible, but it is just as true that deflation is also bad, and that hyper-deflation is disastrous. In economic theory, deflation should have no ill consequences at all, because any upward movement in the value of money can be totally nullified by an equal, compensating reduction in prices and wages. In real life, however, prices are downwardly sticky, while few employees anywhere at any time accept wage cuts without bitter resistance. Even in the United States, with its increasingly flexible labor market and inevitably weak unions, the only reason why wages could decline without resistance from the late 1970s was that inflation made it seem that wages were going up, concealing the loss in real wages.

Hence deflation starves economies, as rigid prices and wages turn the purely nominal fall in demand into an actual one, reducing output and incomes. That is contrary to theory, but it happens every time, most recently in Japan during the post-1990 deflation ('price destruction'). Another purely subjective mechanism also reduces real demand and therefore real production and real employment: when people *feel* poorer, because the nominal value of their houses and other assets is falling, they buy less.

Such being the real world of imperfect humanity, inflation and deflation should be viewed as equally objectionable by politicians and the public; they should sound in our ears as equivalent evils, just as flood and drought, or theft and robbery. It is the greatest triumph of orthodox monetarism that only inflation is viewed as sinful.

When gathering in August 1996 with their host Alan Greenspan, chairman of the Federal Reserve, in Jackson, Wyoming (which thereby instantly became the world's premier resort), the central bankers congratulated themselves at length on their success in reducing inflation by keeping real interest rates high, did not pause to deplore miserable growth rates, and mainly engaged in a sort of reverse auction, competing with each other in calling for even lower inflation rates, at the expense of growth and employment if need be.

Normally it is the chief of the Bundesbank who dominates such occasions. He can thoroughly enjoy himself by sternly preaching fiscal austerity and monetary discipline to errant foreigners everywhere, because Germany was for so long the perpetual winner of the deflation Olympics. In August 1996, however, France was the surprise winner. Untroubled by an economy not merely stagnant but in rigor mortis, with unemployment at 12 per cent, a level unseen since the 1930s, in Jackson the French were enormously proud of their amazingly low 1.3 per cent inflation rate, a full 0.2 per cent below Germany's level. The super-disciplined Dutch did not do quite so well with their 1.8 per cent, but that did not prevent Willem Duisenberg of the Netherlands central bank from sharing with confidants his fears that Germany was showing dangerous signs of laxity.

The Italians, by contrast, refrained from boasting – as befits the gentlemen of the Bank of Italy, which is the country's only elite bureaucracy. Their 2.9 per cent inflation rate was nevertheless a brilliant achievement, given all the banknotes thrown into the economy by a 6.4 per cent budget deficit. The miracle was accomplished with very high interest rates, of course. The fact that low inflation drove up the lira, making Italian exports less competitive, thus further cutting growth and employment in an economy already slowing down, was not the sort of thing that central bankers bother to discuss.

With Duisenberg in the lead, there was heady talk of actually ascending to the paradise of orthodox monetarism, a *zero* inflation rate. It is only a matter of eliminating budget deficits by scrapping more welfare programs, and of interest-rate discipline of course, easily dispensed from the magnificent heights of Jackson, Wyoming, to the vulgar crowd of Europe's eighteen million unemployed. As for Alan Greenspan, he had nothing whatever to worry about, because a 5 per cent unemployment rate and stagnant real wages were accepted by Americans as perfectly normal, or even as good news. In fact, any spurt of faster growth, any fall in unemployment, is very bad news indeed for Wall Street and all of us, because it will only lead the Federal Reserve to increase interest rates, 'to cool down the economy'.

Actually, nobody knows the exact rate of unemployment below which wages start rising, pushing prices upwards. For one thing, everything in the US economy keeps changing, while the government's budget-starved statistical bureaus can only collect the same old increasingly outdated statistical series, in the same old way.

Economists continue to debate the precise level of the NAIRU (the non-accelerating-inflation rate of unemployment), but the Federal Reserve takes no chances. When in doubt, it invariably errs on the side of caution. Thus a million people can lose their jobs because higher interest rates *might* keep inflation at one-tenth of 1 per cent below what it might have been. The Democratic, supposedly pro-labor President Bill Clinton was well advised in 1995 that it would be a good idea to 'test' lower levels of unemployment, but he did not dare to challenge the Federal Reserve. In the event, by 1997 unemployment had fallen below 5 per cent without inducing any inflationary pressures at all, thus disproving the theory – yet without causing the Federal Reserve or its chairman to acknowledge their technical error, which had inflicted the miseries of unemployment on tens of thousands of American families.

The Age of the Central Bankers

How is it that central bankers are now so powerful, more so in many ways than prime ministers or presidents? After all, one heard very little about them in the three postwar decades of rapid economic growth, sharply rising incomes and widening prosperity.

Only during the 1930s, *not* coincidentally the years of the Great Depression, were central bankers as prominent as they are now. A world in crisis waited with baited breath for every pronouncement from the lips of the Bank of England's Montagu Norman, Germany's Hjalmar Schact and their lesser colleagues on both sides of the Atlantic. Firm as rocks they were in their mutual solidarity right through the 1930s, even unto 1939, when the Bank of England dutifully handed over Czechoslovakia's gold deposits to Hitler's Reichsbank, by then the central bank of Bohemia and Moravia as well.

With tragic consequences for tens of millions of unemployed as far away as Argentina and Australia, and far more terrible repercussions in Europe, governments almost everywhere accepted the central bankers' remedy for the Depression. It was of course to deflate, deflate, deflate, by cutting public spending and restricting credit. One result was Hitler's rise to power, propelled by the mass unemployment caused by deflation.

We now know that the central bankers were totally wrong. The only way to refloat the sinking economies of the 1930s was to start off the chain-reaction of demand by sharply increasing government spending, and never mind a bit of inflation. So long as the big boys of the world economy led the way, by inflating and importing first to generate more demand for their own exports, everyone would have come out just fine. But only a few adventurous souls, and only one reputable economist, John Maynard Keynes, dared to contradict what seemed to be common sense, and even they were hesitant. The central bankers, by contrast, were utterly certain that they were right, just as they are now. They gave exactly the same advice – the only advice central bankers ever give – tighten credit, restrict spending, hold back demand.

The power of the central bankers is so great because it is so broadly based. First, they are sustained by almost all respectable professional opinion, as they were in the 1930s. Hence it is foolish to criticize Alan Greenspan personally, or any of his foreign counterparts. They merely exemplify, apply and enunciate a consensual doctrine as unchallengeable as the immaculate conception within its own premises. Moreover, orthodox monetarism attracts both conventional right-wing and conventional left-wing political support, not to speak of the center, whose opinions coincide with the center of gravity of respectable professional opinion.

To bond-holders – that is, the prudent among savers, wealthy or not, but especially the truly rich (as opposed to poor people with money, even much money, who speculate) – the fight against inflation or, better still, the achievement of deflation is self-evidently the only blessed cause. That enlists the center and the moderate Right to the faith. But orthodox monetarism would be politically weak if it did not also attract the support of the passive Left everywhere – the Left that is much concerned with the welfare of ordinary workers, but unwilling to risk any innovative action on their behalf.

For that Left, the mainstream Left everywhere nowadays, splendidly represented by Tony Blair, the only truth is the central bankers' mantra that inflation is the cruellest tax. When prices start rising, the price of real estate goes up, as does that of all long-lived assets. But it goes up more than proportionately, anticipating future inflation; indeed it acquires new value as a hedge against inflation. Hence those who already have assets become richer, while those who do not have them must pay much more if they need such assets – for instance, dwellings to dwell in. And inflation is disorienting, creating fast-buck opportunities for fast people, enriching the mostly richer. By contrast, the salaries and wages of ordinary employees tend to fall behind.

Moreover, the disorientation caused by inflation has worse consequences than the opportunities it creates for undeserving quick-footed speculators. As people lose a clear sense of the relative value of things, inefficient distortions spread across the economy. Finally, when there is outright hyper-inflation, production declines as people become preoccupied with spending their money rather than working.

As against these truths, there is a greater truth. As everyone knows, full employment causes inflation, other things being equal. By the same token, however, money-fuelled demand causes full employment, so long as the spending is sustained, as it was after 1939 with the war's deficit finance. Stagflation, i.e. inflation plus unemployment, comes about only when investment falls off because would-be investors fear a forthcoming strangulation of demand – to stop inflation, of course.

People who believe that the corrosive self-doubt and material impoverishment caused by unemployment is worse than some loss of real gross national product to distortions, and worse than inflation's inconveniences and irritations, should oppose orthodox monetarism during the present deflationary era. As for the iniquities of inflation, whole-wealth or 'excess earnings' taxes can certainly offset the cruellest tax, as they did during the Second World War.

Another perspective maintains that no explanation of the extraordinary power of today's central bankers is needed at all, because it is not they who are powerful, but rather 'the markets'. This refers to the world's financial markets, made up of all who buy and sell currencies as well as stocks, bonds and looser bundles of debt. It is often said that the markets impose stringency anyway, by punishing countries that opt for a soft money policy. They inflict this punishment by marking down the offending country's currency. In these deflationary times of chronic excess capacity, the result however is that cheapened exports rise and dearer imports fall, increasing employment at both ends, in import-substitution as well as export trades.

This is exactly what happened in Italy in 1993–95, after the lira was forced down by both foreigners and Italians who were alarmed that the country's political turmoil would accentuate its fiscal and monetary laxity. As the lira fell, the Italian economy enjoyed an export-led boom, while Germany and other EU countries of exemplary monetary discipline were suffering from increasing unemployment. With the lira then being much in demand to pay for all the exported Ferraris and everything else, it started a slow and continuing climb – even though only the more courageous fraction of investors and currency traders bought lire and lira-denominated bonds and stocks, adding their own capital demand to the trade-generated demand for lire.

At the time, grave warnings were issued that Italy's inflation would soon accelerate because of the rising costs of imports. This is what is written in the textbooks – but then textbook writers do not know very much about Ferragamo shoes. When the cost of dollar-denominated ostrich leather increased, the import content of 400,000 lire shoes went up from 10,000 to 15,000 lire (0.0375 per cent of their total value), and that was just about the extent of Italy's import-induced inflation. Advanced economies are like that.

To be sure, in inflationary times with productive capacity already fully utilized, the downward valuation of the currency by money markets cannot result in increased exports, while rising import prices do accelerate inflation even further. However, this is quite irrelevant to the present situation of chronic deflation and excess capacity. Everyone knows that inflation results from too much money chasing too few goods. Everyone knows that there is now an abundance of capacity to produce more goods, so that more money could be printed without causing much inflation.

A straightforward political explanation is also offered for the rise of the central bankers. In these post-socialist times of ours, the Right everywhere is still unflinching in its allegiance to the bond-holding *rentiers* who oppose inflation above all things, while the idea-less Left is very tired of complaining about unemployment, and frankly bored by the poor. In the United States, the 1996 presidential election rapidly became a contest between a far right and a plain right-wing candidate, except that on public finance the Democrat Bill Clinton actually managed to maneuver himself to the right of the Republican Bob Dole. While Clinton trumpeted as his own achievement the sharp cuts in all non-military public spending imposed by the Republican-dominated Congress (the Federal deficit was down to 1.7 per cent of gross national product, a level unseen in two decades), it was Bob Dole who proposed a tax cut, risking an increasing deficit to stimulate growth.

As for Europe, Britain's Tony Blair is only the most prominent among today's nominally left-wing party leaders in revealing his disdain for the poor and other losers, his desire to sup at the table of financial success, and his contempt for the broad masses of working people with small houses, big mortgages and ugly little cars. He is certainly unequipped to resist the plausibilities of orthodox monetarism. In Germany, Italy and Spain, the ex-socialist and ex-communist parties are not subject to the gravitational pull of fashionable society as in Britain, but they can still do no more than march despairingly to electoral defeat, unless they repudiate their essential schemes of the past. Such is their poverty of ideas that they are now listening attentively to Tony Blair's mutterings about a 'third way' and a 'stakeholder' society – not even getting the stakeholder stuff from the original source, Ryuzaburo Kaku, former chairman of Japan's Canon Inc. Only in France is there a recognizably socialist government in power at this time, but it too accepts orthodox monetarism in full.

In the absence of any intellectual counterweight to orthodox monetarism, even a left-wing electoral victory can yield only right-wing policies, poorly executed by ex-socialists who have no talent or natural affinity for finance. So it was France under Mitterrand, and in Italy, after the 1996 victory of the ex-Communist Party, re-labelled the PDS, 'the democratic party of the left'. Exemplified by its leading government minister, the youngish and fashionable Walter Veltroni, more at home in Manhattan's Madison Avenue than in the slums of the South, the PDS used all its power to sustain Romano Prodi's coalition government. Its overriding goal was not to reduce Italy's unemployment, terribly high in much of the South, or to refashion decaying schools and antiquated universities on modern lines, or to endow Italy with an adequate health-care system, or to raise the government's bureaucracy to European standards. Instead it was to bring Italy into the European Monetary Union – the crowning achievement of Europe's orthodox monetarism.

The March to the Euro

It need not have been so. The perfectly sound project of replacing Europe's confusion of currencies with the euro was born long before monetarism became extremist religion, and did not originally imply the acceptance of deflation and unemployment forever. Even before the Bretton Woods system of fixed exchange rates was undermined by Nixon's 1971 decision to stop the convertibility of dollars into gold, the European Community had already proclaimed the long-term goal of establishing a single European currency.

So long as exchange rates were still fixed, however, except for rare devaluations and revaluations, the multiplicity of European currencies was only a minor inconvenience. Commerce was not disrupted by currency gyrations, or silently inhibited by the fear of possible shifts in exchange rates. Both things, however, happened from 1973 onwards when exchange rates were unfixed, starting the up-and-down floating that has been going on ever since, to the great benefit of the new industry of currency speculation, and at the expense of all other industries.

The project of a single European currency remained on the horizon as the ultimate aim, but in 1979 the European Monetary System (EMS) was introduced as an interim arrangement. Member countries agreed to keep the relative value of their currencies within specific and narrow limits. Under EMS rules, as soon as traders pushed up or marked down a currency anywhere near the set limits, the country in question had to react, chiefly by raising or lowering interest rates – to attract or repel capital inflows, as the case might be.

Central banks have also attempted to control speculation by 'open-market operations', i.e. by out-trading the traders, dumping currencies much in demand, or buying up weak currencies, sometimes acting in concert specifically to ambush speculators. It is most revealing, however, that the central bankers have never been very good at the game. Public and politicians may believe that they are geniuses by job definition, but speculators know better: when they go head to head with the high priests of orthodox monetarism, they regularly leave the table with large winnings, sometimes with enough to keep their great-grandchildren in the pink, from one night's trading.

In any case, interest-rate jiggling and open-market operations could at best cope only with mere fluctuations. Beyond that, if a currency was sliding or ascending because of enduring export and import trends, the only way of staying within the allowed EMS limits was to change the country's taxes and spending as a whole, to raise or lower the economy's overall demand. In the old Bretton Woods days, currency problems could still be dealt with by imposing or relaxing prohibitions on the purchase of foreign currency, and leaving the domestic economy out of it. But such 'exchange controls' have long since been abolished in the European Union – they are, of course, utterly incompatible with a unified market – so that there is no interposed barrier between currencies and economies.

Although the European Monetary System was only an approximation to fixed exchange rates, it already required the currency tail to wag the economic dog, and all that goes with it: demand, employment, taxes, social programs. In other words, the EMS can work only if its own priority outranks all other relevant political priorities, i.e. most of politics, and therefore most of democracy. It therefore presaged what the euro requires of its members.

No democratic hesitations could stop the euro's advance. Meeting in Hanover in June 1988, the European Union's Council of Ministers agreed on the guidelines for the specialist negotiations that led to the Maastricht Treaty, signed in February 1992. This laid down the criteria for admission into the European Monetary Union, future issuer of the euro currency.

In 1998, each candidate's 1997 statistics were examined, to determine which countries could be admitted into the European Monetary Union: all but Greece passed the test. On 1 January 1999, the successful applicants must adopt, totally and irrevocably, fixed exchange rates. In practice that would already bring the euro into existence as Europe's only real money. Although national banknotes and coins would continue in circulation, DMs, francs, guilders and lire would differ only in color and design, being entirely interchangeable at their respective, totally fixed, exchange rates. Finally, by January 2002, national currencies are to be withdrawn, ceasing to be legal tender six months later, and being wholly replaced by euro notes and coins.

It is not the euro itself, however, or even the compulsory, inflexible dates of its adoption (they simply disregard the business cycle) that have transformed 'Maastricht' from the name of one of Europe's most pleasant minor cities into an evocation of well-justified fears. After all, currencies of every sort, including the euro, can be managed in drastically different ways.

The value of sterling, for example, has often been 'defended' (i.e. forced upwards) since the 1920s. This happened to the greater glory of the British empire or the UK, as the case was, to the great benefit of the City, which needed the prestige of a strong currency and/or high interest rates to attract depositors, and to the even greater benefit of wealthy Britons who could thereby invest more advantageously abroad – and all at the expense of British industry, whose exports were systematically overpriced, while competing imports were just as underpriced. In the process, X-thousand City gents were kept happily rich with scant effort, Y-hundreds of ultra-rich Brits cheaply accumulated many broad acres in Canada and Australia, real estate, bonds and shares in America, Europe and Japan, as well as villas on the Côte d'Azur, while Z-millions of disemployed, under-employed, underpaid or never employed British industrial workers, their managers high and low, and all those foolish enough to invest in British industry paid for the fun.

This is what 'the defense of sterling', always much applauded by an innumerate press, has amounted to, from the disastrous decision to revert to the gold standard in 1920 to the Thatcher government's decision to enter the European Monetary System at a 'prestige' level, which guaranteed trade deficits and the further decline of British industry. With equally disastrous results for French industry, the French franc was managed in the same way throughout the 1990s and the DM too was greatly overvalued, leading to the emigration of German industry both eastwards into ex-communist Europe and westwards to the United States. Such are the fruits of orthodox monetarism – a currency that the unemployed can be proud of.

The US dollar, by contrast, has mostly been allowed to float freely since fixed exchange rates were finally renounced in 1973. Far from 'defending' the dollar, successive administrations have intervened in earnest to push it down, nakedly exploiting their geopolitical power over the hard-currency champions but Second World War losers, Germany and Japan, forcing them to revalue their currencies and thereby devalue the dollar. True, US officials have often promised to complaining foreigners that they would try to raise the dollar when it was too grossly undervalued, but they never promised that they would keep their promise. In any case, a very low and still declining propensity to save has ensured chronic US trade deficits, muting currency complaints.

Amidst the total indifference of the public, in spite of some highly specialized Wall Street objections at times, successive US governments have gleefully watched the dollar fall, slide, plunge, plummet, collapse or even sink, for that meant more exports, fewer imports, more work, more output and more profits – reckoned in dollars, and only dollars, of course. At times, American tourists in Switzerland or France would be kicked out of their lodgings or denied a table by innkeepers afraid of being stuck with traveler's checks denominated in rapidly falling dollars. Such news always caused hilarity rather than shame back in the United States, merely prompting suggestions that the unlucky tourists should try Colorado or Florida next time. Orthodox monetarism is not quite so fanatical a faith in the United States, and it has never been coupled with the idiocy of currency-nationalism.

The Euro: A Super-Hard Currency?

It is not therefore the euro itself, but rather its management, that counts. Will it be kept as high as possible, as sterling has been and the French franc too, or will it be allowed to slide now and then, as with the US dollar? Two things guarantee that the euro will be valued too high for the health of Europe's economies, which in 1998 had no jobs for some eighteen million unemployed: the specific Maastricht criteria for admission into the European Monetary Union, and the fact that its monetary policy will be exclusively controlled by the European System of Central Banks, from its inception on 1 January 1999.

The Maastricht criteria in themselves were utterly pervaded, nay inspissated and parboiled, by the spirit of orthodox monetarism. Admission into the European Monetary Union required that for 1997, the year of statistical 'examination', budget deficits be less than 3 per cent of the gross national product; that the inflation rate be within 1.5 per cent of the three least sinful entrants; that long-term interest rates (a measure of the markets' estimate of future inflation) be within 2 per cent of those of the three most virtuous entrants; that applicants be unblemished by the shame of any post-1995 devaluation; and finally, the most difficult of all criteria, that the public debt not exceed 60 per cent of the gross domestic product, a condition that only France and Denmark could easily satisfy. For the Netherlands, at 78 per cent in 1996, or even Spain (80 per cent) and Portugal (71 per cent), let alone Germany (62 per cent), the allowed ratio of debt to gross domestic product was fairly easily attainable by 1997 – all it took was some stiff taxation to pay off some of the bond-holders at home or abroad. This further depressed demand, output and employment, but of course the newly disemployed already had plenty of company. For Belgium at 130 per cent and Italy at 123 per cent (in 1996) the ratio of debt to gross domestic product could not be cut to 60 per cent by 1997 except by unimaginably extreme measures.

In the event, no extreme measures were needed at all. The public debt of Belgium and of Italy was not seriously reduced, but no matter. Just as the Maastricht meeting of the European Union's Council of Ministers inscribed the 60 per cent criterion into the treaty, further meetings nullified its effect. Thus in 1998 Italy as well as Belgium joined the others in the European Monetary Union, by merely deflating already deflated economies to cut their current deficits well below 3 per cent – which was perfectly feasible if even more unemployment was accepted, as it was.

What has not been changed by any meeting of the Council of Ministers, in spite of strenuous French attempts, is the fundamental principle of the European Monetary Union: the *totality* of monetary policy, from interest rates to credit norms, is to be controlled exclusively by the European System of Central Banks. Appropriately enough, this is the conclave of the newly created European Central Bank with the central banks of each country, which are to sit at the European Central Bank's feet to implement its every command. Its first act, as of the start of 1998, was to conduct a statistical inquisition to determine each country's fitness for admission. As noted, all except Greece were admitted. By then too, all central banks not yet deemed 'independent' were to become so by law to ensure their full independence from their own governments and parliaments, as the Bundesbank and Federal Reserve already were.

No independence, however, can be as magnificently absolute as that of the European Central Bank itself: it is to receive *no* instructions from either member countries or *any* institution of the European Union, be it the mandarinate of the Commission, the ex-powers that were of the Council of Ministers, or the grossly overpaid, pathetically underpowered European Parliament. This is truly a sovereign power, given irrevocably to an institution headed by a central banker, selected and advised by other central bankers, who are themselves recruited and trained by their predecessors in their respective central banks. The non-elected European Central Bank will assume total and exclusive control over the monetary policy of all member countries from the formal inception of the union on 1 January 1999. Itself free of any democratic interference, the Bank will be free to interfere at will in all that concerns money in all the member countries.

In theory, the precedents of the Bundesbank and Federal Reserve should certify the democratic legitimacy of the European Central Bank's independence. If Americans and Germans have long been happy to accept the unfettered independence and undemocratic power of their central banks, why should Europeans jointly be less happy with the undemocratic independence of the European Central Bank?

In reality, however, there is no precedent, and no democratic legitimacy by analogy. The Bundesbank and Federal Reserve exist within countries that are democratically governed, whose legislatures could ultimately choose to restrict their independence, or even abolish them outright. Totally independent in legal theory, the heads of the Bundesbank and Federal Reserve must be careful to remain within the boundaries of the prevailing political consensus; they can do whatever they want, so long as they do not displease all-powerful democratic legislatures.

The European Central Bank, by contrast, exists within a European Union that has no all-powerful democratic legislature, or even a moderately powerful one. As for the national governments that ultimately control all European institutions, and which do of course represent their separate democracies at one remove, they are so very likely to block each other over any dispute with the European Central Bank that the latter need not fear their interference at all. Jointly all-powerful, the national governments are severally impotent before it.

No institution has claimed such prerogatives or has had such unlimited actual power since the best days of the medieval Catholic Church, and with all due respect to the importance of religion, the control of money goes a very long way indeed. Beyond the enormous leverage of interest rates across the entire spectrum of economic life, beyond its control of credit in general, the European Central Bank is empowered to invigilate quite a few specific rules, including three sacrosanct prohibitions:

- No financing of state deficits by central banks (back to gold-in, gold-out public treasuries).
- No loans on favorable terms to any public body or state-owned company by any private or public financial institution.
- No guarantees by any member country of any other member country's public debt – the famous 'no bail-out' rule.

Yves-Thibault de Silguy, at the time the European Commissioner in charge of economic, financial and monetary affairs, and an enthusiastic advocate of the European Central Bank, raised and answered The Great Question to his own complete satisfaction:

> Some people claim that the independence of the European System of Central Banks is anti-democratic. That criticism is baseless. The European Central Bank will be subjected to the rules of transparency and open information already imposed on central banks in most industrialized countries.[1]

Who says that French-patrician Eurocrats lack a sense of humor? Even the Federal Reserve is so untransparent that its chairman summons the FBI to investigate leaks of its strictly closed-door meetings. Imminent interest-rate changes and such must, of course, be shielded to avoid leaks to speculators. But all Fed deliberations are secret, even the ones that nobody could dishonestly exploit. Yet because it does supply much statistical data, the Fed is far more open than any European central bank which are as liberal in sharing information about their workings as the North Korean Politburo.

Under the European Central Bank, the euro will most likely be managed like sterling in the 1920s rather than like the US dollar since 1974. It will be the hardest of hard currencies, kept that way by the cruellest, most persistent deflation. What an outcome from all the hopes that European unity once evoked! First, the entire European project is channeled into a project of monetary union, rather than towards a confederation that involves at least a degree of political unity. Then the monetary union is structured to ensure the most tight-fisted monetary policy imaginable, sacrificing everything to the one aim of stopping inflation.

In 1948 the United States reacted to the prostration of immediate postwar Western Europe with the Marshall Plan: billions of dollars were printed to allow Europeans to reconstruct by buying machinery and materials from each other as well as from the United States. In the process, there was some inflation back in the United States, but it was rightly considered a minor shortcoming of a splendidly far-sighted policy. In 1998 a now very wealthy Western Europe reacted to the prostration of post-communist eastern Europe, Russia and central Asia by looking strictly inward, enforcing a policy of extreme

---

[1] 'Vers la monnaie unique', *Commentaire*, vol. 19, no. 74, p. 279; author's translation.

monetary stringency that ruled out any act of far-sighted generosity, let alone anything resembling a Marshall Plan.

With the economies of Western Europe stalled by a chronic insufficiency of demand, with Russians lacking everything except for nuclear weapons, from surgical instruments in hospitals to room heaters in their homes, and with many eastern Europeans almost as badly off, generous printings of euros sent eastwards would immediately return to employ millions in Western Europe, relaunching investment and growth, and engendering bright new hopes in its despondent youth, as well as some inflation no doubt. All it would take is for the European Central Bank to be governed by a board of industrialists and trade unionists, with no central bankers allowed on the premises, and headed by an accountant charged only with keeping inflation at bay by stopping the euro printing presses now and then. As it is, of course, any real help for the other Europeans is ruled out.

Turbo-capitalism is not caused by deflation; its accelerated, societally disruptive structural change in jobs, firms, industries and localities has been brought about by government deregulation and privatization, by a peculiar phase of technological progress, and to a slight degree by globalization. Turbo-charged capitalism merely happens to coincide with the present third-phase deflation in the demand/technology cycle. To change the cycle itself would involve much more interference with world commerce, and much more inefficiency, than replacing orthodox monetarism with full employment, while tolerating the resulting inflation and relying on taxes to negate its inequities. Nowadays, the economics of Democrats or Republicans, Tories or Labour, center-right and center-left everywhere are interchangeable for most purposes; they are all different labels for orthodox monetarism when it comes to employment policies. That suits the Right very well; but no left-wing party, however moderate, should be content to emulate the Right in monetary policy.

TWELVE

Shopping as Therapy

Turbo-capitalism is not only a process, but for many a prescription for success. The United States has the most turbo-capitalist of economies. Is it also the most successful? 1998 was certainly a glorious boom year for the American economy by all accounts. Unemployment and inflation were both as low as they had been in decades, growth was vigorous. Amidst the celebrations, no great fuss was made over the record trade deficit or indeed about the overall deficit in the balance of payments that includes royalties, dividends, tourism accounts and indeed all money flows. That deficit was easily funded because other countries are glad to accept US dollars for their foreign-currency reserves. The additional borrowing of 1998 merely increased the total indebtedness of the American economy to the rest of the world. So long as other countries are willing to accept paper overprinted by the US Treasury in exchange for goods and services, the deficits can continue to accumulate. Of course interest must be paid on the debt, but that too is easily funded with yet more dollars, so that the world's richest economy can continue to be the most indebted by far, with its net debt steadily increasing towards the mythic level of one million million dollars.

This borrowing and debt naturally reflected what was happening within the domestic economy. During 1998, consumption as well as investment spending were also at record levels. Household incomes were rising, but spending was rising even faster, so that total household debt was also increasing. Rising incomes can of course sustain increasing debt, but for a growing number of American households evidently that was not enough: credit-card default rates and personal bankruptcies were also at record levels in 1998. The paradox of increasing insolvency in a booming economy requires explanation. In part, it is simply a matter of highly skewed income distribution: prosperity is so unevenly divided in turbo-capitalist times that more than half of American households did not share in its increase. There was no paradox for them. That, however, still leaves a great deal to be explained. Why do Americans spend so much, and why do those who have less to spend nevertheless go ahead and spend their way into debt and bankruptcy?

Americans protest their love of individual freedom, with much historical justification. Yet they enslave themselves to the Demon Debt to accumulate all sorts of far-from-essentials, from large powerful trucks used as mere cars, down to porcelain baubles advertized on late-night television ('valuable instant heirlooms for only five easy payments of $19.99'). To pay for their buying habit, Americans work more hours during each year than any other advanced population on earth except for the Japanese, and when it comes to vacations even the Japanese manage 25 days per year as against the 23 that Americans average, a miserable portion of free time as compared to the 42 days of the Germans and the 38 that the French find insufficient. True, some people obtain so much satisfaction from their jobs that they live to work. But many of those who work only for money are nevertheless eager to accept overtime and even seek second jobs, sacrificing their personal freedom and family life to consume more. In fact, many Americans do not choose to work in order to buy – they *must* work to pay the interest and repay the principal on what they have already bought.

Frugal East Asians save as much as 40 per cent of their personal income in hard-striving China, and one-third of far larger incomes in Japan. Prudent continental Europeans save roughly one-fifth. (Significantly, the turbo-capitalist British now save only one-tenth of their income.) Americans save very little, and less and less – lately not quite one-twentieth of their personal income. Even that phenomenally low proportion is an average heavily skewed by the large savings of the top slice of highest-earning households. Most Americans save less than nothing, borrowing with abandon from all possible sources, from credit-card issuers at very high interest, from home-equity lenders at the risk of losing their dwellings, from banks and credit unions up to their credit limits – from mortgage lenders for the largest sums down to pawn shops for the smallest.

Americans scarcely invented debt, but three things are unique about their present indebtedness. First, there is its sheer size, which keeps increasing: by mid-1998 the total debt of all American households reached the unprecedented level of 89 per cent of total household income. It is no coincidence that the foreign debt of the United States is now by far the largest ever recorded for any country at any time in history, for domestic savings are so small as compared to both household and government debt. By contrast, Italy's notoriously huge government debt, some 120 per cent of the country's gross national product, is offset by equally large domestic savings, so that Italy is actually a net lender to the rest of the world.

Second, American debt has little to do with poverty, the traditional cause of personal and family debt. The poorest 20 per cent of American households owe very little to anyone, for nobody except petty money-lenders with sturdy enforcers allows such borrowers any credit. The recent increase in 'sub-prime lending', which carries especially high interest rates and is much used in the selling of used automobiles, largely reflects the borrowing of the next-to-poorest 20 per cent of American households – which are far from poor by any historic or international standards. Most American borrowers are not poor at all, or rather they would not be poor but for their borrowing.

The third unique feature of American indebtedness is the particular use made of the immense amounts borrowed. Indian peasants go into debt to feed their families when the monsoon fails, and to wed their daughters; young couples all over the world borrow to buy their first household necessities. A large portion of American household debt likewise consists of home mortgages and college loans, but much of it reflects the purchase of expensive motor vehicles, designer clothing, signature watches, assorted recreation gadgets and all manner of other things that are scarcely necessities of life by anyone's definition. To borrow at 18 per cent or more on a credit card to purchase a fancy bit of clothing is a commonplace of American life; to exhaust the equity limit in a second mortgage to buy a luxury car, leaving no margin of safety from dispossession, is by no means unusual – even Mercedes and BMW dealers encounter few cash buyers.

Fearing the ultimate consequences of savings so small and spending so great that the US foreign debt is approaching $1 trillion, even rigorously value-free academic economists have lately begun to insert *sotto voce* pleas for a bit of frugality. Others more boldly ask for a restoration of all forms of Calvinist restraint. Anti-pornography, anti-

smoking, anti-fat, anti-beach nudity, anti-suga
and anti-alcohol campaigns are vigorously
prison terms, longer prison terms, mandato
of new death penalty statutes, accelerated
prison conditions and even a return of
how the economic insecurities of today's t
expressed.

But one form of Calvinist restraint has ɪ
wall of conventional opinion loudly supports ᴀ
but not even a fringe group has tried to condemn the borrow ᴀ
buy habit that is by far the greatest American addiction. Thus the
most important of all the original Calvinist virtues – saving, capital
accumulation and investment in lieu of consumption – is the only
one that remains forgotten. The proclivities of the professional evangelists who lead many of the 'anti' campaigns are no doubt a factor –
people so eager to buy beach apartments, jewelry and the costliest
cars with the contributions of their devotees are justifiably hesitant to
deplore any form of materialism. Another factor is the deeply American conjunction between moralism and greed, a perverted rendition
of the original Calvinist belief that virtue is rewarded by wealth.

A Cure for Solitude

In fairness to materialistic evangelists and moralists, it must be
recognized that their failure to include the consumer addiction in
their sweeping condemnations of every other form of self-indulgence
has a sound justification. For there is nothing frivolous about the
buying habit. It may still be self-indulgence, but its motives derive
from the most profound of human needs. *Homo Americanus* is genetically
programmed to need the emotional support of a complete family just
as much as *Homo sapiens* in Norway or Italy. But nowadays he usually
finds himself living in a state of emotional solitude to which the
human species has not yet adapted.

In normal human societies, in which extended-family ties are
naturally preserved by geographic proximity from birth till death, or
actively sustained by those who depart to live elsewhere, the annual
calendar is a sequence of birth celebrations, religious or voluptuary
festivals, marriages, anniversaries and funerals, all of which also serve
as clan re-unions. With much hugging and kissing of the very young,
and the tacit pledging of mutual aid and comfort among the less

ily ties are maintained, repaired and strengthened, to
hat uncles and aunts are multiple parents at one remove,
the cousinage of their children is an assemblage of siblings at
remove, that grand-uncles and grand-aunts are supplementary
andparents, and that even second cousins still function as blood
relatives in working order – from all of whom material aid and
emotional support are expected, received and reciprocated.

As against this normal human behavior, most Americans are
emotional destitutes, as poor in their family connections as Afghans
or Sudanese are in money. Many Americans still marry, of course,
but with marriages now fragile even if unbroken, they supply much
anxiety as well as support, failing to serve as even fragmentary
replacements for an entire family in working order. American parents
have their children, of course, but to hug is not the same thing as to
be hugged and, besides, the same ambient conditions that otherwise
leave parents in solitude induce children to live apart from them –
indeed, the youth living at home beyond his teens is considered not
a caring child but a problem, even an embarrassment.

True, this predicament is probably only temporary. In another
20,000 years or so, *Homo sapiens* may well adapt to the present
condition of most American lives. In the meantime, with much
ingenuity, the vast majority of affected Americans have found diverse
ways of evading the suicidal aggression or deadly melancholy of
isolated hyenas and baboons. Having fully participated in the abandonment of family ties by way of missed christenings, weddings or
funerals for ball-game or fishing or golf, by way of departures to
distant places even for fractional economic advancement, by way of
theme-park or resort vacations in lieu of a round of familial visits, by
way of telephone calls unmade, letters unwritten and gifts ungiven,
many Americans find a substitute that may be only processed cheese
rather than Brie or Stilton, but which certainly has the sovereign
American virtue of immediate availability.

Emotional Fast Food

The emotional equivalent of fast food for lives otherwise deprived of
affect is supplied by the chapels, temples, ashrams, sanctuaries and
covens of pseudo-evangelical, New Age, pseudo-Hindu, pseudo-
Christian, pseudo-Buddhist, pseudo-Muslim, catacumenical-catholic,
pseudo-scientific, pseudo-political and many other cults. The United

States is filled with them. Each offers its modestly or expansively charismatic imitation of a father who instructs his children with some admixture of severity and paternal love. Each strives to provide an imitation family, often with much encouragement of hugging, kissing or at least hand holding by the devotees in attendance, though some cults go in for the severe style, stressing the strict obedience of exacting rules, and a few offer only ideological intensity. Most of the cults specifically promote themselves as fostering reciprocal caring, even love, in contrast to the focus of established religions on obedience to a god. Almost all emphasize the emotional warmth of their assemblies, as opposed to the cold ceremonials of established churches.

The combined revenues of today's roster of American cults probably exceed those of the computer industry – some reach $300 million a year, many are in the tens of millions. Going by the only criterion that matters to most of their leader/owners, the cults are certainly a great success. But they are also cost-effective for their devotees in many cases. Money aside – though some cults do demand a great deal of it – the only cost is to the intellect, whose critical faculties must be willfully suspended in order to believe implausible and sometimes exceedingly bizarre doctrines. This sacrifice, however, usually amounts to very much less in terms of time, attention and even money than the years of hugging, kissing, telephoning, writing, giving, travelling, visiting, listening, waiting and attending the sick that the upkeep of natural families requires. Instead of all that, most cultists need only drive a short way to their chosen franchise or corporate headquarters, park their car and plug into a simulated instant family, complete with earnest expressions of loving concern from fellow devotees.

So much success in attracting the lonely crowd could not be ignored by the established churches. Many have reacted as smart competitors always will. They too now favor hand holdings and huggings, with a more or less subtle shift in emphasis from the delivery of obedience and love to the deity, to the supply of love to the congregants themselves, from each other as well as from the deity conscripted to the task. Emotional fast food can now be had from millennial or at least secular churches as well as from a myriad of cults much less antique than IBM.

Other Americans cope in more perilous ways by substituting the private universe of habitual, frequent or occasional alcoholic or narcotic stupefaction for the missing emotional security of a supportive clan. This replacement, too, is mostly successful, contrary to legend.

Emotionally isolated Americans drink, inhale or inject, while effectively pursuing their careers and maintaining their fragment of a nuclear-only family. As for the monetary cost, it is often trivial. Even the fanciest illegal substances hardly make a dent in the budget of many users, some of whom are multi-millionaires, many more of whom are merely affluent. The ruined drug addict on his way to a penniless death in a sordid alley is mostly myth: if it were not so, if the customer base truly consisted of derelicts and the unemployable as well as petty criminals, Colombian drug lords would have to be content with tenements and bicycles instead of palatial mansions and executive jets.

The trouble with cults and psycho-active chemicals is that both provide only intermittent relief from the chronic emotional deficit of a clan species in unnatural solitude. Besides, many Americans refuse both options for reasons of temperament, intellect or prudence. Not all chemical remedies, however, are disruptive or illegal. According to the latest obesity statistics, one-half of all Americans find their emotional fast food *in* fast food, or rather all foods – fast, slow, instant snack or sweet non-foods. Americans are collectively envied in much of the world for their political, economic and military successes, but their silhouettes alone show that many of them (glandular cases excepted) consider themselves to be hopeless failures.

And, of course, there is work and its satisfactions, which can certainly overcome almost any emotional deficit, or even recycle it into an added reason to do more work. Conventionally viewed with more approval than cults, chemicals or overfeeding, work is a peculiar remedy for family ties in disrepair, because it is itself the greatest destroyer of family ties. That does not make it any less effective as a substitute – but only for the minority whose work is persistently exciting, or deeply purposeful, from racing-car drivers to scientists gripped by their research, from tycoons on a roll to genuinely devoted hospice nurses. Play, too, can be a remedy: the lonely can go bowling, even if alone.[1]

Each remedy is effective up to a point, but the most common and important of remedies is morale boosting by a constant stream of presents. It is always very nice to receive presents, but the presents in question are not *gifts*. They are not given by others. Americans instead buy presents for themselves, in shops and department stores, by responding to advertizing, mass-mailed catalogs and direct-mail and

---

[1] Robert Putnam, 'Bowling alone', *Journal of Democracy*, vol. 6, no. 1 (1995), pp. 65–78.

telephone solicitations, by calling to order objects displayed on television shopping programs and lately on-line through the Internet, on a colossal, multi-trillion-dollar scale. One shopper, interviewed by a *Wall Street Journal* reporter for an article on marketing trends,[2] had bought thirteen Christmas presents: two for her boyfriend, eleven for herself. 'I deserve them all' was her comment.

Because such an extraordinary proportion of what is bought by Americans consists of presents, including some gifts to others, the essential character of the consumer goods on offer has become steadily less functional. Much of what Americans buy nowadays amounts to baroque elaborations in which the original functional purposes are submerged by excesses, fripperies, frills or simply overdesign. There are entire categories of once practical products, from baggage to writing implements, that now appear in the guise of 'executive toys'. Any puritanical outrage at other people's enjoyment of fancy goods is really beside the point: the peculiar preferences of American buyers have enormous economic consequences, because they cripple US exports of consumer goods. Buyers around the world who are not in need of boosting their morale refuse to buy 'gift' versions of the objects they seek. Most notably, the US automobile industry nowadays produces very few unadorned vehicles meant to provide a means of transportation. Instead it turns out heavyweight luxury passenger 'trucks', enormous 'family vans', coupés of deliberately reduced functionality (they cost more for less room), convertibles and sports cars, as well as a mass of super-lavish and intermediate-lavish sedans.

Shopping and the Trade Balance

Great fun is had by all, but foreign car-buyers reject the results for reasons of fuel economy, plain economy, environmental economy or just good taste. The result is manifest in US trade figures. Instead of contributing to a favorable trade balance, the automobile industry, by far the largest of all US manufacturing industries, is so weak an exporter that the sector accounts for the single biggest item in persistent US trade deficits. Between January and July 1997 the United States imported motor vehicles for a total of $65.3 billion as opposed to $31.8 billion of exports, resulting in a deficit of $33.5

[2] Cynthia Crossen, ' "Merry Christmas to moi" shoppers say', *Wall Street Journal*, 11 December 1997, p. B1.

billion, almost one-third of the overall trade deficit of $108.4 billion during that period.

The same is true of other categories of consumer goods; so much so that the United States is now primarily an exporter of capital equipment – notably, passenger aircraft, precision machinery and power-generation equipment – as well as chemicals. All these are sectors uncontaminated by the baroque propensities of American consumers out to buy presents for themselves.

The larger economic picture reveals larger consequences. In the booming US economy of 1996, whose gross domestic product reached $6.9 trillion, personal consumption expenditures for goods and increasingly for services reached the level of $4,700 billion – at 68 per cent, an extraordinarily high proportion by world standards. The consumption of some services is, of course, entirely involuntary, as in the case of emergency, chronic and terminal medical care, as well as the legal services that all too many Americans must have to defend themselves against lawsuits. None of these expenditures reflects a hidden emotional agenda. At the opposite extreme, however, there are highly personal services that are largely bought as self-given presents (hair care, massage, manicure, etc.). In between these two limiting cases, there are two interesting categories of consumption expenditures: services for the elderly, and tourist travel.

Americans are spending more and more on old-people's homes, 'assisted-living' residences and similar euphemistic variants. Conventionally, the increasing consumption of such services is readily explained as a straightforward demographic phenomenon. That it is, but greatly modified by the consequences of family breakdown – except that the families in question consider themselves to be perfectly normal and unbroken, even admirable models of family life. Matters have evolved so far that the phrase 'family breakdown' invariably refers to underclass non-families, wherein women without husbands are left to care for children and grandchildren, with public assistance sparingly given, and lately often denied. On the other hand, affluent couples who live in spacious suburban homes and yet consign their own parents to the care of strangers are nevertheless considered 'unbroken'. The fact that many elderly parents may actually prefer to live apart from their children, and out of reach of their grandchildren except for more or less occasional visits, indicates nothing except the degree to which family breakdown has been internalized as normal. One of the perversities of national accounting, incidentally, is that the US gross national product is all the greater for the fact that the care of the elderly devolves into commercial transactions that generate recorded sales; in contrast, the gross national product of Spain, for example, is diminished because grandparents live with their children and grandchildren, generating no numbers that statisticians can collect, but providing the firmest possible basis for the emotional security of all involved.

As for tourist travel expenditures, Americans are notably modest as compared to Europeans, who in addition to a great deal of family visiting are far more inclined to travel to exotic destinations at any given level of disposable income. This is an interesting exception because tourist travel is rarely individual; it is most unusual for couples not to travel together, with or without children. One consequence is that this category of expenditure does not afford much opportunity for self-given presents, meant to assuage feelings of emotional solitude.

In any case, what is squeezed out by so much personal consumption of goods and services is government expenditure and investment (at $1.2 trillion in 1996) and private investment (at $1 trillion in 1996, which was actually a boom year). This is in spite of the modest but useful contribution of the outside world by way of a $144 billion trade deficit in goods and services, which was on credit of course, so that during 1996 the United States once again added to its total foreign debt by overconsuming.

The low level of government expenditure and investment yields the paradox of a very rich country with poor Federal, State and local authorities, which cannot afford to provide health care to every citizen, as every other developed country is doing in one way or another, or to assist the poor as they are assisted in every other affluent country. As for the low level of private investment, it at least contributes to the much-debated and much-deplored lag in labor 'productivity' – the very slow (1 per cent per annum) rate of increase in the total product obtainable from given amounts of labor.

The great claim that is made for the 'flexibility' of Americans and hence of the US labor market – the willingness of Americans to move from place to place, to change their trade or even profession, and to accept lower wages to keep working – is, of course, its economic efficiency. Nobody pretends that the personal and social consequences of so much mobility and adaptability are positively desirable in themselves.

However, once the chain of repercussions is followed step by step from an economic system that achieves efficiency by imposing constant structural change, to the fragmentation of family life that is thereby caused, to the resulting psychological consequences, to the consumption habits they induce, and then to the impact of those habits on the economic system by way of low savings and baroque consumer preferences, it may be concluded that a more rigid but more stable economy could be even more efficient. Labor costs would be higher, but so would savings rates because less mobile, more secure employees would be that much more likely to plan ahead and to sustain reassuring family ties, reducing emotionally motivated consumption expenditures. Higher savings rates would increase the supply of capital, which would in turn increase the productivity of labor, offsetting higher labor costs.

At a time when the dynamic turbo-capitalism of today's deregulated, globalized US economy is so greatly celebrated, it is instructive to recall that until the late 1970s the US economy *was* more rigid and much more stable, because a great many industries, from airlines and natural gas to Savings and Loan associations were subject to detailed regulation and thus stabilized, as was their labor force. Consumption spending absorbed a lower proportion of incomes, so that savings rates were higher. Growth, too, was higher, in spite of all the inefficiencies of regulation. There were fewer opportunities for financial acrobats to accumulate enormous wealth, but most employees were relatively well paid and economically secure, because stable industries meant stable jobs. Judging by the lower voluptuary spending of the period, Americans may also have been happier.

THIRTEEN

The Great Dilemma

In Venice, Italy, tourism is booming as never before now that eastern Europeans too can visit, but young Venetians setting out to earn a living in that most romantic of cities encounter almost insurmountable obstacles. The motor boats that serve as taxis yield very good incomes, but each requires a license issued by the municipality, which has not issued any new licenses in years. The only way to get one is to buy it from a current holder, for the going price of roughly $300,000. Almost every adult Venetian is a skilled oarsman, and many could handle a gondola and even do a bit of the required singing; but *gondolieri* too must have a license, which now costs more than $200,000.

Tourists buy millions of postcards and great quantities of souvenirs, from elaborate creations in hand-blown Murano glass to small plastic frogs. But a young person cannot just rent a space and start off with a stock of postcards and frogs hoping to build up his business, because every shop must have a license, which might cost half a million dollars, if it can be had at all. Pharmacies have their own separate licensing system, and because they sell costly drugs to an ageing population much given to medication, their licenses can cost a million dollars or more even in impoverished small towns, let alone Venice. Postcards and frogs can also be sold to the passing crowds from street stands, but for that too a license is needed. Last issued long ago, they are now passed from father to son as the family treasures they are.

Amazingly, in Venice as all over Italy, a specific and extremely restricted license is needed even to sell newspapers and magazines; they are not to be found in the many convenience stores, supermarkets and corner groceries, only in a few booths and fewer shops that sell only newspapers, magazines and perhaps pornographic videotapes. This not only deprives young Venetians and all young Italians of an easy-entry starter business; it also affects the nation's literacy by crippling the distribution of newspapers, whose circulation is very low compared to the size of the population and its standard of living.

Young people in the United States can get by as part-time waiters while awaiting some better opportunity, counting on tips to make up for small wages or none. But in Italy, where a strong trade union ensures rather good wages and generous benefits for all waiters, there are severe restrictions on the employment of part-time workers, and tips-only jobs are strictly illegal. Hence the cafés and restaurants of Venice, each of which has to have its own license, cannot offer transitional youth jobs, and must count on their patrons' patience at peak times. That leaves only the hotel trade for Venetian job-seekers who lack professional qualifications. But because hotel licenses are also severely restricted, the huge expansion of tourism of recent years has led to sharply increased room rates, rather than the conversion of more vacant palaces into hotels – again denying many potential jobs to young Venetians.

All would be different under turbo-capitalism in the American style, with competition unrestricted by laws, regulations, costly licenses, trade-union rates or local traditions. The number of taxi-boats, gondolas, shops, street stalls, cafés, restaurants and hotels would greatly increase, allowing that proliferation of service jobs that is so typical of economies undergoing turbo-capitalist change, and the key to their lower unemployment rates. Young Venetians entering the labor force would find many more job openings, while others would be free to create their own jobs and a few more besides, by starting new ventures in trades no longer restricted, from street stalls to hotels. For both job-seeking youngsters and entrepreneurs of all ages, the arrival of turbo-capitalism in Venice would amount to a liberating revolution.

Tourists would also benefit immensely. With more taxi-boats, gondolas, shops, street stalls, cafés, restaurants and hotels to choose from, there would be more competition. With that, Venice's notoriously high prices would fall, perhaps sharply. But total tourism revenues would almost certainly increase considerably, because the many tourists who now flee back to the cheaper mainland after a day trip would be more likely to stay overnight, or for more nights (what that would do to a city already sinking under the weight of mass tourism is another matter). That too is typical of turbo-capitalist change in everything from airlines to telephone services: deregulation unleashes competition, which lowers prices, which increases demand, which expands total sales to levels much higher than before. All this is to the great benefit of consumers, who desire to consume more cheaply and to consume more and more. But only retired consumers are not producers as well. And for the consumer who is also a producer, the same process amounts to running faster merely to stay in the same place.

For revolutions are not all gain. For the privileged of the *ancien régime* they can be all loss, even if they are not aristocrats but merely modest middle-class people in the service trades. The owner-operators of the existing taxi-boats, gondolas, shops, stalls, cafés, restaurants and hotels, all of them now shielded from competition by licensing barriers, would see their earnings decline just as sharply – unless they were willing and able to offset lower prices by selling more, by working longer hours at their boats, stalls, cafés and so forth.

Not only owners would lose out, but employees too in most cases. With union wage rates abolished and all entry restrictions removed, the labor market would also be opened up to competition – so that employers, forced to cut costs to match new competitors, would find cheaper labor to do it with, in part by hiring part-timers and seasonal workers in place of career employees. That is what happened in the entire American economy once it was deregulated, leading to the enormous expansion of the manpower outfits that provide temporary employees of every sort, from fully qualified accountants to cleaning staff. In Venice the shift away from stable career employment would be even more pronounced, because the tourism industry is more seasonal than most, and both the eating and lodging trades can be run most efficiently with part-timers around a core of skilled full-time employees.

For employees who have no special skills, who cannot climb the economic ladder by moving right out of the Venice tourist trades (Treviso, twenty miles away, the home of Benetton and hundreds of successful export firms, offers many opportunities), the final outcome is likely to be a pattern of stagnant or declining wage rates. Yet their total family income could still increase in turbo-capitalist conditions, because there would be more jobs for themselves, their spouses and their children of working age, more opportunities for second jobs, and for overtime. This is the trade-off that many Americans have had to accept since the 1970s: more money earned by working more hours for lower hourly rates – at the expense of family life, of course.

As of the end of 1997, the overall impact of turbo-capitalism on wage rates, hours worked and unemployment emerges very clearly in the following comparison, specifically of so-called 'production workers' in manufacturing, but in fact indicative of a broader trend that applies to the lower half of the entire labor force in every economic sector, from highly skilled industrial workers to part-time shop assistants:

Hours worked, wages and unemployment, 1997

| | ← Least turbo-capitalist | | | Most turbo-capitalist → | |
	France	Germany	Italy	UK	USA
Average weekly hours worked	31.7	29.0	35.0	35.6	37.9
Average total earnings/hour ($)	19.34	31.87	18.08	14.19	17.74
National rate of unemployment (%)	13	12	12	5	4.9

Source: US Department of Labor, Bureau of Labor Statistics; DRI/McGraw-Hill, cited in *The International Herald Tribune* (Tokyo edition), 13 November 1997, p. 5.

In the greatly admired, long-booming American economy, in which four million people can now call themselves millionaires, and no fewer than 170 people have net worths in excess of $1,000 million, sixty million or so rank-and-file employees have not done so well, as we have seen: in real dollars net of inflation, their hourly earnings were actually higher in the early 1970s, when the United States still had a heavily regulated economy. And more than seventeen million, fully employed 40 hours per week, 50 weeks a year, remain below the poverty line.

This is only a correlation, of course, not proof of a cause-and-effect connection between the enrichment of some and the impoverishment of many. It might, therefore, be a mere coincidence that masks a very different cause for what has happened, or several of them. Globalization cannot be the main reason why hourly wages have declined, because foreign trade does not account for enough of all that goes on in advanced economies, with their large public sectors and their preponderance of services not much exposed to foreign low-wage competition.

Free-market enthusiasts, unwilling to believe that deregulation may not be all peaches and cream, offer an alternative explanation: the accidental course of technological innovation did it, they say, by offering computers this time around, and so many new ways of automating the work of mere humans. This nicely transfers responsibility from themselves to 'technology', depicted as a transcendental force beyond all human control – even though new technologies *never* just happen, their introduction always depends on a receptive environment. In this instance, it was the very human politics of deregulation that opened the way for many innovations, in the telecommunications industry for example, once everywhere a state or regulated monopoly, now almost everywhere private, increasingly competitive and of course increasingly unstable.

Dynamism and Insecurity

There is one result of turbo-capitalism that cannot be blamed on anything else: the greater instability of firms and of jobs in a far more fluid economy, even in times of great prosperity, such instability being caused by the accelerated structural change that deregulation allows, technological change promotes and globalization favors. Every day of the week, corporations large and small merge to achieve economies of scale and eliminate duplication – headquarters staffs are 'consolidated', geographically overlapping bank branches or retail outlets are closed, and excess capacity in combined production plant, warehouses and distribution chains is eliminated. All this increases efficiency and wealth. But we have no measure for how people *feel* when they might lose their current jobs at any time, even though there may be more jobs to be had overall. And, indeed, it is obvious that personal economic insecurity is the other side of the coin of turbo-capitalist opportunity. While most young Venetians would benefit from a turbo-capitalist revolution, their parents would lose their own economic security, now solidly protected by a myriad barriers to competition in all its forms.

Shopkeepers would face a special problem. At present, opening hours are severely restricted in Venice, as they are in much of Western Europe, with a compulsory lunch-time closure for all shops from 1 p.m. to 3 p.m. at least, Saturday closure by 4 p.m., a further half-day off during the week, no Sunday opening hours at all, and weekday-evening opening hours restricted to 8 p.m. at the latest. This is very inconvenient for shoppers who themselves work – in Germany the limit was only extended to 8 p.m. in 1996; it had been 6.30 p.m. But these laws which perpetuate medieval guild rules do allow married couples to own and operate shops while still leading a normal family life, and effectively protect small shops from the competition of supermarkets and chain stores, which cannot function efficiently with only sixty selling hours per week.

On top of that, supermarkets and department stores of any kind require special licenses in several European countries including Germany, rarely granted in large cities and not at all in most smaller places – specifically to prevent the kind of destruction that has been visited on hundreds of American market towns by a single, gigantic chain of all-purpose discount stores, Wal-Mart, whose phenomenally low prices are the joy of consumers, the doom of traditional shop-keepers. Under turbo-capitalist rules, all such restrictions would be abolished, allowing large-scale retailers to serve customers more cheaply at all hours, driving traditional family-run shops right out of business. In the United States, the only small shops that survive, in city or country, aside from specialty boutiques and eating establishments, are the so-called 'convenience' retailers that mostly belong to the 7–11 or other giant chains, and are staffed by low-paid employees on shift work.

In due course, professionally managed corporations with much more capital and lower costs all round would take over most of the Venetian trades, not just shopkeeping. A few large taxi-boat and gondola outfits would replace today's owner-operated boats, chains would displace many family-run cafés and restaurants, and as in tourist destinations all over the world, multinational corporations would take over most of the hotels, not just the five-star category they already own.

Naturally, income distribution would also change, inevitably becoming more unequal as in the United States, where the 5 per cent of all families at the top of the pyramid have relentlessly increased their share of total family income, from some 15–16 per cent in the 1970s, to 17–18 per cent in the early 1980s, to 21.4 per cent by 1996, a most spectacular shift that leaves the top-earning five million families with just about as much income as the bottom fifty million families.[1]

---

[1] US Bureau of the Census, *Share of Aggregate Income Received by Each Fifth and Top 5% of Families: Processed* (1996: 101 million families by Census definition).

In Venice too, turbo-capitalist change would allow entrepreneurial acrobats to accumulate spectacular fortunes, while the top managers of the new breed of large-scale firms would be at least well paid. At the same time, the present middle class of independent owner-operators and shopkeepers would be forced to work for other people for whatever they could get, while most of today's unionized employees would also see their earnings decline – though there would be more jobs for those of them who are now unemployed.

Venetian society would also change in all sorts of ways. Young people would be much less dependent on their parents, better able to make their own way with all the new opportunities to work and to start new businesses. The many youngsters now forced to live at home into their late twenties and beyond for strictly monetary reasons would have the means to move out and live on their own, perhaps marrying and starting their families at a younger age than now – thus increasing the birth rate, which is now just about the lowest in the world. In a Venice less stultified by entrenched interests at every turn, no longer dominated by those already in possession of licenses and secure jobs, much less resistant to change in all its forms, the overall balance of power between young and old would shift in favor of the former, increasing the sheer vitality of its now very staid society.

Less pleasantly, the social distance between employers and employees would greatly increase, sometimes to intercontinental proportions when the new employers are multinational corporations. Even in firms remaining under Venetian ownership, purely contractual arm's-length arrangements would replace the familial relationships between employers and employees that now prevail, which now range all the way from warm amity and a deep sense of mutual responsibility to a resentful sense of dependence. In this, of course, the Venetian tourist trades would be undergoing most belatedly a transformation that started almost two centuries ago elsewhere in Western Europe, when familial artisan workshops gave way to factories. Now an impossible trauma for many employers, legally very difficult if not outright impossible, and costly in the extreme because of high severance payments, the abrupt firing of long-serving employees to cut costs would become mere routine, as in the States. So would the hiring of new career employees, of course, now greatly inhibited by the very same retrictive obligations that safeguard those already in possession of a job.

Most fortunately for Venice, it lacks a native stigmatized underclass, the accumulated result of job deprivation that leads to family disintegration, which in turn leads to the breeding of non-educable, non-employable youths ready for the streets, drugs, guns and the criminal academies of juvenile detention. Hence the greater social distancing that comes with turbo-capitalism could not reach American dimensions – or British ones for that matter – so that there would be no need to start building prisons to warehouse underclass men and youths, who are deemed less worthy of society's consideration than the trees of the Amazon or Africa's endangered species.

A turbo-capitalist revolution would thus do far more than bring the efficiency of free markets to Venice. As befits a true revolution, sweeping changes would reshape Venetian life, with more economic opportunity, more economic insecurity, more money, and a wider gap between rich and poor. Given the choice, how many Venetians would prefer all that to today's Venice, for all its stultified conservatism? True, if there were a choice at all, it would be biased in the extreme by the age-composition of the present population, the combined result of Italy's extraordinarily low birth rate and extraordinarily long life expectancy, in both of which Venice exceeds the national averages. The preponderant mass of the old might thus selfishly choose to deny a widening of economic opportunities to the young, their own children and grandchildren. But of course there is no choice, there is only the tidal wave of turbo-capitalism, now only feebly resisted in the absence of any plausible alternative vision of how economies might be run.

What is true of Venice is true of the entire world, only more so. For there are many countries, including Italy itself, where publicly owned industries and services are still in the process of being sold off to private owners, where turbo-capitalism is advancing on a national scale. And globally, countless barriers to international commerce are still being removed, allowing a yet broader advance. Everywhere the logic of turbo-capitalism is that nothing should stand in the way of economic efficiency, neither obstructive government regulations nor traditional habits, neither entrenched interests nor feelings of solidarity for the less fortunate, neither arbitrary privileges nor the normal human desire for stability. For nothing must hinder competition, which alone enforces efficiency by impoverishing less efficient individuals, firms, industries, localities or countries – and sometimes all of them at once.

Some of the results can be seen with the naked eye. In American cities, the urban landscape is constantly changing, as old buildings are demolished to make room for more efficient uses of their sites, as failing offices and shops are replaced by successful newcomers, as restaurants and cafés come and go. With none of the restrictive licensing still widespread in Europe and Japan, which protects old commerce by suppressing the new, with construction permits easily granted, few public institutions exempt from market forces and hardly any buildings protected by architectural preservation orders, American cities very readily adapt to shifting economic pressures, both large and very small. Overall this makes them much more efficient as places of work and business than European cities – and much less of a home for their inhabitants. Turbo-capitalism leaves no room for emotional attachments to old buildings, old bookshops, old neighbourhood venues, or anything else for that matter. Not surprisingly, Americans are greatly attracted to such places as Paris, Rome and Kyoto, so much less adaptable and efficient than New York, Chicago or Los Angeles, so much more hospitable to human life. Parisians, Romans or even Kyoto's famously traditionalist citizens hardly lead lives of unexamined tranquillity, but among them one constantly feels that their strong sense of belonging to their cities leaves their happiness far less dependent on the size of their disposable income.

Under turbo-capitalist rules, individuals must also adapt to constant change or suffer the consequences. Ideally, they should re-examine their options twice a day, to decide whether to remain in the same trade, profession or job, or promptly switch to whatever alternative offers higher rewards, perhaps in a different locality, country or continent. So much turbulence may seem a fantastical departure from normal human proclivities. But for the employees of Wall Street investment banks, at the very heart of turbo-capitalist change, utterly unstable professional lives are already a prosaic reality. They 'network', as they call it, on an almost daily basis to find better jobs, with no misplaced sense of loyalty to their current employers, who are in turn constantly re-evaluating the cost/benefit ratios of their continued employment. Wall Street investment banks pay phenomenally well, with million-dollar salaries very common for middling executives in their forties – and even lowly clericals are paid well enough to sustain the world's richest cocaine market. But they offer no secure jobs to anyone, no venues for life-long careers, no reassuring sense of mutual obligation. It is employment in its purest form that they offer, reduced to its strictly mercenary essence, offering no satisfactions except for money.

The Destruction of Authenticity

The human consequences of turbo-capitalism are both liberating and profoundly disorienting. The loss of individual authenticity that Friedrich Nietzsche predicted is now upon us in full force. It starts with the unconscious absorption of meretricious language – from the 'Thank you for flying ... airlines' to the now almost customary 'I love you all' of public speech – and ends with outright depersonalization, the loss of one's own genuine humanity. Having lied all day at the office in order to sell goods, services or oneself, the lying continues after hours to 'network' more effectively at social gatherings in search of business, then persists even at home by sheer habit, until finally reaching the point of lying to oneself.

This process of depersonalization is visibly complete in the modern television politician, who speaks of his most intimate sorrows on the public stage in order to claim that he, too, has genuine feelings – feelings which would impose a total silence upon him if actually felt. Instead of authentic emotions, such politicians offer theatrical simulations – but in all sincerity, for that is all they have. The much-noted confluence of politics with mass entertainment is certainly a feature of our turbo-capitalist times, symbolized, it is said, by the advent of Ronald Reagan, a professional actor, as President of the United States – undoubtedly his best role. But this symbolic example is misleading, for the theatrical performances of professional politicians are far more common than the successful entry of professional actors into politics.

It is true, of course, that leaders courting public support have always tried to illustrate their statesmanship with as much theatrical skill as they could muster – from ancient times rhetoric was declaimed, not merely spoken. Yet there is a fundamental difference between the acting of a Lincoln or Churchill and that of Tony Blair or Bill Clinton. The former expressed their leadership by gesture and words as well as by deeds. The latter emote in public as a *substitute* for what they cannot accomplish. Clinton outmaneuvers a budget-cutting Congress by proffering his own welfare cuts, all the while warmly empathizing with the poor, actively seeking occasions to hug and palpate them by visiting public-housing projects and inner-city schools. Blair likewise perpetuates cold-hearted Thatcherite policies towards turbo-capitalism's losers, while missing no opportunity to express the intensity of his feelings for the less fortunate.[2]

[2] His televised jacketless, on-the-verge-of-tears response to the news of Princess Diana's death evoked the admiration of professional actors everywhere.

It is unfair to compare war-leaders, who could do much every day, with their peacetime successors in budget-cutting times, who can do very little. But it is hard not to conclude that image has displaced substance. Twenty years ago, for example, the worthy visitor who met a president or prime minister for a chat would subsequently receive a commemorative photograph of his encounter with the great one, duly signed or even dedicated. Today, many visitors are scheduled to go in and out within 120 seconds or so, strictly for 'photo opportunities', subsequently receiving a machine-signed photograph that commemorates a conversation that never actually took place.

Turbo-capitalism's competitive compulsions do not positively require this particular instance of the destruction of authenticity. But it could hardly have become an established practice if all concerned were not already thoroughly habituated by commercial manipulations to accept meretricious images in place of substance – indeed, as substance. In some trades, this has become standard operating procedure, such as the marketing of perfume bottles labelled by famous *clothing* designers, as if the ability to design attractive clothing were in any way a qualification for concocting smells, or the marketing of plain $2 cotton T-shirts for $10 or $20 by printing the name of high-fashion designers across their front, and the marketing of anything and everything by utterly irrelevant 'tie-ins' with celebrity names. Already indoctrinated by these displacements of reality, the protagonists of 120-second White House non-meetings, for which many travel from afar, do not complain. On the contrary, they happily exhibit the well-framed picture to admiring visitors; not a few find themselves enlarging on the themes of their discussion with the President, until in some cases the photograph may seem to be commemorating an entire day or even a weekend of intimate talk. After a while, many inevitably come to believe the photographic lie themselves.

The loss of personal authenticity is to a degree deliberate. For most people, a willful retreat from consciousness into a sleepwalker's existence of play-acting one role after another is actually the best remaining option. And for tycoons, top corporate chiefs, leading politicians and other high achievers, it is the best prescription for success, because to think of ultimate purposes or simply of true personal desires – as opposed to impressing other people – would only spoil their performance.[3]

---

[3] In a common enough sequence, a successful investment banker who joined the present writer for a trip into the jungles of Bolivia abruptly resigned upon returning to New

The destruction of authenticity goes well beyond individual lives to deform vocations – entire categories of them. Turbo-capitalism not only conquers markets and economic relationships, but also extends the reach of the market into every sphere of human activity. In the process, the *contents* of medicine, art, literature and sport, for example, are utterly deformed by the removal of their original personal satisfactions, of all disinterested motives and ethical boundaries, being replaced with money, often lots of it, though not necessarily for the protagonists.

Little need be said of turbo-capitalism's pervasive conquest of medicine in the United States, now that cost accountants outweigh doctors in prescribing treatments for each specific category of patients, while surgeons seek mid-career business degrees instead of specialist surgical training. And with good reason: while the chief executives of health-maintenance and hospital corporations receive millions in stock options, the average earnings of medical professionals have been stagnant or declining.

The overall result of turbo-capitalist medicine is often said to be the erosion of trust, or rather its further erosion. For nothing has changed in private medicine since the profession first emerged in antiquity. Patients who pay their own bills, especially if known to have money to spare, can never know if some therapy, test or elective surgery prescribed for them is meant to improve their own health, or add to their doctor's income. Although this is true in varying degree throughout the world, not by coincidence it was in the United States, the country of frankly businesslike doctors, that the practice of systematically seeking 'second opinions' before accepting costly (or dangerous) treatments was invented. Now widely followed, the practice is certainly prudent. It also implies a lack of trust in regard to either competence or honesty.

What is new with turbo-capitalism is yet one more example of its many structural changes: the wholesale conversion of medical *institutions* into profit-maximizing corporations. University teaching hospitals are in severe difficulty, partly because they provide the most advanced and thus often the most costly care to their patients, in excess of repayment limits if deemed necessary, and partly because much of their research cannot be packaged and sold. Public hospitals are under pressure all over the world in deflationary, budget-cutting

York. Disconnected from the whirl of the office, cell-phone, e-mail and fax, he had been both free and forced to reflect on his own existence.

times – including American municipal hospitals, whose emergency rooms replace family doctors for the disorganized, transient and bewildered. Non-profit mutual insurance associations such as Blue Cross/Blue Shield in the United States, are also in decline, because the proliferation of ultra-costly treatments and tests have invalidated their original method of leaving medicine to doctors, simply paying their fees within set limits.

In place of these variously benevolent institutions, medical corporations much beloved by Wall Street and its investors have risen instead: for-profit hospitals that systematically overtreat patients who are automatically covered by the US government's Medicare payments for the aged and Medicaid for the poor,[4] and 'health maintenance organizations' that systematically undertreat their subscribers because they pay a flat annual fee. When one of their doctors pronounces a therapy, test or surgical operation unnecessary, the patient cannot know if the reason is his own unexpectedly good health, or the organization's relentless pressure to cut costs. Hence patients cannot trust their doctors, while doctors cannot trust themselves to act in their patients' best interests: if they exceed set cost limits, if they are thought excessively prudent with their patients' health, they lose their jobs. Trust is a word of large meaning, but not large enough in this case, for in reality it is the entire human relationship between doctor and patient that is fatally corroded by the interposition of monetary calculations between them.

Sport was always entertainment as well as competition and the pursuit of personal satisfactions; and a few sports have long been a source of income and profits. Scandalized comments about money changing hands in supposedly amateur sport competitions start with the Panhellenic Games of Olympia, Delphi, Corinth and Argos, underway from 776 BC, commercialized and worse by the fifth century BC: Pausanias amusingly reports a boxing bribery scandal of the first century AD. Football throughout Europe and in much of the world, ice-hockey in Canada, baseball, American football and basketball in the United States, and its own baseball in Japan, were both popular passions and big business long before the arrival of turbo-capitalism. But now any sport however recondite and specialized, for teams or single athletes, for professionals or even young children that can

---

[4] Few private patients are both rich enough to have high-paying insurance plans and stupid enough to accept treatment in the average for-profit hospital, in which no research is conducted.

attract a paying audience and/or sponsorships and/or paid television coverage is not allowed to remain just sport; it must become a revenue-maximizing spectacle.

The extent to which turbo-capitalist practices deform the essential content of sport can be illustrated by the example of marathon and other long-distance running. One would have thought that, of all sports, they would be the least amenable to commercialization. There is no closed stadium, hence the public can be neither excluded nor forced to buy tickets; sponsorship is always possible for anything at all, of course, but there is no visually interesting focus for television coverage except in the finale.

None of this prevented the abolition of the very first rule of any athletic competition: the winner, not one of the losers, must win the race. Kenyans from their country's highlands are the problem, excessively well suited to long-distance running by their native terrain and habits. Ever since Kip Keino won a gold medal in the 1968 Mexico City Olympics, highland Kenyans have overcome every obstacle of poverty (an air fare is a rich man's fortune locally) to enter long-distance competitions everywhere that pay prize money – a few thousand dollars go a long way in Kenya. In the 1997–8 season, Kenyans came first in six out of the eight races of the US Professional Road Racing Circuit. Kenyans won the 1997 marathons of New York City, Boston and Honolulu, as they have won long-distance races all over the world from Mexico to Morocco.

The Kenyans evidently are splendid runners. But they have grave shortcomings: they are taciturn, some do not speak good English, others simply answer questions by providing the requisite information. TV journalists complain that there is no 'story' anymore because they do not know 'who the Kenyans are', and cannot 'communicate with them'. Naturally, the media story of a long-distance race cannot be the race – it has to be the human-interest angle, the sweaty-runner interview.

The result was catastrophic: a reduction in media coverage. This, in turn, seriously displeased the corporate sponsors, which provide the prize money. Racing organizers were thus caught in a dilemma: abandon the essential rule of all sports, or else lose corporate contributions. Given the present order of values, the outcome was inevitable:

• In 1997, six Kenyans came in the first eight in the Boulder–Boulder race; from 1998 only three Kenyan citizens can compete, and any

American who finishes within the top five receives double prize money.

- The George Sheehan race in New Jersey adopted a five-man team format specifically to exclude Kenyans, who cannot afford five air fares to win one prize.
- The organizers of the Pittsburgh Marathon have found a simpler solution: they now award prize money only to Americans.
- Many race organizers have switched their affiliation to the USA Circuit, which attracts no Kenyans because it awards prize money only to American citizens.
- The Harvard Pilgrim race in Cape Cod pays special bonuses to American runners – in 1997 the top US citizen received $4,000 for placing 11th.
- The organizers of the Gate River race in Jacksonville, Florida, sponsored by Gate Petroleum, were the pioneer innovators: after several Kenyan victories, in 1994 they stopped awarding prizes to non-Americans.

Doug Alred, the Gate race director, told a reporter that the exclusion policy was vindicated when Todd Williams, American winner of the 1998 race, did so much better than his Kenyan predecessors. True, he was slower. But in a TV interview Alred proudly announced that Todd Williams had said: 'I love Jacksonville, and I love Gate.'[5] That is what sportsmanship is about for Mr Alred, and for Gate Petroleum.

It is hardly surprising that the ultra-lucrative sport of American football is so thoroughly deformed that its games are tacitly interrupted every twelve minutes or so in coordination with television advertizements – all dutifully pretend that the game 'pauses' by mere coincidence, in every game without fail. Football *is* big business in its essence, and pretence is just one of the requirements of any sort of merchandising. It is more remarkable, however, that even the economic insignificance of long-distance running was not enough to protect it from the deforming effect of turbo-capitalist pressures.

The much broader significance of this sordid betrayal is to be found in an entire mentality that is really quite new. Two things are being accepted: the displacement of essential content by incidental and even quite trivial money making; and the elevation of the incidental money making into the overriding value that legitimizes decisions. Thus the

[5] Marc Bloom, 'Kenyan runners in the US find bitter taste of success', *New York Times*, 16 April 1998, p. 1, D27.

exclusion of Kenyan runners is validated by the funding thereby obtained from corporate sponsors. In other words, whatever brings in money, even in a primarily non-economic activity, takes precedence over all other considerations. Naturally, the principle applies to things far greater in combination than long-distance running, than all of sport for that matter.

Rembrandt was a keen if unsuccessful businessman, and long before him, artists had tried to earn as much as they could for the work they produced. It is only now, however, that X is respected as an artist because his paintings sell very well, while Y's inability to sell his sculptures is deemed sufficient evidence of *artistic* failure. Inevitably, artists respond. Instead of trying to sell what their inner voice tells them to create, they try to create what gallery owners tell them they can best sell. This has always happened, of course. The difference is one of degree: is essential content displaced in some art-work, much of it, or virtually all? The shipwreck of currently produced art suggests that the degree of displacement has much increased. But the making of art is perhaps too evanescent a subject to allow persuasive conclusions. There is a better example: published literature.

The book-publishing industry was once notoriously inefficient. The returns on equity earned by most publishing houses were so low that they could not raise capital as other businesses did, by issuing shares bought by arm's-length investors. Wall Street despised the industry, as did the City of London. Capital was provided instead by long-suffering families that tolerated low returns on their investment, and by wealthy individuals who had made their money elsewhere and wanted the prestige of publishing books. The result was that most publishing houses were visibly undercapitalized, reflected in shoddy furniture and worn carpets in shabby, overcrowded premises. Cash flow was a disaster because all the costs of making books come early, and booksellers pay late. Net income being low, bankruptcy was avoided by underpaying staff. Poorly paid managers were notably unbusinesslike, often remiss in hunting out waste, in searching for staff economies, in marketing. Worse paid, editors were even less businesslike. Their most damaging eccentricity was their insistence on publishing what they called 'important' works − books that they arrogantly deemed necessary to advance culture, even if few copies could be sold.

While some eccentric editors do survive, much of the industry has now been transformed by turbo-capitalist change. It is now elevated into an efficient industry dominated by gigantic conglomerates which earn returns on capital deemed acceptable by Wall Street. And something else: the content having being deformed, the publishing industry is much degraded culturally. We are not dealing with the unfathomables of art; there are facts that can be proved.

Before the transformation, stocks of unsold books were usually kept for several years ('the back-list'), to supply ten or twenty copies per year to eager if lonely readers, to scholars in urgent need of them. Since the transformation, the practice is to 'remainder' books quickly after a short season of full-price marketing, i.e. sell them off in bulk at deep discounts. Whatever is left over is pulped. One result is that great savings are made. Another is to eliminate the physical embodiment of culture (and rubbish) once constituted by publishers' back-lists. Books now go in and out of print very fast. If a passionately interested *aficionado* wants to read the still unpopular poet, let him photocopy a library holding. If a scholar needs that three-volume work much too large to be photocopied, too bad.

Growth For Ever

Its advocates are painfully aware of the greatest shortcoming of turbo-capitalism: while it imposes its disruptions on all in perfect equality, its rewards are disproportionally given to the few. Controlled capitalism in all its variants functioned very differently, for it brought societies together by lifting the poor and semi-poor into the middle class, while depressing incomes only at the very top. Of the many around the world who want to follow the American example by dismantling the many restraints of controlled capitalism, few are aware of the consequences of fracturing their nations by reverting to pre-industrial extremes of inequality. Such anxieties do not worry the true believers, for they are convinced that turbo-capitalism has a solution for inequality too: ever faster economic growth for ever and ever, by yet more technology, more deregulation and more globalization.

About future technology, nothing whatever can be said with confidence. Advances depend on unpredictable and never rightly predicted scientific breakthroughs, while their economic consequences are just as unpredictable. When electric motors first arrived on the scene to propel all types of industrial machinery, they displaced a great deal of manual work as well as steam engines. At the same time, however, electric motors gave birth to a huge variety of new products, from tramways to ventilators, which in turn gave employ-

231

ment to many people. Above all, by sharply increasing the productivity of labor that used them, electric motors generated new wealth, which in turn was used in part to transform kitchens and homes by equipping them with domestic appliances, in part propelled by electric motors. Once all the ripple effects and counter-effects worked themselves out, electric motors turned out to be important job creators. Information technology, by contrast, has been a job destroyer so far. It is impossible to tell how things might work out in the future, once further effects and counter-effects interact. Still less can anything be said about technologies as yet unknown.

No such caution needs be exercised when it comes to growth as a cure-all prescription. Even at rates much lower than in the past – roughly 2.5 per cent per year as opposed to the 4 per cent of the 1950s and 1960s – the economy of the United States has cumulatively grown a great deal since 1978. Yet it is perfectly evident that under turbo-capitalist conditions growth yields more inequality, not less. True, the prescription is for *faster* growth, though it is explained neither how faster growth might be sustained nor why it should reduce inequality rather than increase it even more. It was structural change that caused the problem in the first place; with faster growth, structural change would become even more rapid, thus presumably increasing inequality still further.

It is counter-logical to believe that a process that has produced a given result, in this case increasing inequality, would suddenly start producing an opposite result if it were faster. True, such things are not unknown under the sun: there *are* paradoxical processes whose effects reach a culminating point, only to reverse themselves. In fact, as we have seen, the logic of conflict is always paradoxical, so that opposites end up coinciding after their culminating point is passed. However, it is not just ordinary logic that goes against the faster-growth prescription of the ruling orthodoxy, but also the specifics of the case: inequality increases under turbo-capitalism because it accelerates both the opening of new opportunities and the destruction of established jobs and other sources of income. Hence it rewards agility, punishes stolidity. Faster growth would accelerate that acceleration, leaving behind static workers even more than now, favoring the acrobats best able to exploit fleeting opportunities to an even greater extent.

With no other solution in sight, it must be accepted that there are *no* remedies for the increased and increasing income and wealth inequalities other than political remedies – the use of state power to change either turbo-capitalism itself or its results, by redistributing incomes. The former has been done before, by way of regulations, or indicative planning, or outright public ownership. The latter is being done all the time by the progressive income taxes of every developed country in the world. Yet in today's climate, the notion that the state should tame the market, instead of trying further to unleash its dynamic workings, has become unmentionable, almost unthinkable. As for redistribution after the fact, for libertarians the very idea of it is absurd: income is earned by individuals, wealth is accumulated by individuals. As they see it, the state has no more right to take away an individual's income or wealth than to take his life.

For conservatives, the principal reason to participate in politics is to prevent what they see as its abuse for the purpose of redistribution. While the Left of all stripes and species in all countries has no such objection, it is now largely paralyzed by the argument that redistributing incomes reduces the incentive to earn high incomes by striving to produce more; and that redistributing wealth reduces the incentive to create it, which is precisely the individual accumulation of wealth.

When the Great Depression of the 1930s ravaged the lives of people in all parts of the world that were sufficiently advanced to partake of the international economy, almost all business people, bankers and academic economists were in perfect agreement that the only possible remedy was to cut government expenditures. We now know that the exact opposite was true. Much could have been done by simply printing money to finance public works that would put people back to work, thus giving them incomes that would be spent, in turn putting other people back to work. If all the major countries had done it together, increasing imports from each other more or less in step, the entire world economy would have been relaunched on an upward path. Such cooperation would have allowed single countries to engage in deficit spending without exhausting their foreign exchange reserves, and without having to impose import limits.

Even without so much harmony, it would have been better to restrict imports rather than to tolerate the persistence of devastating rates of unemployment, as much as 30 per cent in the United States, United Kingdom and Germany during the worst years. This would have reduced the standard of living of 'all', while increasing the standard of living of more people than not; for in those days a large portion of the labor force would have seen its wages rise because of the added demand of import-substitution industries. In the event, world trade was wrecked anyway by proliferating exchange controls, import licensing, quotas, outright import prohibitions and high tariffs. That made a bad situation much worse, by diminishing employment in everyone's export industries. But precisely because of their inefficiency, import-substitution industries would have employed even more people to make what was previously imported – had the monetarism of those days not strangled demand, adding contrived deflation to the natural deflation of the times.

Finally it was only the Second World War that solved the problem, which was only fair because mass unemployment in Germany and Japan had done much to cause the war in the first place. Wartime exigencies forced governments to do what the orthodox economics of those years had forbidden, to print money and employ people with it. Yet until military necessities intervened, the respectable politicians of the age could only agree with respectable professional opinion, leaving it to a few radical fringe politicians to challenge the ruling orthodoxy – Oswald Mosley in the UK, unsuccessfully; Hitler in Germany, all too successfully.

In our own days, Democrats and Republicans in the United States, Tories and Labour in the United Kingdom, Gaullists and Socialists in France, Christian Democrats and Social Democrats in Germany, right and left in Italy, and all other established political parties throughout Western Europe are equally incapable of coping with the challenges of turbo-capitalism. They have no answers at all for the acute sense of personal economic insecurity that afflicts so many of their electors, or for the grim realization of their worst fears in the structural unemployment widespread in Western Europe.

Instead they can only vainly promise more growth through the magic of a yet more dynamic economy. While conservative parties contradict themselves by preaching both unchanging 'family values' and more dynamic economic change, leftist parties can offer only improved social programs and more dynamic economic change – except that lately both the US Democrats and the UK's New Labour have cut social programs *and* embraced 'family values'. In other words, everyone's remedy for turbo-capitalism is more turbo-capitalism, even though most people, ordinary strivers rather than acrobats, would rather have secure jobs than the possibility of higher incomes through dynamic economic growth – for they correctly suspect that *their* earnings would not increase by much, if at all.

Although all respectable political parties are equally bereft, the parties of the Left are worst off, because the one thing that the majority of voters in the United States, Europe and Japan emphatically do not want is their standard product. People who are employed and who are earning, and perhaps very well, but who fear for their economic future, have no use for political parties that only want to tax away more of their uncertain incomes in order to assist those who do not work, and to feed the huge bureaucracies that stand between them and the assisted. That is why the Democrat Bill Clinton became the leading advocate of 'welfare reform', i.e. the reduction of aid to mothers with dependent children, while New Labour's Tony Blair inaugurated his rule by proposing restrictions on long-term unemployment benefits, and Italy's Ulivo coalition made cuts in government pensions its highest priority. As other left-wing parties followed in their wake, only the French Socialists of Jospin stood out by proposing unemployment relief through public spending, and they too did so with a diminishing degree of conviction.

A vast segment of the political spectrum is thus left vacant by the conservative contradiction on the one hand, and by leftist paralysis on the other. If a new political economy cannot emerge to tame the new force of turbo-capitalism, the wave of the future could be populism. Its local forms differ from country to country, but the essence is always the same: a revolt of the less educated against elite rule, elite opinions, elite values, and the elite's consensus on how government and the economy should be run. The United States has known its own version of populism in third-party candidates such as Perot in 1992 and Buchanan in 1996. France has Le Pen, who exemplifies the type.

Without specifying how the feat might be accomplished, populism in all its versions offers the promise of more personal economic security to the broad masses of office workers, shopkeepers, industrial workers and government employees now threatened by efficiency and unemployment. In some countries, and most prominently in France and Austria, populism acquires more than a tint of fascism by racist invective, anti-immigration proposals and an authoritarian stance. It is, in effect, a product-improved version of fascism, though we would be spared the frantic militarism of the original version because there are very few expendable youths in today's small families. No longer do father and mother confront a table full of children, only a few of whom can find work on the family farm or in the parental trade; no longer do they accept their sons' departure for war, or tolerate the idea that they might not survive to return home. With the emotional capital of families invested in a single male child on average (USA,

Russia) or less than one (Western Europe, Japan), populists and right-wingers in general are no more willing to accept the casualties of war than liberals or leftists. So militarist populism is not a threat, but the plain variety still is, if only because today's Great Deflation will not end soon.

The Great Dilemma

Allowing turbo-capitalism to have its way, as in the United States and the United Kingdom, results in widening income differentials in exchange for not-so-rapid economic growth. Resisting turbo-capitalism, by preserving labor-protection laws and stabilizing commercial regulations or even public ownership, as in France, overburdens employers, suppresses entrepreneurship and retards technological progress, resulting in even slower growth and considerable structural unemployment.

Allowing turbo-capitalism to advance unresisted disintegrates societies into a small elite of winners, a mass of losers of varying affluence or poverty, and rebellious law-breaking rebels. Not only social fellow-feeling is eroded, but even family bonds – people running ever faster to keep up are too busy to tend to them. The resulting social breakdown must then be countered by harsh laws, savage sentencing and mass imprisonment, to remove from circulation disaffected losers. But to resist turbo-capitalist change and its destructive efficiencies in a competitive world economy can result only in a progressive relative impoverishment for the nation as a whole, sadly diminishing prospects for young people just starting on their working lives.

Allowing turbo-capitalism to convert all institutions – from hospitals and publishing houses to long-distance races – into profit-maximizing enterprises, deforms or even perverts their essential content, while improving their economic performance. To resist the transformation leads to the impoverishment and eventual annihilation of institutions in societies that can no longer sustain them or anything else, since they themselves have been conquered by their respective economies. This, after all, is the turbo-capitalist reversal: societies serve economies, not the other way around. When all capital is allocated efficiently to whatever entities earn the highest returns, there is none to spare for institutions that do unprofitable things because of felt moral obligations or moralistic pretensions, professional ethics or professional conceits, high ideals or mere habit.

This, therefore, is the great dilemma of our times. So far, almost all Western governments have had no better plan than to allow turbo-capitalism to advance without limit, while hoping that faster growth will remedy all its shortcomings. That it will instead accelerate the fracturing of their societies into Silicon Valley heroes and vales of despond is suggested by all logic, but ignored by all mainstream politics.

As compared to the slavery of the defunct communist economies, despiriting bureaucratic socialism and the grotesque failures of nationalist economics, turbo-capitalism is materially altogether superior, and morally at least not inferior, in spite of all its corrosive effects on society, families and culture itself. Yet to accept its empire over every aspect of life, from art to sport in addition to all forms of business, cannot be the culminating achievement of human existence. Turbo-capitalism, too, shall pass.

APPENDIX

The Global Advance of Turbo-Capitalism

Turbo-capitalism is advancing on every continent, but its conquest of the world is far from complete.

In the Americas, it is excluded only in Cuba by the deliberate old-communist policies of Fidel Castro, and in Haiti by irremediably chaotic conditions, but there are still important though eroding barriers to trade, investment and internal competition in Brazil, Colombia, Mexico and Venezuela as well as in the lesser economies of the Dominican Republic, Honduras, Nicaragua, Guyana and Surinam. Each retains some or many of the features of the distinctive Latin American brand of statism, with its combination of the public ownership of key industries and the bureaucratic regulation of many more, as well as the import and investment barriers that go with both. Paradoxically, it is in Argentina, where the formula was invented in the immediate postwar years by Juan Perón and his celebrated Evita, and in Chile where it was most fully imitated, that statism has now been eradicated most decisively, with their example followed by Bolivia, Peru and Ecuador. Now all these rank as free-market economies alongside Costa Rica and Panama, which were never statist to begin with.

In Europe, turbo-capitalism is now excluded only in Belarus by a dictatorship unwilling to take the indispensable first step of privatization, and in Bosnia, Macedonia and Serbia-Montenegro as well as in Armenia, Azerbaijan and Georgia by the effects of ethnic wars and their disordered aftermath of banditry, war-lordism or plain destruction. But in spite of its fairly steady advance almost everywhere, there are still many barriers to foreign investment, imports and internal market competition in the ex-communist countries except for the Czech Republic, Estonia, Hungary, Latvia and Poland. By an amazingly rapid transformation, the Russian Federation had become a market economy by 1994, as the most farsighted of all its economic observers was to claim,[1] but it will be many years yet before the remaining impediments to plain business dealings are removed. As for the other ex-communist countries, Bulgaria, Lithuania, Moldova, Romania, Slovakia and the Ukraine, they are each liberalizing at their own pace, according to their peculiar circumstances.

In France at the time of writing, the advance of turbo-capitalism is still being strongly resisted by the policies of a Socialist-Communist coalition government, which has slowed or stopped the privatization of state-owned enterprises, including the aerospace conglomerate Aerospatiale and the Renault automobile company, and which shows no signs of dismantling elaborate job-protection laws, including a newly legislated 35-hour limit on the working week. In Italy, resistance is far more subtle. Privatizations are underway for the state-owned ENI oil and gas firm, the Stet telephone monopoly, the ENEL electrical-power monopoly, the *Autostrade* toll-roads and more, but this is being done by establishing 'public companies', which the government will still control even after more than 51 per cent of the shares are sold off to private investors. Likewise, deregulation is definitely underway, but very much faster for shopkeepers, who are to lose their precious licenses (very few of them voted for the ruling center-left government), than for key industries or the labor market, which will seemingly remain heavily regulated. In fact, in Italy too a 35-hour working week limit was legislated in 1998, in head-on collision with the European consensus that unemployment can be reduced only by more 'flexibility', i.e. lower wages and/or longer hours and/or shift work, as well as that impossible American virtue of easy mobility.

While in France the local version of controlled capitalism is still being overtly defended with grim determination, in Italy all the talk is of radical innovation, including the transformation of the chronically depressed South into Europe's 'Florida'. In Florida USA, however, many employees in the tourist trades work 70-hour weeks or more during the high season, and not many of its motels, eateries, theme

---

[1] Anders Åslund, *How Russia Became a Market Economy* (The Brookings Institution, Washington DC, 1995).

parks, gas stations or sales outlets would hire employees prohibited from working more than five hours a day every day, or five seven-hour days a week with two days off.

In Germany, big business is energetically pressing for liberalization all round, but especially for the dismantling of the employee safeguards that defined the country's own brand of controlled capitalism: the 'social market' economy. Trade unions are of course resisting the process, but are regularly outmaneuvered by the transfer of industrial production to plants outside Germany. The management of the largest of all industrial companies, Daimler-Benz, specifically acquired Chrysler to share in the benefits of turbo-capitalism, from American-style salaries for executives (Chrysler, the smaller company by far, paid much more to its top management) to a 'flexible' labor force.

In Spain, the many barriers to free competition left behind by the Franco regime are not yet fully dismantled, but the process is far advanced. The long-lived socialist government of Felipe Gonzales did its part by abolishing many of the corporatist elements of the Franco system, but not the strict job-protection laws, vigorously defended by the trade unions who spoke for many socialist voters. The conservative government now in office has no such inhibitions.

In Scandinavia, oil-rich Norway can afford to resist turbo-capitalist change and does so rather firmly, while Sweden is in the process of dismantling its once much admired version of controlled capitalism. Few privatizations are required because state ownership was not a significant part of the system. Not much deregulation is under way, for the same reason. In Sweden's case a social-democratic government is instead diminishing the scope of the welfare programs established over the decades by successive social-democratic governments, in order to reduce the taxes they had increased.

Elsewhere in Western Europe, liberalization is under way to open up fully economies that are already much advanced in a turbo-capitalist direction. But from Finland to Portugal, from Holland to Greece there are still significant restrictions on everything from retailing (opening hours) to banking, so that only Switzerland and the United Kingdom rank as ultra-free economies alongside the United States and New Zealand (Australia is catching up), as well as the entrepôt city-states of Hong Kong, Singapore and Bahrain.

In Asia, turbo-capitalism is totally excluded by government policy only in North Korea, but it is still very largely blocked by both deliberate policies and prevailing political conditions in quite a few other countries: perpetually conflicted Cambodia, Myanmar (Burma) and Sri Lanka, where there is too much violence for any significant investment or anything much beyond cash-and-carry trade; semi-communist Vietnam, where privatization and deregulation started off with much energy, only to slow down drastically; and all five of the ex-Soviet Central Asian republics: vast, oil-rich Kazakhstan, remote mountainous Kyrgyzstan, war-ridden Tajikistan, thinly populated, gas-rich Turkmenistan, and Uzbekistan, which has more people than all of the rest combined, but is rather poor in natural resources. Nor does it help matters that in none of the five has democratic government taken hold, with parliaments hardly more than nominal assemblies, no real free press anywhere, and chief executives ruling in a more or less openly dictatorial style.

Two more black holes for turbo-capitalism could not be more different: Afghanistan, captive to its own chronic ethnic, religious and tribal warfare, which has proved far more destructive than the Afghan–Soviet fighting ever was; and the remote Himalayan kingdom of Bhutan, whose Buddhist ruling family very firmly keeps out whatever might disturb an ancient isolated serenity, from mass tourism to foreign businessmen offering modernities. As for Iran, it has been opening up for the investment of returning exiles at least, but largely remains forbidden ground for the industrialists and traders of the world, except for the likes of the state-owned French oil company Total, which has an even stronger stomach than its American counterparts when it comes to coexisting with the brutalities of fanatical rulers.

Turbo-capitalism is steadily advancing in the insular and peninsular South East Asian countries traditionally more open to external influences: Indonesia, South Korea, Malaysia, the Philippines and Taiwan, as well as Japan, a case by itself. In all of them, the dramatic 1997 external-debt crisis only served to break down yet more barriers to foreign investment and internal competition, notably the peculiar East Asian propensity for under-the-table arrangements that tacitly award market shares or even entire industries to favored corporations, families or individuals.

Everywhere else in Asia, major policy barriers remain in effect at the time of writing, though very few new barriers are being added, while the old ones are eroding, if only slowly. This is true of both the giants China and India as well as of Bangladesh, Mongolia, Nepal and Pakistan. The Chinese may indeed be natural-born capitalists, but much of the economy is still state-owned, and foreign investors are still being forced to enter into joint ventures with local companies if they want to start a major industrial enterprise, such as car-assembly plants.

The up-front deal is that the foreigners must share their precious technology with the local partner in exchange for access to the Chinese market; and they cannot own a majority of the joint company. But while the system is still old-communist enough to impose these requirements, the local partners are new-capitalist enough to draw off sales and profits for themselves, while sharing costs all too evenly. The result is that as of 1998 every one of the new entrants in China's automobile market was losing money. Their chief executives proudly publicized their Chinese assembly plants and their pioneering break-throughs into the enormously promising China market of the future (so far, Brazil's is still much larger), while their accountants weep over the results. Even Volkswagen/Audi, the most seemingly successful of the Western makes (200,000 cars in 1997) found that Audi's local partner, First Auto Works, insisted on independently producing Audis at the joint venture's Changchun assembly plant, for sale under its own Red Flag badge. Thus Audi–Audi revenues are split as per the joint venture, while 100 per cent of Red Flag–Audi revenues go to First Auto Works. Peugeot was already producing 20,000 cars a year by 1992 with a Guangzhou partner, but discovered that its 22 per cent share yielded only losses, and abandoned its investment in 1997. Chrysler is still turning out its Jeep Cherokees in China (a much-publicized, very early 'breakthrough'), while refusing to disclose its local financial results. In the light of what has happened, the major Japanese automobile companies may be thankful that the Chinese government kept them out (small Daihatsu was allowed a plant) except for component production, in line with the anti-Japanese campaign vigorously sponsored to stimulate a pan-Chinese national-ism.

None of the above applies to the great bulk of foreign investment in China, which comes from overseas Chinese who are perfectly capable of coping with imposed joint ventures. After agreeing to whatever conditions are set by the designated state-owned company, local or regional authority or the central government's appropriate ministry, they make their own side-deals with the individual officials who are supposed to represent any or all of the above. Instead of paying 50 per cent of the profits into the coffers of the public entity, they give 10 per cent in cash directly into the hands of the entity's ranking officials, along with lavish dinners complete with *dessert* (the pan-Chinese loan word for agreeable companions who come in after the last course), keeping 90 per cent for themselves. True, resentful lower-ranking officials, denied both cash and fun, are apt to denounce these goings-on. But the resulting unpleasantness is soon settled with some more cash, and the replacement officials selected for their assured incorruptibility rarely resist when offered twenty years' worth of salary in a single bribe.

Things are very different in India, where both the social-democratic ideology of much of the educated elite and the Hindu populism of their opponents have proved far more resilient obstacles to turbo-capitalism than China's corrupt remnants of communism. For years now, successive Indian prime ministers of all parties have proclaimed their eagerness to liberalize what is one of the world's most regulated economies, to encourage both local enterprise and foreign investment. And for just as many years, many attempts to take them at their word have failed, after colliding with the stubborn resistance of bureaucrats, lesser politicians and public opinion. Bangalore has become the center of an expanding software and programming-services industry that serves the world, a garment export boom is underway in Tamil Nadu, and there are other islands of globalization. But these are still exceptions.

Major infrastructure projects financed by foreign investors are resisted with nationalist arguments, lesser foreign investments in fast-food or consumer-goods outlets are resisted with the egalitarian argument that they take away the livelihood of traditional food stalls and petty merchants, and local enterprise that seeks to exploit new opportunities opened up by deregulation is confronted by bureaucrats who are very creative in discovering new regulatory obstacles. It is not enterprise as such that is opposed, or even foreign enterprise, but rather *modern* private enterprise of any sort. For most Indians calculate that, if public industries and services are replaced by private ones, if traditional suppliers are replaced by modern ones, their world-class quality will come with world-class prices, far beyond the reach of most Indian incomes. Much the same is true of Bangladesh and Pakistan as well. That in both countries, as in India, fierce resistance to new inequalities coexists with the tranquil acceptance of old ones is certainly illogical, but a fact of life nevertheless.

In the Middle East, only the arbitrary dictatorships of Iraq, Syria and Yemen are still denied territories for turbo-capitalism, but in all other countries without exception barriers to foreign investment or trade or internal competition are still extensive and sometimes absolute. Their nature varies greatly, however, from Israel's state-owned banks and industries, whose privatization is very slow in an otherwise open economy, to the unwritten rules that shield the numerous business enterprises of some 5,000 ranking Saudi princes from the hardships of fair competition. In law, nothing prevents a local or foreign investor from starting a new enterprise of any kind in Saudi Arabia, so long as it does not sell forbidden goods such as alcohol or uncensored videotapes or books. In practice, nobody would be naive enough to start competing with a business owned by a powerful prince. But matters become complicated if the princely interest is a well-kept secret, or retroactive: for a local businessman facing the threat of a more efficient new entrant, one solution is to give away an ownership share to a man of power who can shut down the competition. The same is true in the United Arab Emirates and Qatar, though not Dubai, the ultimate free market of Arabia along with Bahrain.

Egypt, far different in nature as well as magnitude, has no ruling house with a population explosion of extortionate princes, but it too is largely denied to turbo-capitalism by the state-ownership residues of Gamal Abdel Nasser's 'Arab socialism', as well as by the impeding medium of the world's oldest and most entrenched bureaucracy – which was already generating masses of papyrus-work 3,000 years ago (Hellenistic and Roman historiography would be bereft without its documentary detail, on everything from the supply of fish sauce for visiting imperial retinues to tax appeals). Permits are required at every turn to import, export, produce or sell anything, but the permit-issuing officials believe in long intervals of reflection before responding to permit applications, and they know that only a denial will safeguard them from accusations of laxity or corruption – so that they much prefer rather small bribes to *consider* applications rather than large ones actually to grant them.

In all of Africa, only Morocco, Tunisia and the South African sphere (which also embraces Botswana, Lesotho, Namibia and Swaziland), offer favorable conditions for turbo-capitalism, to which they have opened most doors. In all of them, both local and foreign enterprise can act with almost as much legal freedom as in Europe, and not much less security, having moreover the added strength that comes from the great scarcity of capital and the great abundance of labor, which ensures its humble acceptance of low wages.

This is just as true almost everywhere else in the African continent except for Libya, which has much oil and few people, but to little avail. For what the market would offer – the world's cheapest labor and an abundance of natural resources – is taken away by governments addicted to arbitrary prohibitions, outright confiscations, impossible regulations and unsystematic extortion. Whatever good was done by colonial powers in their best moments is easily offset by the evils perpetrated by the state structures they left behind. Since independence, some African rulers have been bloodthirsty monsters or mega-thieves, or both. A few have been saintly figures of disinterested benevolence. Most have not differed all that much from their counterparts all over the world, in trying to rule as effectively as they could at least some of the time, enriching themselves in the process to be sure, but not to a far greater extent than political leaders elsewhere. All of them, however, monsters and saints included, have been incapacitated by state structures designed in Europe on the premise that they would be run by tolerably efficient, reasonably honest and generally loyal personnel, but which are in fact replete with administrators who fail to process the paperwork they demand except for cash, soldiers who defend nothing except their right to eat without working, policemen who moonlight as highway robbers, and customs officers and tax collectors who collect more bribes for themselves than revenues for the public coffers. Insofar as any actual policies can be pursued through these distorting mechanisms, they tend to be statist: rulers who own the state for all practical purposes naturally prefer the state ownership of whatever infrastructures and industries might exist.

Under this general dispensation, actual conditions vary from place to place and from time to time. At the time of writing, for example, Benin, Gabon and much-ravaged Uganda are pursuing free-market policies under their current rulers, while Ghana, Cameroon, the Ivory Coast, Kenya, Senegal and Zimbabwe are all variously statist, but otherwise offer tolerable circumstances for many kinds of local and even foreign enterprise. By contrast, in Algeria, Angola, Burundi, Congo-Brazzavile, Congo (ex-Zaire), Liberia, Mozambique, Rawanda, Sierra Leone, Sudan and Somalia, the devastations of recent or still-persisting violence preclude virtually all forms of large-scale business except for extractive industries with their own security forces. In between, a long list of African countries from the Central African Republic to Zambia is neither in nor out of the global economy, for while economic activities are possible, only those with the highest margins can overcome the impediments of crumbling infrastructures or extortionate governments, or both. By and large, policy changes could swiftly remove most of the obstacles to turbo-capitalism in ex-communist Europe, Latin America and Asia; in Africa, however, it is ancestral cultural traits that would have to change.

SELECTED COUNTRIES: 1985 and 1998

Ex-State Capitalist ('Communist') Countries Being Privatized

China   Czech Republic (process complete)
Hungary   Poland
Romania   Russian Federation
Slovenia   Ukraine (process only started)

Residual State-Capitalist ('Communist') Economies

Belarus   Cuba
North Korea   Vietnam

Controlled Economies Being Privatized/Deregulated

Argentina   Australia
Chile   France
India   Italy
Japan   Korea (South)
Mexico   Peru
Spain   Turkey

Fully 'Turbo-Capitalist' Economies

Hong Kong   New Zealand
Singapore   Taiwan
United Kingdom   United States

China

	1985	1998
Role of state, regional and/or local authorities in the economy		
Ownership of industry	Almost total	V. extensive
Privatization underway?	V. slowly/v. partially*	Advancing
Ownership of services	Total	Almost total
Privatization underway?	No	Slowly/partially*
Ownership of agric. land	In dissolution	Residual
Privatization underway?	Yes	Almost complete
Barriers to international commerce		
Tariffs	n/a**	V. high***
Licenses required?	n/a**	Yes, v. restrictive
Quotas	n/a**	Yes, v. restrictive
Vexatious non-tariff barriers	n/a**	Yes***
Investment restrictions	V. many	Many
Limits on service imports	n/a**	V. many
Barriers to internal competition		
Bank ownership public	Total	Almost total
Bank ownership private	No	V. small
Bank privatization underway?	No	Announced
Restrictions on bank activities	n/a	Yes
Stock-market activities	None	Emerging market
Central planning of the economy	Yes	No
Degree of regulation by:		
Bureaucratic controls	Total	High***
Licensing	High	High***

*Private capital (almost totally foreign) allowed only in joint ventures controlled by state/regional/local entities.

**Foreign commerce and external finance were still almost entirely initiated by state/regional bodies.

***Except in designated 'Free Trade Zones'.

1998 Heritage Foundation/Wall Street Journal, *Index of Economic Freedom* overall multisector rating, including taxation levels, price controls, inflation, etc., on a 5–0 (0 = 100% free) scale: **3.75**.

Czech Republic

	1985	1998
Role of state, regional and/or local authorities in the economy		
Ownership of industry	Total	None
Privatization underway?	No	Completed
Ownership of services	Total	V. little
Privatization underway?	No	Yes
Ownership of agric. land	Total	None
Privatization underway?	n/a	Completed
Barriers to international commerce		
Tariffs	n/a*	V. low
Licenses required?	n/a*	No
Quotas	n/a*	None
Vexatious non-tariff barriers	n/a*	None
Investment restrictions	n/a*	V. few
Limits on service imports	n/a*	No
Barriers to internal competition		
Bank ownership public	Total	None
Bank ownership private	None	Yes
Bank privatization underway?	n/a*	Completed
Restrictions on bank activities	n/a*	V. few
Stock-market activities	None	Emerging market
Central planning of the economy	Yes	No
Degree of regulation by:		
Bureaucratic controls	Total	V. low
Licensing	n/a*	V. low

*Total state control of the entire legal economy.

1998 Heritage Foundation/Wall Street Journal, *Index of Economic Freedom* overall multisector rating, including taxation levels, price controls, inflation, etc., on a 5–0 (0 = 100% free) scale: **2.20**.

Hungary

	1985	1998
Role of state, regional and/or local authorities in the economy		
Ownership of industry	Almost total	Substantial
Privatization underway?	No	Yes
Ownership of services	Almost total	Substantial
Privatization underway?	No	Yes
Ownership of agric. land	Total	None
Privatization underway?	n/a	Completed
Barriers to international commerce		
Tariffs	n/a*	Medium-high
Licenses required?	n/a*	No
Quotas	n/a*	Some
Vexatious non-tariff barriers	n/a*	Few
Investment restrictions	n/a*	V. few
Limits on service imports	n/a*	No
Barriers to internal competition		
Bank ownership public	Total	Some
Bank ownership private	None	Yes
Bank privatization underway?	n/a*	Yes
Restrictions on bank activities	n/a*	Few
Stock-market activities	None	Emerging market
Central planning of the economy	Yes	No
Degree of regulation by:		
Bureaucratic controls	Total	Low
Licensing	n/a*	Low

*Total state control of most of the legal economy.

1998 Heritage Foundation/Wall Street Journal, *Index of Economic Freedom* overall multisector rating, including taxation levels, price controls, inflation, etc., on a 5–0 (0 = 100% free) scale: **2.90**.

Poland

	1985	1998
Role of state, regional and/or local authorities in the economy		
Ownership of industry	Total	Considerable
Privatization underway?	No	Yes
Ownership of services	Total	Considerable
Privatization underway?	No	Yes
Ownership of agric. land	V. little	None
Privatization underway?	n/a	n/a
Barriers to international commerce		
Tariffs	n/a*	Medium-high
Licenses required?	n/a*	No
Quotas	n/a*	No
Vexatious non-tariff barriers	n/a*	None
Investment restrictions	n/a*	V. few
Limits on service imports	n/a*	Some
Barriers to internal competition		
Bank ownership public	Total	Some
Bank ownership private	None	Yes
Bank privatization underway?	n/a*	Yes
Restrictions on bank activities	n/a*	V. few
Stock-market activities	None	Emerging market
Central planning of the economy	Yes	No
Degree of regulation by:		
Bureaucratic controls	Total	Low
Licensing	n/a*	V. low

*State control of much of the legal economy.

1998 Heritage Foundation/Wall Street Journal, *Index of Economic Freedom* overall multisector rating, including taxation levels, price controls, inflation, etc., on a 5–0 (0 = 100% free) scale: **2.95**.

Romania

	1985	1998
Role of state, regional and/or local authorities in the economy		
Ownership of industry	Total	V. large
Privatization underway?	No	Slowly
Ownership of services	Total	Substantial
Privatization underway?	No	Slowly
Ownership of agric. land	Almost total	Considerable
Privatization underway?	No	Yes
Barriers to international commerce		
Tariffs	n/a*	Low-medium
Licenses required?	n/a*	Some
Quotas	n/a*	No
Vexatious non-tariff barriers	n/a*	Some
Investment restrictions	n/a*	V. few
Limits on service imports	n/a*	Some
Barriers to internal competition		
Bank ownership public	Total	V. considerable
Bank ownership private	None	Rapidly expanding
Bank privatization underway?	n/a*	Slowly
Restrictions on bank activities	n/a*	Some
Stock-market activities	None	Informal only
Central planning of the economy	Yes	No
Degree of regulation by:		
Bureaucratic controls	Total	Medium
Licensing	n/a*	Low

*State control of the entire legal economy except some crafts.

1998 Heritage Foundation/Wall Street Journal, *Index of Economic Freedom* overall multisector rating, including taxation levels, price controls, inflation, etc., on a 5–0 (0 = 100% free) scale: **3.30**.

Russian Federation

	1985	1998
Role of state, regional and/or local authorities in the economy		
Ownership of industry	Total	Substantial
Privatization underway?	No	Slowly
Ownership of services	Total	Substantial
Privatization underway?	No	Slowly
Ownership of agric. land	Almost total	Considerable
Privatization underway?	No	Slowly
Barriers to international commerce		
Tariffs	n/a*	Medium-high
Licenses required?	n/a*	No
Quotas	n/a*	No
Vexatious non-tariff barriers	n/a*	Yes
Investment restrictions	n/a*	Few
Limits on service imports	n/a*	Some
Barriers to internal competition		
Bank ownership public	Total	Some
Bank ownership private	None	Substantial
Bank privatization underway?	n/a*	Slowly
Restrictions on bank activities	n/a*	Some
Stock-market activities	None	Emerging market
Central planning of the economy	Yes	No
Degree of regulation by:		
Bureaucratic controls	Total	Low
Licensing	n/a*	Low

*Total state control of the entire legal economy.

1998 Heritage Foundation/Wall Street Journal, *Index of Economic Freedom* overall multisector rating, including taxation levels, price controls, inflation, etc., on a 5–0 (0 = 100% free) scale: **3.45**.

Slovenia

	1985	1998
Role of state, regional and/or local authorities in the economy		
Ownership of industry	Almost total**	Residual
Privatization underway?	No	Yes
Ownership of services	Almost total**	Considerable
Privatization underway?	No	Yes
Ownership of agric. land	No	No
Privatization underway?	No	n/a
Barriers to international commerce		
Tariffs	High	Medium-high
Licenses required?	Yes	Some
Quotas	Some	Some
Vexatious non-tariff barriers	Yes	No
Investment restrictions	Yes	Many remain
Limits on service imports	Yes	Some
Barriers to internal competition		
Bank ownership public	Total	Residual
Bank ownership private	None	Yes
Bank privatization underway?	No	Almost complete
Restrictions on bank activities	n/a*	Few
Stock-market activities	None	Informal only
Central planning of the economy	No	No
Degree of regulation by:		
Bureaucratic controls	High	Low
Licensing	High	Low

*As part of Yugoslavia.
**Under the specific Yugoslav system of so-called 'worker control'.

1998 Heritage Foundation/Wall Street Journal, *Index of Economic Freedom* overall multisector rating, including taxation levels, price controls, inflation, etc., on a 5–0 (0 = 100% free) scale: **3.10**.

Ukraine

	1985	1998
Role of state, regional and/or local authorities in the economy		
Ownership of industry	Total	V. extensive
Privatization underway?	No	Slowly
Ownership of services	Total	V. large
Privatization underway?	No	V. slowly
Ownership of agric. land	Total	Residual
Privatization underway?	n/a	Yes
Barriers to international commerce		
Tariffs	n/a*	High
Licenses required?	n/a*	No
Quotas	n/a*	No
Vexatious non-tariff barriers	n/a*	Some
Investment restrictions	n/a*	Few
Limits on service imports	n/a*	Yes
Barriers to internal competition		
Bank ownership public	Total	Extensive
Bank ownership private	None	Growing
Bank privatization underway?	n/a*	Slowly
Restrictions on bank activities	n/a*	Some
Stock-market activities	None	Informal only
Central planning of the economy	Yes	No
Degree of regulation by:		
Bureaucratic controls	Total	Medium-high
Licensing	n/a*	Medium-high

*Total state control of the entire legal economy.

1998 Heritage Foundation/Wall Street Journal, *Index of Economic Freedom* overall multisector rating, including taxation levels, price controls, inflation, etc., on a 5–0 (0 = 100% free) scale: **3.80**.

Belarus

	1985	1998
Role of state, regional and/or local authorities in the economy		
Ownership of industry	Total	Almost total
Privatization underway?	No	V. slowly
Ownership of services	Total	Extensive
Privatization underway?	No	V. slowly
Ownership of agric. land	Total	Extensive
Privatization underway?	n/a	Yes
Barriers to international commerce		
Tariffs	n/a*	High
Licenses required?	n/a*	User fees
Quotas	n/a*	Yes
Vexatious non-tariff barriers	n/a*	Some
Investment restrictions	n/a*	Unstable
Limits on service imports	n/a*	Yes
Barriers to internal competition		
Bank ownership public	Total	None
Bank ownership private	None	Yes
Bank privatization underway?	n/a*	Completed
Restrictions on bank activities	n/a*	Some
Stock-market activities	None	None
Central planning of the economy	Yes	No
Degree of regulation by:		
Bureaucratic controls	Total	High
Licensing	n/a*	Medium

*Total state control of the entire legal economy.

1998 Heritage Foundation/Wall Street Journal, *Index of Economic Freedom* overall multisector rating, including taxation levels, price controls, inflation, etc., on a 5–0 (0 = 100% free) scale: **4.05**.

Cuba

	1985	1998
Role of state, regional and/or local authorities in the economy		
Ownership of industry	Total	Total
Privatization underway?	No	No
Ownership of services	Total	Almost total
Privatization underway?	No	V. limited, v. slowly
Ownership of agric. land	Total	Total
Privatization underway?	No	No
Barriers to international commerce		
Tariffs	n/a	n/a
Licenses required?	n/a	n/a
Quotas	n/a	n/a
Vexatious non-tariff barriers	n/a	Yes*
Investment restrictions	Absolute	Some JVs allowed
Limits on service imports	Absolute	Absolute
Barriers to internal competition		
Bank ownership public	Total	Total
Bank ownership private	None	None
Bank privatization underway?	No	No
Restrictions on bank activities	n/a	n/a
Stock-market activities	None	None
Central planning of the economy	Yes	Yes
Degree of regulation by:		
Bureaucratic controls	Total	Total
Licensing	n/a	n/a

*On unrequited gifts from abroad.

1998 Heritage Foundation/Wall Street Journal, *Index of Economic Freedom* overall multisector rating, including taxation levels, price controls, inflation, etc., on a 5–0 (0 = 100% free) scale: **5.00**.

North Korea (Democratic People's Republic of Korea)

	1985	1998
Role of state, regional and/or local authorities in the economy		
Ownership of industry	Total	Total
Privatization underway?	No	No
Ownership of services	Total	Total
Privatization underway?	No	No
Ownership of agric. land	Total	Total
Privatization underway?	No	No
Barriers to international commerce		
Tariffs	n/a*	n/a*
Licenses required?	n/a*	n/a*
Quotas	n/a*	n/a*
Vexatious non-tariff barriers	n/a*	n/a*
Investment restrictions	n/a*	Almost total**
Limits on service imports	n/a*	Total
Barriers to internal competition		
Bank ownership public	Total	Total
Bank ownership private	None	None
Bank privatization underway?	No	No
Restrictions on bank activities	n/a*	n/a*
Stock-market activities	None	None
Central planning of the economy	Yes	Yes
Degree of regulation by:		
Bureaucratic controls	Total	Total
Licensing	n/a*	n/a*

*Except for very limited transborder commerce, it is a pure state economy.
**North Korea has invited foreign investment in a Free Trade Zone and for specific projects, without effect so far.

1998 Heritage Foundation/Wall Street Journal, *Index of Economic Freedom* overall multisector rating, including taxation levels, price controls, inflation, etc., on a 5–0 (0 = 100% free) scale: **5.00**.

Vietnam

	1985	1998

Role of state, regional and/or local authorities in the economy

Ownership of industry	Total	Almost total*
Privatization underway?	No	V. slowly
Ownership of services	Total	Almost total*
Privatization underway?	No	V. slowly
Ownership of agric. land	Yes	Yes
Privatization underway?	No	V. slowly

Barriers to international commerce

Tariffs	n/a**	V. high
Licenses required?	n/a**	Yes
Quotas	n/a**	Yes
Vexatious non-tariff barriers	n/a**	Yes
Investment restrictions	n/a**	Many*
Limits on service imports	n/a**	Many

Barriers to internal competition

Bank ownership public	Total	Almost total
Bank ownership private	No	Yes
Bank privatization underway?	No	No
Restrictions on bank activities	n/a**	Yes
Stock-market activities	None	None
Central planning of the economy	Yes	Yes
Degree of regulation by:		
Bureaucratic controls	Total	V. high
Licensing	n/a*	V. high

*Joint ventures with foreign investors (up to 50% ownership) are increasing; local private enterprise is largely limited to crafts and retail trade.
**State control of the entire legal economy.

1998 Heritage Foundation/Wall Street Journal, *Index of Economic Freedom* overall multisector rating, including taxation levels, price controls, inflation, etc., on a 5–0 (0 = 100% free) scale: **4.70**.

Argentina

	1985	1998
Role of state, regional and/or local authorities in the economy		
Ownership of industry	Extensive	Residual
Privatization underway?	No	Yes
Ownership of services	Extensive	Residual
Privatization underway?	No	Yes
Ownership of agric. land	None	None
Privatization underway?	n/a	n/a
Barriers to international commerce		
Tariffs	High	Medium-high
Licenses required?	Yes	No
Quotas	Some	Few
Vexatious non-tariff barriers	Many	V. few
Investment restrictions	Many	Few
Limits on service imports	Many	Few
Barriers to internal competition		
Bank ownership public	Extensive	Residual
Bank ownership private	Yes	Yes
Bank privatization underway?	No	Yes
Restrictions on bank activities	Some	Some
Stock-market activities	Limited	Emerging market
Central planning of the economy	No	No
Degree of regulation by:		
Bureaucratic controls	High	Low
Licensing	High	Low

1998 Heritage Foundation/Wall Street Journal, *Index of Economic Freedom* overall multisector rating, including taxation levels, price controls, inflation, etc., on a 5–0 (0 = 100% free) scale: **2.60**.

Australia

	1985	1998

Role of state, regional and/or local authorities in the economy

Ownership of industry	Residual	None
Privatization underway?	Yes	n/a
Ownership of services	Extensive	Considerable
Privatization underway?	No	Yes
Ownership of agric. land	None	None
Privatization underway?	n/a	n/a

Barriers to international commerce

Tariffs	High	Low
Licenses required?	Yes	No
Quotas	Yes	Yes
Vexatious non-tariff barriers	No	No
Investment restrictions	Many	None
Limits on service imports	Many	V. few

Barriers to internal competition

Bank ownership public	No	No
Bank ownership private	Yes	Yes
Bank privatization underway?	n/a	n/a
Restrictions on bank activities	Some	Few
Stock-market activities	Developed	Fully developed
Central planning of the economy	No	No
Degree of regulation by:		
Bureaucratic controls	High	V. low
Licensing	Low	V. low

1998 Heritage Foundation/Wall Street Journal, *Index of Economic Freedom* overall multisector rating, including taxation levels, price controls, inflation, etc., on a 5–0 (0 = 100% free) scale: **2.05**.

Chile

	1985	1998

Role of state, regional and/or local authorities in the economy

	1985	1998
Ownership of industry	Considerable	None
Privatization underway?	Yes	Completed
Ownership of services	Considerable	Residual
Privatization underway?	No	Almost completed
Ownership of agric. land	None	None
Privatization underway?	n/a	n/a

Barriers to international commerce

Tariffs	Medium-high	Medium-low
Licenses required?	No	No
Quotas	None	None
Vexatious non-tariff barriers	Some	None
Investment restrictions	Many	Some
Limits on service imports	Many	Few

Barriers to internal competition

Bank ownership public	Extensive	Considerable
Bank ownership private	Yes	Yes
Bank privatization underway?	No	No
Restrictions on bank activities	Some	Some
Stock-market activities	Small/limited	Emerging market
Central planning of the economy	No	No
Degree of regulation by:		
Bureaucratic controls	Medium-high	Only high in few sectors
Licensing	Medium-low	Low

1998 Heritage Foundation/Wall Street Journal, *Index of Economic Freedom* overall multisector rating, including taxation levels, price controls, inflation, etc., on a 5–0 (0 = 100% free) scale: **2.15**.

France

	1985	1998

Role of state, regional and/or local authorities in the economy

Ownership of industry	Extensive	Extensive
Privatization underway?	Yes	Slowly
Ownership of services	Extensive	Extensive
Privatization underway?	No	V. slowly
Ownership of agric. land	None	None
Privatization underway?	n/a	n/a

Barriers to international commerce

Tariffs	Low	3.6% EU ave.
Licenses required?	Some	Few
Quotas	Some (EU)	Some (EU)
Vexatious non-tariff barriers	Some	Some
Investment restrictions	Some	Some
Limits on service imports	Some	Some

Barriers to internal competition

Bank ownership public	Substantial	Still considerable
Bank ownership private	Yes	Yes
Bank privatization underway?	No	Interrupted
Restrictions on bank activities	Yes	Yes
Stock-market activities	Fully developed	Fully developed
Central planning of the economy	No	No
Degree of regulation by:		
Bureaucratic controls	High	High
Licensing	High	Medium-high

1998 Heritage Foundation/Wall Street Journal, *Index of Economic Freedom* overall multisector rating, including taxation levels, price controls, inflation, etc., on a 5–0 (0 = 100% free) scale: **2.50**.

India

	1985	1998
Role of state, regional and/or local authorities in the economy		
Ownership of industry	Extensive	Considerable
Privatization underway?	No	Yes
Ownership of services	Extensive	Considerable
Privatization underway?	No	Yes
Ownership of agric. land	No	No
Privatization underway?	n/a	n/a
Barriers to international commerce		
Tariffs	V. high	V. high
Licenses required?	Yes	Yes
Quotas	Yes	Yes
Vexatious non-tariff barriers	Yes	Some
Investment restrictions	Many	Few
Limits on service imports	Many	Many
Barriers to internal competition		
Bank ownership public	V. extensive	V. extensive
Bank ownership private	V. small	Small
Bank privatization underway?	No	No*
Restrictions on bank activities	Yes	Yes
Stock-market activities	Limited	Emerging market
Central planning of the economy	Yes	No
Degree of regulation by:		
Bureaucratic controls	V. high	Medium-high
Licensing	V. high	V. high

*But some foreign banks are being allowed to open local branches.

1998 Heritage Foundation/Wall Street Journal, *Index of Economic Freedom* overall multisector rating, including taxation levels, price controls, inflation, etc., on a 5–0 (0 = 100% free) scale: **3.70**.

Italy

	1985	1998

Role of state, regional and/or local authorities in the economy

Ownership of industry	Extensive	Substantial
Privatization underway?	Yes	Yes
Ownership of services	Extensive	Substantial
Privatization underway?	No	Yes
Ownership of agric. land	None	None
Privatization underway?	n/a	n/a

Barriers to international commerce

Tariffs	Low	3.6% EU ave.
Licenses required?	No	No
Quotas	Some (EU)	Some (EU)
Vexatious non-tariff barriers	Few	Few
Investment restrictions	Some	Some
Limits on service imports	Some	Some

Barriers to internal competition

Bank ownership public	Substantial	Considerable
Bank ownership private	Yes	Yes
Bank privatization underway?	No	Yes
Restrictions on bank activities	Some	Some
Stock-market activities	Developed	Fully developed
Central planning of the economy	No	No
Degree of regulation by:		
Bureaucratic controls	High	Diminishing
Licensing	High	High

1998 Heritage Foundation/Wall Street Journal, *Index of Economic Freedom* overall multisector rating, including taxation levels, price controls, inflation, etc., on a 5–0 (0 = 100% free) scale: **2.50**.

Japan

	1985	1998
Role of state, regional and/or local authorities in the economy		
Ownership of industry	None	None
Privatization underway?	n/a	n/a
Ownership of services	Considerable	Residual
Privatization underway?	Yes	Yes
Ownership of agric. land	No	No
Privatization underway?	n/a	n/a
Barriers to international commerce		
Tariffs	Low	V. low
Licenses required?	No	No
Quotas	Prohibitions	Prohibitions
Vexatious non-tariff barriers	V. many	Yes
Investment restrictions	V. many	Many
Limits on service imports	V. many	Many
Barriers to internal competition		
Bank ownership public	Yes*	Yes*
Bank ownership private	Yes	Yes
Bank privatization underway?	No	No
Restrictions on bank activities	Yes	Fewer
Stock-market activities	Fully developed	Fully developed
Central planning of the economy	No	No
Degree of regulation by:		
Bureaucratic controls	V. high**	Diminishing
Licensing	V. high**	Medium-low

*Post Office Savings Bank, the world's largest collector of personal savings.
**Largely by informal 'administrative guidance' from ministries, not legally compulsory, but still obeyed.

1998 Heritage Foundation/Wall Street Journal, *Index of Economic Freedom* overall multisector rating, including taxation levels, price controls, inflation, etc., on a 5–0 (0 = 100% free) scale: **2.05**.

South Korea (Republic of Korea)

	1985	1998
Role of state, regional and/or local authorities in the economy		
Ownership of industry	Considerable*	Considerable*
Privatization underway?	Yes	Yes
Ownership of services	Considerable*	Considerable*
Privatization underway?	Yes	Yes
Ownership of agric. land	No	No
Privatization underway?	n/a	n/a
Barriers to international commerce		
Tariffs	High	Medium-low
Licenses required?	No	No
Quotas	Some	Some
Vexatious non-tariff barriers	Yes	Yes
Investment restrictions	Many	Diminishing
Limits on service imports	Many	Some
Barriers to internal competition		
Bank ownership public	Considerable	None
Bank ownership private	Yes	Yes
Bank privatization underway?	No	Completed
Restrictions on bank activities	Yes	Few
Stock-market activities	Limited	Emerging market
Central planning of the economy	No	No
Degree of regulation by:		
Bureaucratic controls	V. high	High
Licensing	V. high	High

De facto ownership of nominally private entities by optional direct/indirect bureaucratic or political intervention, including expropriation.

1998 Heritage Foundation/Wall Street Journal, *Index of Economic Freedom* overall multisector rating, including taxation levels, price controls, inflation, etc., on a 5–0 (0 = 100% free) scale: **2.30**.

Mexico

	1985	1998
Role of state, regional and/or local authorities in the economy		
Ownership of industry	Extensive	Considerable
Privatization underway?	No	Yes
Ownership of services	Extensive	Residual
Privatization underway?	No	Yes
Ownership of agric. land	Community ownership	Community ownership
Privatization underway?	n/a	Yes
Barriers to international commerce		
Tariffs	V. high	Medium-low
Licenses required?	Yes	Yes
Quotas	None	None
Vexatious non-tariff barriers	Many	Few
Investment restrictions	Many	Some for non-NAFTA
Limits on service imports	Many	Some
Barriers to internal competition		
Bank ownership public	Extensive	Residual
Bank ownership private	Yes	Yes
Bank privatization underway?	No	Yes
Restrictions on bank activities	Some	Few
Stock-market activities	Limited	Emerging market
Central planning of the economy	No	No
Degree of regulation by:		
Bureaucratic controls	Medium-high	Low
Licensing	V. high	High

1998 Heritage Foundation/Wall Street Journal, *Index of Economic Freedom* overall multisector rating, including taxation levels, price controls, inflation, etc., on a 5–0 (0 = 100% free) scale: **3.25**.

Peru

	1985	1998
Role of state, regional and/or local authorities in the economy		
Ownership of industry	Extensive	Residual
Privatization underway?	No	Yes
Ownership of services	Extensive	Still considerable
Privatization underway?	No	Yes
Ownership of agric. land	None	None
Privatization underway?	n/a	n/a
Barriers to international commerce		
Tariffs	V. high	Medium-high
Licenses required?	Yes	No
Quotas	Yes	No
Vexatious non-tariff barriers	Yes	No
Investment restrictions	Some	V. few
Limits on service imports	Many	V. few
Barriers to internal competition		
Bank ownership public	Extensive	None
Bank ownership private	Yes	Yes
Bank privatization underway?	No	Completed
Restrictions on bank activities	Many	V. few
Stock-market activities	Informal only	Emerging market
Central planning of the economy	No	No
Degree of regulation by:		
Bureaucratic controls	Low	V. low
Licensing	Very high	Medium-high

1998 Heritage Foundation/Wall Street Journal, *Index of Economic Freedom* overall multisector rating, including taxation levels, price controls, inflation, etc., on a 5–0 (0 = 100% free) scale: **2.80**.

Spain

	1985	1998
Role of state, regional and/or local authorities in the economy		
Ownership of industry	Extensive	Substantial
Privatization underway?	Yes	Yes
Ownership of services	Extensive	Substantial
Privatization underway?	No	Yes
Ownership of agric. land	None	None
Privatization underway?	n/a	n/a
Barriers to international commerce		
Tariffs	Low	3.6% EU ave.
Licenses required?	No	No
Quotas	Some (EU)	Some (EU)
Vexatious non-tariff barriers	Many	Some
Investment restrictions	Many	Few
Limits on service imports	Some	Few
Barriers to internal competition		
Bank ownership public	Substantial	Residual
Bank ownership private	Yes	Yes
Bank privatization underway?	No	Yes
Restrictions on bank activities	Some	Some
Stock-market activities	Developed	Fully developed
Central planning of the economy	No	No
Degree of regulation by:		
Bureaucratic controls	High	Diminishing
Licensing	High	High

1998 Heritage Foundation/Wall Street Journal, *Index of Economic Freedom* overall multisector rating, including taxation levels, price controls, inflation, etc., on a 5–0 (0 = 100% free) scale: **2.50**.

Turkey

	1985	1998
Role of state, regional and/or local authorities in the economy		
Ownership of industry	Extensive	Extensive
Privatization underway?	No	Yes
Ownership of services	Extensive	Extensive
Privatization underway?	No	Yes
Ownership of agric. land	None	None
Privatization underway?	n/a	n/a
Barriers to international commerce		
Tariffs	Medium-high	Converging to 3.6% EU ave.
Licenses required?	Yes	Some
Quotas	No	No
Vexatious non-tariff barriers	No	Few
Investment restrictions	Yes	Few
Limits on service imports	Yes	Few
Barriers to internal competition		
Bank ownership public	Extensive	Still considerable
Bank ownership private	Yes	Yes
Bank privatization underway?	No	V. slowly
Restrictions on bank activities	Some	Few
Stock-market activities	Limited	Emerging market
Central planning of the economy	No	No
Degree of regulation by:		
Bureaucratic controls	Medium-high	Diminishing
Licensing	Low	Low

1998 Heritage Foundation/Wall Street Journal, *Index of Economic Freedom* overall multisector rating, including taxation levels, price controls, inflation, etc., on a 5–0 (0 = 100% free) scale: **2.80**.

Hong Kong (Special Administrative Region of the People's Republic of China)

	1985	1998
Role of state, regional and/or local authorities in the economy		
Ownership of industry	None	None
Privatization underway?	n/a	n/a
Ownership of services	None	None
Privatization underway?	n/a	n/a
Ownership of agric. land	Crown (urban) lands	State (urban) lands
Privatization underway?	V. slowly	No
Barriers to international commerce		
Tariffs	On only a few items	On only a few items
Licenses required?	No	No
Quotas	No	No
Vexatious non-tariff barriers	None	None
Investment restrictions	None	On all media
Limits on service imports	None	None
Barriers to internal competition		
Bank ownership public	None	None
Bank ownership private	Yes	Yes
Bank privatization underway?	n/a	n/a
Restrictions on bank activities	None	None
Stock-market activities	Fully developed	Fully developed
Central planning of the economy	No	No
Degree of regulation by:		
Bureaucratic controls	Almost none	PRC influence*
Licensing	None	None

*De facto forced sales of UK-owned enterprises to PRC entities.

1998 Heritage Foundation/Wall Street Journal, *Index of Economic Freedom* overall multisector rating, including taxation levels, price controls, inflation, etc., on a 5–0 (0 = 100% free) scale: **1.25**.

New Zealand

	1985	1998
Role of state, regional and/or local authorities in the economy		
Ownership of industry	Extensive	None
Privatization underway?	Starting	Yes
Ownership of services	Extensive	Some
Privatization underway?	No	Yes
Ownership of agric. land	None	None
Privatization underway?	n/a	n/a
Barriers to international commerce		
Tariffs	High	V. low
Licenses required?	Yes	No
Quotas	Yes	V. few
Vexatious non-tariff barriers	Yes	No
Investment restrictions	Many	Few
Limits on service imports	Many	V. few
Barriers to internal competition		
Bank ownership public	No	No
Bank ownership private	Yes	Yes
Bank privatization underway?	n/a	n/a
Restrictions on bank activities	Some	Almost none
Stock-market activities	Limited	Emerging market
Central planning of the economy	No	No
Degree of regulation by:		
Bureaucratic controls	High	V. low
Licensing	Low	V. low

1998 Heritage Foundation/Wall Street Journal, *Index of Economic Freedom* overall multisector rating, including taxation levels, price controls, inflation, etc., on a 5–0 (0 = 100% free) scale: **1.75**.

Singapore

	1985	1998
Role of state, regional and/or local authorities in the economy		
Ownership of industry	Some	Some
Privatization underway?	No	No
Ownership of services	Considerable	Considerable
Privatization underway?	n/a	n/a
Ownership of agric. land	No	No
Privatization underway?	n/a	n/a
Barriers to international commerce		
Tariffs	Low	V. low
Licenses required?	No	No
Quotas	No	No
Vexatious non-tariff barriers	None	None
Investment restrictions	None	None
Limits on service imports	None	None
Barriers to internal competition		
Bank ownership public	None	None
Bank ownership private	Yes	Yes
Bank privatization underway?	n/a	n/a
Restrictions on bank activities	V. few	V. few
Stock-market activities	Developed	Fully developed
Central planning of the economy	No	No
Degree of regulation by:		
Bureaucratic controls	Low	V. low
Licensing	None	None

1998 Heritage Foundation/Wall Street Journal, *Index of Economic Freedom* overall multisector rating, including taxation levels, price controls, inflation, etc., on a 5–0 (0 = 100% free) scale: **1.30**.

Taiwan (Republic of China)

	1985	1998
Role of state, regional and/or local authorities in the economy		
Ownership of industry	Considerable	Residual
Privatization underway?	Yes	Yes
Ownership of services	Considerable	Residual
Privatization underway?	No	Yes
Ownership of agric. land	No	No
Privatization underway?	n/a	n/a
Barriers to international commerce		
Tariffs	High	Low, except agricultural
Licenses required?	Some	None
Quotas	Some	None
Vexatious non-tariff barriers	Yes	Yes
Investment restrictions	Many	Many
Limits on service imports	Many	Some
Barriers to internal competition		
Bank ownership public	Considerable	Residual
Bank ownership private	Yes	Yes
Bank privatization underway?	Slowly	Yes
Restrictions on bank activities	Yes	Yes
Stock-market activities	Limited	Emerging market
Central planning of the economy	No	No
Degree of regulation by:		
Bureaucratic controls	High	Low
Licensing	High	Low

1998 Heritage Foundation/Wall Street Journal, *Index of Economic Freedom* overall multisector rating, including taxation levels, price controls, inflation, etc., on a 5–0 (0 = 100% free) scale: **1.95.**

United Kingdom

	1985	1998
Role of state, regional and/or local authorities in the economy		
Ownership of industry	Residual	No
Privatization underway?	Yes	Yes
Ownership of services	Extensive	Residual
Privatization underway?	Yes	Yes
Ownership of agric. land	None	None
Privatization underway?	n/a	n/a
Barriers to international commerce		
Tariffs	Low	3.6% EU ave.
Licenses required?	No	No
Quotas	Some (EU)	Some (EU)
Vexatious non-tariff barriers	No	No
Investment restrictions	Few	V. few
Limits on service imports	Few	V. few
Barriers to internal competition		
Bank ownership public	No	No
Bank ownership private	Yes	Yes
Bank privatization underway?	n/a	n/a
Restrictions on bank activities	Few	Almost none
Stock-market activities	Fully developed	Fully developed
Central planning of the economy	No	No
Degree of regulation by:		
Bureaucratic controls	Agriculture only	Agriculture only
Licensing	V. low	V. low

1998 Heritage Foundation/Wall Street Journal, *Index of Economic Freedom* overall multisector rating, including taxation levels, price controls, inflation, etc., on a 5–0 (0 = 100% free) scale: **1.95**.

United States

	1985	1998

Role of state, regional and/or local authorities in the economy

Ownership of industry	V. limited*	V. limited*
Privatization underway?	Yes	Yes
Ownership of services	V. limited**	V. limited**
Privatization underway?	No	Yes
Ownership of agric. land	None	None
Privatization underway?	n/a	n/a

Barriers to international commerce

Tariffs	Low	V. low
Licenses required?	No	No
Quotas	Yes	Yes
Vexatious non-tariff barriers	Some***	Some***
Investment restrictions	Some	Few
Limits on service imports	Some	Few

Barriers to internal competition

Bank ownership public	None	None
Bank ownership private	Yes	Yes
Bank privatization underway?	n/a	n/a
Restrictions on bank activities	Many	Few
Stock-market activities	Fully developed	Fully developed
Central planning of the economy	No	No
Degree of regulation by:		
Bureaucratic controls	Eliminated	None
Licensing	V. low	V. low

*Some nuclear/other military production facilities operated by private contractors.

**The Amtrak rail services are *de facto* governmental.

***The US applies very restrictive health standards on food imports and is an aggressive user of anti-dumping fines.

1998 Heritage Foundation/Wall Street Journal, *Index of Economic Freedom* overall multisector rating, including taxation levels, price controls, inflation, etc., on a 5–0 (0 = 100% free) scale: **1.90**.

DEFINITIONS AND SOURCES FOR APPENDIX TABLES

Definitions

Role of State, Regional and/or Local Authorities in the Economy

Public ownership: *extensive* = >50%; *considerable* = >25%; *some* = >10%; *residual* = <10% and/or being privatized.

Services: = public services/infrastructures, i.e. power generation, telecommunications, air, rail and road transport, shipping, and mass media.

Ownership of agricultural land: collective farms are equated to local authority ownership.

Barriers to International Commerce

Tariffs: *v. high* = >20%; *high* = >10%; *low* = >5%; *v. low*.

Licenses: requirement to obtain import permits for specific shipments.

Quotas: periodic quantitative limits, by kind and/or origin, including kind/origin prohibitions (= zero quotas).

Vexatious non-tariff barriers: inappropriate inspection and/or certification requirements and/or health/safety norms abused to keep out imports; local content requirements, e.g. on imported vehicles; arbitrary pricing for *ad valorem* calculations; discriminatory taxation of imported goods, or discriminatory income taxation of purchasers of imported goods; extortion by customs-house officials; anti-dumping fines.

Investment restrictions: restrictions on foreign investment by economic sector; the imposition of technology transfers; compulsion to form joint ventures with local entities.

278

Limits on service imports: insurance policies; financial services; shipping; legal, accounting, engineering, architectural or labor services provided by foreign firms or foreign citizens.

Barriers to Internal Competition

Restrictions on bank activities: prohibitions of, or limits on: equity investments; real estate investments; securities trading; sale of insurance policies.

Licensing: permits required to open businesses and/or engage in specific activities.

Notes on Sources

US Department of Commerce, *National Trade Data Bank* and *Country Commercial Guide* (by single countries).

Office of the US Trade Representative, *Report on Foreign Trade Barriers.*

Bryan T. Johnson, Kim R. Holmes and Melanie Kirkpatrick (eds) for the Heritage Foundation/Wall Street Journal, *1998 Index of Economic Freedom* (Washington DC/New York, 1998). Its overall rating is based on the unweighted average of 'scores' from 1 (very low) to 5 (very high) attributed to the following:

- Trade policy, including non-tariff barriers, extortion, etc.
- Taxation levels, without reference to the nature of expenditures.
- Government intervention in the economy.
- Monetary policy (inflation as a *de facto* tax).
- Capital flows and foreign investment policy (restrictions on).
- Banking (government ownership/restrictions on activities).
- Wage and price controls, including minimum wage if any.
- Property rights (protection of).
- Regulation (administrative regulation and informal interference).
- Black market (with emphasis on piracy of intellectual property).

INDEX